A Law unto Itself?

A LAW UNTO ITSELF?

Essays in the New Louisiana Legal History

EDITED BY *Warren M. Billings and Mark F. Fernandez*

LOUISIANA STATE UNIVERSITY PRESS
Baton Rouge

10   09   08   07   06   05 04 03 02   01
5   4   3   2   1

Designer: Amanda McDonald Scallan
Typeface: Granjon
Typesetter: Crane Composition, Inc.
Printer and binder: Thomson-Shore, Inc.

Library of Congress Cataloging-in-Publication Data
A law unto itself? : essays in the new Louisiana legal history / edited by Warren M. Billings and Mark F. Fernandez.
          p. cm.
Includes index.
  ISBN 0-8071-2583-0
  1. Law—Louisiana—History. I. Billings, Warren M., 1940– II. Fernandez, Mark F., 1958–
  KFL78. L39 2000
  349.763'09—dc21

                                                        00-009838

The paper in this book meets the guidelines for permanence and durability of the Committee on Production Guidelines for Book Longevity of the Council on Library Resources. ∞

For Marie E. Windell
in grateful appreciation for her many
contributions to Louisiana legal history

Contents

Preface

Some twenty-five years have passed since that day when my late friend Albert Tate sought my advice about preserving some old records. Tate was then an associate justice of the Supreme Court of Louisiana, and he was concerned about the future of his court's ancient archives. Logically, the appropriate course would have been to effect their transfer to the custody of the state archives; however, two obstacles blocked that route. The court sits in New Orleans, as it has since it first opened its doors to litigants in 1813, whereas the rest of the Louisiana government, including the state archives, resides eighty miles upriver in Baton Rouge. Tate and his colleagues were reluctant to see the court records go there, especially because in 1976 the state archives was without an adequate facility or sufficient staff. The judge therefore searched for another remedy, which was why he approached me.

Although I knew little of Louisiana's history at the time, and even less about the court's past, I agreed to look at the collection and to come up with some recommendations, without realizing what I was about to see. A trip to the storage facility in the basement of the courthouse immediately revealed an enormous accumulation of documents, all seemingly packaged neatly in manila envelopes and in an orderly array of range on range of pigeon-hole shelving. Here, I realized, was perhaps the greatest untapped resource of Louisiana history, and it lay in imminent need of preservation.

Tate and I discussed alternatives. The first consideration was locating a depository that would afford a secure, proper archival environment. Given the court's reluctance to see the records go off to Baton Rouge, I approached the late Dr. Gerald J. Eberle, then director of the Earl K. Long Library at the University of New Orleans—my home institution—about the library taking physical custody of the manuscripts. Here, I said, was an opportunity to acquire a huge collection of undoubted historical significance, which would obviously enhance the library's research holdings. Eberle was at first skeptical, but he soon encouraged me to explore the possibility further, which pleased Judge Tate no end. In due course Tate and I crafted a memorandum of agreement that the court promulgated by rule in November 1976. Accordingly, the library became the court's official repository of its records from 1813 to 1921 and agreed to provide care and access.

Such an arrangement between court and campus, so far as I am aware, is unique. It came to be because of Tate's foresight and because UNO, as it is known locally, was the urban entity of the Louisiana State University system. As a public institution, UNO could assist the court in a way that did not minimize the judiciary's fiduciary responsibility for maintaining its records in perpetuity.

What seemed a well-ordered accumulation turned out to be badly deranged. Some disorder had occurred during and after the Civil War, but the worst of it, ironically, resulted from a previous attempt at preservation. In 1958, when the court moved from its former location at 400 Royal Street in the Vieux Carré to its present quarters at 301 Loyola Avenue, court staff packed documents in those neat-appearing manila envelopes. Knowing little of the original order, they put everything in what to them was a proper numerical sequence. Thus, any papers that bore a number "1" went into an envelope marked "#1," and so on. No one distinguished between piece and docket numbers, nor did anyone realize that the court had utilized more than one docket numbering system between 1813 and

1958. The result of a well-intended effort was a jumbled mass of papers that required untangling before scholars could make use of it.

A modest grant from the National Historic Publications and Records Commission enabled Dr. Eberle to engage a consulting archivist, who recommended employing a knowledgeable person to tackle the task of reordering the collection. Marie E. Windell was appointed for that assignment in October 1979, and ever since she has worked unstintingly to reconcile the manuscripts, to solve complex problems of description, and to raise the requisite financial support.

As for me, I intended to fade into the background once the transfer had been accomplished, but that was not to be. For one thing, the justices soon came to regard me as the "expert" in anything to do with the records, and I was often asked to answer questions about the collection or about the early court. Whether I wanted to or not, I found myself learning more about both. For another thing, as Mrs. Windell rearranged the records, I began to encourage students in my graduate research seminars to explore them. Their searches required my greater familiarity with the collection, so I spent more time rummaging it to learn its contents. For yet another thing, Tate and several of his colleagues kept urging me to study the court. I grew more receptive to that possibility once I saw a way of merging it with my interest in colonial Virginia legal developments, and I eventually accepted an invitation in 1982 from then Chief Justice John A. Dixon, Jr., to become the court's historian.

By that time, a door was opening to a major reexamination of Louisiana's distinctive legal order. Edward F. Haas, a former director of the historical center at the Louisiana State Museum, convened a symposium that brought together an array of law professors, judges, and historians that culminated in an influential collection of published essays. Richard Holcombe Kilbourne, Jr., was amidst his pioneering studies of the Louisiana civil and commercial codes. Judith Kelleher Schafer had undertaken the first dissertation-length enquiry based wholly on the supreme court collection. The Louisiana Historical Association was allocating sessions devoted to legal subjects at its annual meetings. A number of my own graduate students translated their seminar work into theses, conference papers, and articles.

What started as a trickle of new scholarship has grown to a small, though steady, stream over the past decade. That being so, it seemed appropriate to gather a representative sampler in book form. The idea for such a volume originated with Elizabeth Gaspard, once a student of mine, and the ensuing anthology is its realization. Of its nine essays, seven were especially commissioned for the collection, whereas the remaining two first appeared in *Louisiana History* in 1988 and 1992, respectively.

One of the authors is an acquaintance. I first met another when she was doing her dissertation research. Thereafter, we developed an abiding friendship and a great fondness for Louisiana legal history as our affinities intensified during many trips to and from annual conferences of the Louisiana Historical Association or its board meetings. Her son and my daughter brought us closer together still.

Six writers are my former students. I am pleased above words that this volume binds us to one another in a special way. Beyond that tie, it was my privilege to instruct them. Often, they challenged me to think my best thoughts; I learned much from their enquiries, and I hope they learned a thing or two from me. Best of all, we had, and continue to have, much intellectual fun together.

Warren M. Billings

ACKNOWLEDGMENTS

The editors are indebted to their respective universities for various forms of assistance throughout the gestation of this volume. Thanks are due Carol Dunlap Billings, law librarian of Louisiana, for her help in tracking down citations and for the loan of several antique legal texts. Anastasia L. Karson gave the manuscript a careful reading at a crucial juncture.

An earlier draft of the essay in chapter 4 was presented at the annual meeting of the Louisiana Historical Association in March 1992. Mark F. Fernandez wishes to thank the members of that panel, Warren M. Billings, James Étienne Viator, and Richard Holcombe Kilbourne, Jr., for their comments and support. Some of the research for the essay was supported by a faculty development grant from Loyola University. The author is also indebted to Jon Kukla for assistance in locating some of the unpublished rules of the Superior Court for the Territory of Orleans. Carl A. Brasseaux, editor of *Louisiana History,* graciously permitted the reprinting of articles by Sheridan E. Young and Thomas W. Helis, which appear as chapters 5 and 6, respectively. Both pieces have been slightly edited to achieve stylistic uniformity. Judith Kelleher Schafer wishes to thank Bennett H. Wall and the editors for their comments on an earlier draft of her paper; she is also grateful to her son, T. Gregory Schafer, for his good looks and charm, which enabled her to gain access to the records used in her essay. Kathyrn Page thanks Karen Trahan Leathem for her reading of and insightful comments about the author's essay, an earlier

version of which was read at the annual meeting of the Louisiana
Historical Association in 1986 in Shreveport.

Our late colleague and friend Judge George Arceneaux of the United
States District Court for the Eastern District of Louisiana took a keen interest in the initial research that resulted in several of the essays, and he
was singularly helpful in securing use of some relevant manuscripts from
the Federal Records Center in Ft. Worth, Texas. Sadly, he did not live to
see this book come to print, but we think that he would have been pleased
by it.

Sylvia Frank and Maureen Hewitt, our editors at Louisiana State University Press, have offered wonderful assistance and encouragement. Our
copy editors, Elizabeth Simon and Gerry Anders, provided expert and
careful service. We also thank the anonymous readers for their careful
criticism and suggestions.

We single out Marie E. Windell for especial recognition. Since 1979,
when she assumed her duties as archivist of the Supreme Court of
Louisiana Collection, Mrs. Windell has labored tirelessly to render the
documents in that magnificent deposit ever more useful to judges, attorneys, graduate students, and scholars alike. Her abiding commitment to
the records makes research in them not only easy but also immensely plea-
surable. Therefore, we the editors, joined by our fellow essayists, dedicate
this book to her as a souvenir of our affection for her and our esteem for
her gifts to the New Louisiana Legal History.

A Law unto Itself?

Mark F. Fernandez

INTRODUCTION

Louisiana Legal History: Past, Present, and Future

Louisiana's legal heritage has long been a source of fascination, curiosity, and, sadly, misinformation. Outsiders have viewed the legal system as an anomaly, an odd appendage at the mouth of the Mississippi, and they have shunned its study because of this perceived quirkiness. Consequently, Louisiana has been generally ignored in treatments of American or southern legal history, whereas past writings about the state's legal structure were largely inward looking. Much of that literature also focused on the minutiae of Louisiana's civil law origins, thereby adding to an image of peculiarity that usually scared outlanders away. Recently, that vision has begun to yield to another—"the New Louisiana Legal History." The product of an energetic cadre of writers, this rendering not only expands on previous work, but it also explores new methods and arenas of research with the aim of tying the state's legal history more closely to that of the South and of the nation as a whole. Where in the past Louisiana's legal historians consciously cultivated an approach that was sui generis, the New Louisiana Legal Historians root their work in the main themes of southern and legal history. To understand the relationship between these writers and their predecessors, it is imperative to review both related trends in American and southern history and the sum of Louisiana's legal historiography: its past, present, and future.[1]

Over the last forty years, scholars have made significant strides in developing a legal history for the South. Their efforts stemmed from two primary influences: a desire to explore the ideology of American constitutionalism and the embrace of social science method as a means of historical enquiry. In the 1960s, students of the American Revolution discovered the insights of anthropologist Clifford Geertz, which they incorporated into their explanation of the nexus between ideas and revolutions. Thus began an ideological approach that has dominated discussions of the rise of American constitutionalism ever since. Even recent fascination with postmodernist discourse theory, and its attack on viewing ideology as a means to understanding culture, have failed to unseat ideology as the mainstream approach to the study of constitutionalism.[2]

Concurrent with the advent of the ideological school, a scholarly critique of judicial ignorance of history combined with an emphasis on fundamental social institutions to spawn a closer attention to legal and constitutional studies. By the end of the 1960s, university history departments

1. Warren M. Billings invented the phrase "New Louisiana Legal History" in his review of Richard Holcombe Kilbourne, Jr.'s *History of the Louisiana Civil Code: The Formative Years, 1803–1839,* in *Louisiana History* 30 (1989): 324–5.

2. The fundamental works of the ideological school flow from the anthropological investigations of Clifford Geertz, "Ideology as a Cultural System," in David E. Apter, ed., *Ideology and Discontent* (London, 1964), 47–77; and Geertz, *The Interpretation of Culture: Selected Essays* (London, 1975). American historians of the Revolutionary and post-Revolutionary period adopted the Geertzian approach and incorporated it into their scholarship on the ideology of republicanism; major works in this genre include Bernard Bailyn, *The Ideological Origins of the American Revolution* (Cambridge, Mass., 1967); Gordon S. Wood, *The Creation of the American Republic* (Chapel Hill, 1969); Lance Banning, *The Jeffersonian Persuasion: Evolution of a Party Ideology* (Ithaca, N.Y., 1978); John M. Murrin, "The Great Inversion; or, Court versus Country: A Comparison of the Revolution Settlements in England (1688–1721) and America (1776–1816)," in J. G. A. Pocock, ed., *Three British Revolutions: 1641, 1688, and 1776* (Princeton, 1980); Pocock, *The Machiavellian Moment: Florentine Political Thought and the Atlantic Republican Tradition* (Princeton, 1975); Isaac Kramnick, *Republicanism and Bourgeois Radicalism: Political Ideology in Late Eighteenth Century England and America* (Ithaca, N.Y., 1990). Perhaps the most effective adaptation of the ideological approach to the study of legal systems is A. G. Roeber's *Faithful Magistrates and Republican Lawyers: Creators of Virginia Legal Culture, 1680–1810* (Chapel Hill, 1981). The practical criticism that spawned the reinvigoration of the field of legal history arose after the publication of Paul Murphy's influential essay "A Time to Reclaim: The Current Challenge of American Constitutional History,"*American Historical Review* 69 (October 1963): 64–80.

responded to this challenge by developing specific curricula in legal history. These courses and the historians who taught them embraced a conceptual approach to legal studies that drew on traditional methodologies by emphasizing the development of law, legal institutions, economic and social trends, and the intellectual nature of the law as well as constitutional themes and case studies. Within a decade, several specialized approaches to legal history began to emerge as the "law and society" school, the "law and culture school," and "critical legal studies." The law and society and law and culture schools emphasized the intersection of law and legal institutions with social and cultural history. Critical legal studies focused more precisely on viewing law in a vacuum. Clashes among these methodologies have dominated the field of legal history ever since.[3]

Such developments within the specialized field of legal studies dovetailed nicely with the advent of "history from the bottom up." Social historians relied chiefly on documentary sources where so-called inarticulate voices could be heard. Legal records such as trial transcripts, depositions, tax lists, wills, and inventories emerged as convenient repositories where the words and deeds of the "speechless" could be researched, and a natural marriage of legal history and social history ensued.[4]

Southern historians responded to all three of these trends in exciting and influential ways. Rhys Isaac's Pulitzer Prize–winning study *The Transformation of Virginia,* for example, successfully wedded the ideological approach to the techniques of social and cultural history. Legal scholars, while not nearly as imaginative as Isaac, also incorporated current methods into their writings. Constitutional historians examined the role of southern thinkers in the development of federalist and antifederalist ideology, as well as the role of prominent southerners as pragmatic politi-

---

3. One of the best essays both on the salient trends in modern legal history and the advent of Critical Legal Studies and what some call the "New Legal History" is Stanley N. Katz, "The Problem of a Colonial Legal History," in Jack P. Greene and J. R. Pole, eds., *Colonial British America: Essays in the New History of the Early Modern Era* (Baltimore, 1984), 457–91. Although Katz is primarily concerned with developing a rationale for studies in colonial legal history, his analysis of the various schools of American legal historiography is a solid primer on twentieth-century legal historiography.

4. For an excellent essay on the development, methodology, and problems of the New Social History, see Alice Kessler-Harris, "Social History," in Eric Foner, ed., *The New American History* (Philadelphia, 1990), 163–84.

cal practitioners of republicanism. In fact, no figures loom larger in the study of early constitutional thought than Thomas Jefferson and James Madison. At the opening of the nineteenth century, indeed, the influential constitutional ideas of southerners such as John C. Calhoun, John Taylor of Caroline, and John Randolph of Roanoke formed the very foundation of states' rights ideology.[5]

Studies in American constitutional history in general and southern history in particular also attended to the articulation of state constitutions and governments, as well as the relation of both to the larger national and regional ideological trends. The net effect of these findings was a heightened interest in the evolution of southern courts. Moreover, this literature effectively joins the intellectual contributions of the ideological analysis with legal and social history.[6]

A growing concern with the history of the book in American society has invigorated history and American studies in the past thirty years. This trend is especially important to legal scholars as it has forced them to take a closer look at legal literature and publication. Investigation of legal literature has greatly improved legal scholars' understanding of the intellectual life of early American lawyers. At the same time, investigation of legal publishing, especially court reporting, demonstrates much about the nineteenth-century modernization of the legal community.[7]

5. Rhys Isaac, *The Transformation of Virginia: 1740–1790* (Chapel Hill, 1982).

6. Kermit L. Hall and James W. Ely, Jr., eds., *An Uncertain Tradition: Constitutionalism and the History of the South* (Athens, Ga., 1989) and Peter S. Onuf, "State Sovereignty and the Making of the Constitution," in Terence Ball and J. G. A. Pocock, eds., *Conceptual Change and the Constitution* (Lawrence, Kans., 1988); F. Thornton Miller, *Juries and Judges Versus the Law* (Charlottesville, 1994); Timothy J. Huebner, "Divided Loyalties: Justice William Johnson and the Rise of Disunion in South Carolina, 1822–1834," *Journal of Supreme Court History* (1995): 19–30; Huebner, "The Consolidation of State Judicial Power: Spencer Roane, Virginia Legal Culture and the Southern Judicial Tradition," *Virginia Magazine of History and Biography* 102 (1994): 47–72; Huebner, "Encouraging Economic Development: Joseph Henry Lumpkin and the Law of Contract, 1846–1860," *Journal of Southern Legal History* 1 (1991): 357–75; Huebner, "Joseph Henry Lumpkin and Evangelical Reform in Georgia: Temperance, Education and Industrialization, 1830–1860," *Georgia Historical Quarterly* 75 (1991): 254–74.

7. Robin Myers and Michael Harris, eds., *Aspects of Printing from 1600* (Winchester, U.K., 1987); Myers and Harris, eds., *Pioneers in Bibliography* (Winchester, U.K., 1988); Myers and Harris, eds., *Fakes and Frauds: Varieties of Deception in Print and Manuscript* (Winchester, U.K., 1989); Myers and Harris, eds., *Spreading the Word: The Distribution Networks of Print, 1550–1850* (Winchester, U.K., 1990); Myers and Harris, eds., *Property of a Gentleman: The Formation, Organisation, and Dispersal of*

Perhaps the most visible result of the social history on southern legal studies is a growing literature on the relationship between the law and slavery and on the legal rights of southern women. Works on slavery and the law have focused on two primary themes: the economics of slavery and the treatment and living conditions of slaves. Important work on the profitability of slavery continues to be a vibrant aspect of southern historiography, though more recent works have centered on the influence of plantation economics on the development of slave culture and the treatment of slaves. Historians have also questioned whether slaves were treated more harshly in the lower South than in other parts of the region. Legal records of business transactions involving slaves and the treatment of slaves as well as criminal proceedings against slaves have garnered a great deal of attention.[8]

To establish a historical context from which to view the following essays, however, it is first necessary to relate them to existing work on

of the Private Library, 1620–1920 (Winchester, U.K., 1991); Myers and Harris, eds., Censorship and the Control of Print in England and France, 1600–1910 (Winchester, U.K., 1992); Myers and Harris, eds., Serials and their Readers, 1620–1914 (Winchester, U.K., 1993); Myers and Harris, eds., A Millennium of the Book: Production, Design, and Illustration in Manuscript and Print 900–1900 (Winchester, U.K., 1994); Myers and Harris, eds., A Genius for Letters: Booksellers and Bookselling from the 16th to the 20th Century (Winchester, U.K., 1995); Myers and Harris, eds., Antiquarians, Book Collectors and the Circle of Learning (Winchester, U.K., 1996); Giles Mandelbrote, Arnold Hunt, and Alison Shell, eds., The Book Trade and Its Customers, 1450–1900: Historical Essays for Robin Myers (Winchester, U.K., 1997); Mandelbrote, Hunt, and Shell, eds., Stationers Company and the Book Trade (Winchester, U.K., 1997); Robin Myers, ed., Medicine, Mortality, and the Book Trade (Winchester, U.K., 1998); Bernard Bailyn and John B. Hench, The Press and the American Revolution (Boston, 1981); Pierce W. Gaines, William Cobbett and the United States (Winchester, U.K., 1971); William L. Joyce, David D. Hall, Richard D. Brown, and John B. Hench, Printing and Society in Early America (Worcester, Mass., 1983); Warren M. Billings, "English Legal Literature as a Source of Law and Practice for Seventeenth-Century Virginia," Virginia Magazine of History and Biography 87 (1979): 403–17; Billings, "Law and Culture in the Colonial Chesapeake," Southern Studies 17 (1978), 333–49; Billings, "Justices, Books, Laws, and Courts in Seventeenth-Century Virginia," Law Library Journal 85 (1993): 277–96; Florence M. Jumonville, Bibliography of New Orleans Imprints, 1764–1864 (New Orleans, 1989).

8. E.g., Eugene D. Genovese, Roll, Jordan, Roll: The World the Slaves Made (New York, 1974); Loren Schweninger, Black Property Owners in the South, 1790–1915 (Urbana, Ill., 1990); Paul G. Finkelman, ed., Fugitive Slaves (New York, 1989); Finkelman, ed., Free Blacks in a Slave Society (New York, 1989); Finkelman, ed., Law, the Constitution, and Slavery (New York, 1989); Finkelman, ed., Southern Slavery at the State and Local Level (New York, 1989); Victoria E. Bynum, Unruly Women: The Politics of Social and Sexual Control in the Old South (Chapel Hill, 1992); Kathleen M. Brown, Good Wives, Nasty Wenches, and Anxious Patriarchs: Gender, Race, and Power in Colonial Virginia (Chapel Hill, 1996).

Louisiana's legal development. The question mark in the title of this book relates directly to the New Louisiana Legal Historians' placement of the state's legal history into a larger southern and national context, an attempt that, for diverse reasons, was not important to earlier scholars. Thus, it is imperative to relate how Louisiana came to be understood as having "a law unto itself."

A unique vision of Louisiana's legal heritage developed almost coincidentally with the dawning of statehood. As the first large territorial acquisition of the United States, Louisiana entered the Union as something of an anomaly. Never part of English America, Louisiana with its continental flavor, foreign populace, and civilian legal arrangements struck early-nineteenth-century Americans as a peculiar piece of real estate. Shortly after the Purchase, Congress met to debate the organization of the territory, and some congressmen argued that the inhabitants were incapable of governing themselves. Fortunately, others, such as George Washington Campbell of Tennessee, disagreed. "One gentleman observes," he noted, "that we ought to regard the people of Louisiana as totally distinct from, and as not possessed of any similar habits with ourselves. I trust however, we shall consider them as a part of the human species . . . I trust, therefore, that we shall extend to them the same rights as are enjoyed by the other territories." To Campbell's credit, Louisianians were at least human. Early historians, however, had difficulty identifying them as "American."[9]

Those first writers were "gentlemen-scholars" who crafted history in addition to their other, more lucrative, occupations. As the nineteenth century progressed, the introduction of the German seminar style fostered the emergence of professional historians who thrived in university settings. The interpretation of the American past that prevailed among both of these groups was Whiggish in origin and essentially Anglocentric. It influenced both gentleman-scholar and professional alike, when each wrote about Louisiana, to look at the deviations from these traditions. Thus, the state's first historians focused on its continental origins. As they dealt with the law, they explored its civilian roots and differences and, to a large extent, they ignored or dismissed the similarities. Unlike their Whig

---

9. Quoted in Winthrop D. Jordan, *White over Black: American Attitudes toward the Negro, 1550–1812* (New York, 1968), 389.

counterparts, they celebrated Louisiana's French and Spanish heritage. When these writers described Louisiana culture, they identified it with creole rather than American lineage.

Gentlemen-scholars who wrote the first histories of Louisiana were barristers and judges, most of whom lacked academic training in law or history. Even so, their handling of the subject frequently was of the first rank, and their work remains exceedingly reliable, sometimes eclipsing that of more modern academicians. Writers like François-Xavier Martin, Charles E. A. Gayarré, Alceé Fortier, and Henry Plauché Dart, among others, provided sensible, accurate portrayals of the state's legal past, though they cast the results of their research in a narrative style that shied away from profound historical analysis.

Judge Martin's *History of Louisiana from the Earliest Period* still contains one of the best examinations of the judicial structure from the colonial period to the early nineteenth century. Unlike others of his day, Martin avoided florid prose or heroic speculation to buttress his discussions or as a substitute for close readings of the documentary record. Accordingly, his *History of Louisiana* has withstood the test of time, becoming not only a useful secondary source but an important primary document as well. Indeed, it is more reliable than those of Gayarré or Fortier.[10]

Other lawyers and judges wrote on specific aspects of the law and the legal profession, tackling subjects such as criminal jurisprudence, judicial biography, and the early history of the Supreme Court of Louisiana. Their work grew into an impressive body of narrative literature. Like similar contemporary histories of the era elsewhere, it emphasized the intrepid deeds of the "great white men" who founded and nurtured bench and bar. Equally evident in their writings were the authors' ardently nationalist orientations and their tendency to overlook the shortcomings of their "distinguished" subjects.[11]

Lawyers also produced another type of Louisiana legal history. This

10. François-Xavier Martin, *The History of Louisiana from the Earliest Period,* 2 vols. (New Orleans, 1827–1829); Charles E. A. Gayarré, *History of Louisiana,* 4 vols. (New Orleans, 1885); Alcée Fortier, *A History of Louisiana* (New Orleans, 1904).

11. Albert Voorhies, *A Treatise on the Criminal Jurisprudence of Louisiana* (New Orleans, 1860); Lewis Kerr, *An Exposition of the Criminal Laws of the Territory of Orleans: The Practice of the Courts of*

enormous species, some of which has become available to study only now, is what some call "law office history." Attorneys prepared law office histories to support their arguments when trying to win cases. Obviously, with large sums of money or even lives at stake, these gentlemen-scholars employed history for a didactic purpose: to reinforce the arguments in their briefs. Thus, the genre lacked the critical and analytical foci of academic legal history, a conception of rather recent origin.

Frederic William Maitland, the sire of modern legal historical studies, distinguished between law office history and legal history in a turn-of-the-century address to his colleagues at the University of Cambridge. Lawyers, he remarked, write history to win cases, period. That goal distorts analysis and smacks of presentism. Indeed, Maitland argued, implicit presentism was ahistorical, and he called for a more consistent, documentary, and objective approach. Many are those who have heeded Maitland's call since the first decade of the twentieth century. Nonetheless, law office history remains something of a constant for the practicing bar, which gives it a unique place in the history of Louisiana law. What is distressing is that this approach all too frequently remains the most popular way of disseminating legal history to the general public. The peril of its methodology is its capacity to misinform. Fortunately, by the early 1900s the vitality of the amateur tradition that favored narrative history tempered the most distracting elements of the law office approach.[12]

Despite the hazards, modern legal historians can learn much from the law office histories of the past if they approach them as primary documents. Consider, for instance, the case of *State* v. *McLean*. In 1849 an anonymous Louisiana attorney prepared a detailed legislative history of

---

Criminal Jurisdiction, the Duties of Their Officers, With a Collection of Forms for the Use of Magistrates and Others (New Orleans, 1806). Henry Plauché Dart, "The History of the Supreme Court of Louisiana," 133 La. xxx–lxi (1914) subsequently reprinted in *Louisiana Historical Quarterly* 4 (1921): 5–112. Dart's output, which ran the gamut from lectures to edited translations of colonial judicial records, spoke to the multiplicity of his research interests (*Dictionary of Louisiana Biography*, s.v. "Dart, Henry Plauché"; William Kernan Dart, "The Justices of the Supreme Court," 133 La. lxxxiv–xc (1914), also reprinted in *LHQ* 4 (1921): 113–24. A representative sampling of their works appears in Judith Kelleher Schafer and Warren M. Billings , eds., *An Uncommon Experience: Law and Legal Institutions in Louisiana, 1803–2003* (Lafayette, La., 1996).

12. Fredric William Maitland, "Inaugural Lecture," delivered 13 October 1888, in *Collected Papers of Fredric William Maitland,* ed. H. A. L. Fisher (Cambridge, U.K., 1911), 1: 480–97.

criminal law. In his brief he chronicled the problematic nature of the territorial crimes acts of 1805 (the basis of all penal law in the state), he analyzed the penal jurisdiction of the courts, and he presented a handy comparison of the view of informations and indictments in England and the United States. As history, *State* v. *McLean* contained its inaccuracies, but as an example of nineteenth-century views of the state's criminal system, the brief stands as a useful source for present-day scholars.

As the twentieth century wore on, Louisiana's legal history came increasingly under the purview of judges and law professors like Albert Tate, Jr., Joseph Dainow, or Robert Fisher. They and similarly minded colleagues drew increasingly on the findings and methods of academic historians. One of the most striking aspects of this tendency was growing specialization, which led to more focused studies and a keener sense of periodization, and that trend marked a coming of age, of sorts. Although the range of their scholarship is too wide to recount in full here, several major themes emerged to influence much of the modern scholarship on Louisiana's law.[13]

By midcentury, academic historians began to turn their attention to Louisiana's legal arrangements. Writers in this vein drew heavily on the work of those who had previously investigated questions regarding the origins of the legal order. These historians studied the rise of the colonial Cabildo and Superior Council, and they made important contributions, though their studies lacked any specific interpretive theme. As these works appeared, however, another band of lawyers, judges, and historians developed a healthy literature that posited a "clash of legal traditions" thesis. That interpretation generated the most influential and prolific corpus of writing on the history of the law in the Bayou State before the New Louisiana Legal Historians came on the scene.[14]

The "clash of legal traditions" interpretation originated in the ruminations of social and political historians about a "creole-American conflict,"

13. Mark F. Fernandez, "*State* v. *McLean:* Louisiana's First History of Criminal Law," *Louisiana History* 34 (1995): 313–25.

14. Albert Tate, Jr., "The Role of the Judge in Mixed Jurisdictions: The Louisiana Experience," in Joseph Dainow, ed., *The Role of Judicial Decisions and Doctrine in Civil Law and in Mixed Jurisdictions* (Baton Rouge, 1974), 23–38; Dainow, ed., *The Role of Judicial Decisions and Doctrine in Civil Law and in Mixed Jurisdictions;* Robert B. Fisher, Jr., "The Louisiana Supreme Court, 1812–1846: Strangers in a Strange Land," *Tulane Civil Law Forum* (New Orleans, 1973).

and it eventually filtered into the arena of legal studies. Much of the analysis rested on commonsense reasoning: Put two diverse ethnic groups in the same territory and they are bound to quarrel. Evidence for such a thesis was readily found in travel journals or histories such as Gayarré's, as well as in the fiction of George Washington Cable and Kate Chopin; Progressive historiography, which emphasized social conflict; the so-called "Civilian Renaissance" of the 1920s, 1930s, and 1940s; the social register; and the wishful thinking of Louisianians.

When, for example, George Washington Cable criticized creole culture in *The Grandissimes,* he was ostracized from New Orleans society. Kate Chopin suffered similar attacks after publishing *The Awakening,* a novella about a young American wife seduced by the sanguinary delights of creole culture. Chopin's protagonist, Edna Pontellier, awakened to her inner feelings and sexual desires as a result of her contact with creole culture; however, her actions then placed her outside the confines of polite society and drove her ultimately to suicide amid the breakers at Grand Isle. Lawyers and legal historians experienced similar pressures to conform to traditional standards. In the 1930s both began to realize how the natural progression of their legal system had led Louisiana to evolve into a common-law jurisdiction. The result was an intellectual cul-de-sac called the "Civilian Renaissance" that sprang from an attempt to re-create state law into a more representative civilian jurisdiction. To this day, certain legal scholars still focus on the minutiae of civil traditions and the impact of the clash of cultures and neglect the similarities between Louisiana's legal customs and other American jurisdictions.[15]

As the field continued to develop, a few historians started reviewing

15. Jerry A. Micelle, "From Law Court to Local Government: Metamorphosis of the Superior Council of French Louisiana," *Louisiana History* 9 (1968): 189–218; Jean Tarrade, "L'administration colonial en France à la fin de l'ancienne régime: projets de reforme," *Revue Historique* 229 (January–March 1963): 103–22; Donald Lemieux, "The Office of *Commissaire Ordannateur* in French Louisiana, 1731–1763" (Ph.D. diss., Louisiana State University, 1972); Raphael Morazon, "Letters, Petitions, and Decrees of the Cabildo of New Orleans, 1800–1803" (Ph.D. diss., Louisiana State University, 1972); Charles O'Neill, *Church and State in French Colonial Louisiana; Policy and Politics to 1732* (New Haven, 1966); Francis McDermott, ed., *Frenchmen and French Ways in the Mississippi Valley* (Urbana, Ill., 1969); Ben Robertson Miller, *The Louisiana Judiciary* (Baton Rouge, 1932); and John Preston Moore, *Revolt in Louisiana: The Spanish Occupation, 1766–1770* (Baton Rouge, 1976) analyze the conciliar system, Ulloa's ill-fated attempt at reform, and O'Reilly's successful reform of the legal system.

the state's legal heritage. Most merely appropriated the idea of the clash of cultures as the organizing premise of their findings.

By the late 1940s and early 1950s, Louisiana historians were appropriating the clash of cultures concept. Building on what they perceived as inherent cultural rivalries between Creole and Anglo-American inhabitants of the territorial period, these scholars superimposed this cultural battle on their analysis of legal development. To them, the civil and common-law traditions were constantly butting heads, with the civil law always winning out. This view narrowed the focus to the origins of Louisiana's substantive law and ultimately hinged on a single, overwhelming question: were those origins French or Spanish? These authors acknowledged the Anglo-American presence in Louisiana, but deemphasized its impact on the legal order. Thus, the clash of cultures thesis mapped out a terrain that would become familiar to a generation of Louisiana scholars, who romanticized the civil law as a victor in a "Creole-American" cultural conflict. Those who sailed this tack grossly overestimated the importance of the *Digest of the Civil Laws Now in Force in the Territory of Orleans,* which they viewed as a triumph for "creole" legions rather than for what it was—merely a compilation of laws in force. At the same time they ignored the impact of English and American legal traditions, especially judge-made law.[16]

This emphasis on the "Creole" aspects of the Creole-American conflict stamped its mark on subsequent research on substantive law that law professors were publishing as seminal research in the *Tulane Law Review,* the *Louisiana Law Review,* the *Loyola Law Review,* and similar journals. That line of inquiry reached its zenith in the celebrated "Tournament of Scholars" issue of the *Tulane Law Review.* At the heart of the joust was a pointed argument between Rodolpho Batiza of the Tulane Law School and Robert Pascal of the Louisiana State University Law School over the sources of the civil code. Were they Spanish law? Were they French? Answers to those questions sparked controversies that dominated the dialogue from the 1960s to the 1980s. Discussions were erudite, passionate, and sometimes downright nasty. More importantly, the Tournament of

16. Leonard Greenberg, "Must Louisiana Resign to the Common Law?" *Tulane Law Review* 11 (1936–37): 598–601, and Gordon Ireland, "Louisiana's Legal System Reappraised," ibid., 585–98; 236 La. Rep. 5–119 (1959).

Scholars inspired additional research not only on the code but also on other substantive aspects of the civil law.[17]

These forays culminated in the most enduring work of the genre, George Dargo's authoritative volume *Jefferson's Louisiana: Politics and the Clash of Legal Traditions*. There Dargo incorporated the clash of legal traditions thesis with what stands to this day as the best sociopolitical analysis of territorial Louisiana. He sketched out the socioethnic matrix of early Louisiana in the first part of the book. The second half embraced Groner and Brown and rested on his own research on Edward Livingston. His analysis of the social settlement in territorial Louisiana provided a genuinely reliable treatment, but the emphasis on dueling legal systems stressed too heavily the disputes between Livingston and the federal government over possession of batture lands.[18] Dargo's book polished the Creole-American conflict thesis and made it available to a wide scholarly audience. But like his intellectual predecessors, he failed to attend to conflicting evidence regarding Anglo-American influences on Louisiana's law and its judiciary.[19]

As this lively emphasis on the clash of legal traditions unfolded, certain jurists and others walked a different route. They drew notice to a blend between civil and common law that made Louisiana a "mixed jurisdiction." For the most part, however, they concentrated primarily on contemporary judicial practices, not legal history. One of these theorists, Judge Albert Tate, Jr., however, wrote a page of his own in Louisiana's legal history. In 1976 he persuaded his brother justices of the Supreme

17. Samuel B. Groner, "Louisiana Law: Its Development in the First Quarter Century of American Rule," *Louisiana Law Review* 8 (1948): 350–82; Elizabeth Gaspar Brown, "Law and Government in the Louisiana Purchase: 1803–1804," *Wayne Law Review* 2 (1956): 169–89; Brown, "Legal Systems in Conflict: Orleans Territory, 1804–1812," *American Journal of Legal History* 1 (1957): 35–75; Rodolpho Batiza, "The Louisiana Code of 1808: Its Actual Sources and Present Relevance," *Tulane Law Review* 48 (1972): 4–164; Robert A. Pascal, "Sources of the Digest of 1808: A Reply to Professor Batiza," *Tulane Law Review* 48 (1972): 603–52; Batiza, "Sources of the Civil Code of 1808, Facts and Speculation: A Rejoinder," *Tulane Law Review* 48 (1972): 628; Batiza, "Origins of Modern Codification," *Tulane Law Review* 58 (1982): 477–601.

18. Batture lands are alluvial soil deposits in front of levees along the Mississippi River. The dispute between Livingston and the federal government was over the question of who owned the land thus created. That controversy is detailed in William B. Hatcher, *Edward Livingston: Jeffersonian Republican and Jacksonian Democrat* (Baton Rouge, 1940), chapter 8.

19. Tate, "Role of the Judge," *Loyola Law Review* 20: 231–44.

Court of Louisiana to designate the University of New Orleans as the depository for the court's archives. As a result, the court's historic records—then the largest untapped source of Louisiana history—were opened to systematic scholarly enquiry. Thereafter, Tate encouraged friends and acquaintances among Louisiana historians to exploit the collection. Among other things, his encouragement led the Louisiana State Museum to sponsor a symposium of law professors, judges, and historians from across the state and region, who pondered the effect of law on Louisiana's heritage. Selected papers from the conference subsequently appeared in an anthology edited by then–museum historian Edward F. Haas under the title *Louisiana's Legal Heritage.* Most articles in that compilation echoed the clash of legal traditions thesis, but Warren M. Billings's essay "Louisiana Legal History and its Sources: Needs, Opportunities, and Approaches" struck off in a different direction. Billings surveyed the intellectual and documentary landscape of Louisiana's legal literature and challenged his readers to employ the newly opened supreme court records in conjunction with other neglected sources, and he called for new approaches to interpreting the state's unusual legal past.[20]

Almost at once, the essay inspired a cadre of researchers, whose investigations over the past decade have resulted in theses, dissertations, conference papers, articles, and books that turned Louisiana legal historiography on its head. That evolving body of work constitutes the New Louisiana Legal History.

One could argue that the New Louisiana Legal History was born in Warren Billings's graduate American history seminars at the University of New Orleans. There Sybil A. Boudreaux, Thomas W. Helis, Elizabeth Gaspard, Sheridan E. Young, and Mark F. Fernandez wrote what were essentially the first works of the genre. Among others, they developed topics as diverse as the origin and meaning of Union army courts during the federal occupation of New Orleans, the complexion of the state's antebellum bar, courts and procedures, the supreme court, and the clash of legal traditions. Billings himself looked at supreme court rules, criminal law, and legal education. Independent of these seminal studies the equally

20. Warren M. Billings, "Confessions of a Court Historian," *Louisiana History* 35 (1994): 261–4; Edward F. Haas, ed., *Louisiana's Legal Heritage* (Pensacola, Fla.: 1983); Billings, "Louisiana Legal History and its Sources," in Haas, ed., *Louisiana's Legal Heritage,* 189–203.

important work of Judith Kelleher Schafer on slave law, books by Richard Holcombe Kilbourne, Jr., on the civil code and on post–Civil War
debt collection, as well as essays by James Étienne Viator on tort law and
Joseph W. McKnight on the dispersion of law books along the Hispanic
frontier extended the new lines of enquiry.[21]

The tie that binds these diverse scholars together is a common search
for imaginative approaches to the study of legal history and a determination to integrate Louisiana into the mainstream of American legal history,
southern history, and American history in general. For example, Helis, in
his discussion of the Union military tribunals in New Orleans, dared to
suggest that "justice" during the federal occupation under the direction of
Generals Benjamin "Beast" Butler and Nathaniel Banks was not only
possible but also the norm. Likewise, Richard Kilbourne's treatment of
local credit networks and bankruptcy in the post–Civil War era adds a

21. Sybil A. Boudreaux, "The First Minute Book of the Supreme Court of Louisiana, March
1813 to May 1818: An Annotated Edition" (M.A. thesis, University of New Orleans, 1983); see chapter 6 of the present volume; Elizabeth Gaspard, "Rise of the Louisiana Bar," *Louisiana History* 28
(1987): 183–93; see chapter 5 of the present volume; Mark F. Fernandez, "From Chaos to
Continuity: Early Reforms of the Supreme Court of Louisiana, 1845–1852," *Louisiana History* 28
(1987): 19–41; Fernandez, "The Appellate Question: A Comparative Analysis of Supreme Courts of
Appeal in Virginia and Louisiana, 1776–1840" (Ph.D. diss., College of William and Mary in
Virginia, 1991); Fernandez, "*State* v. *McLean et al.*, 313–25; Warren M. Billings, "A Judicial Legacy:
The Last Will and Testament of François-Xavier Martin," *Louisiana History* 25 (1984): 277–89;
Billings, "The Supreme Court and the Education of Louisiana Lawyers," *Louisiana Bar Journal* 33
(1985): 74–80; Billings, "Origins of Criminal Law in Louisiana," *Louisiana History* 31 (1991): 63–76;
Billings, ed., *The Historic Rules of the Supreme Court of Louisiana, 1813–1879* (Lafayette, La., 1985);
Judith Kelleher Schafer, "Slavery and the Supreme Court in Antebellum Louisiana, 1809–1862"
(Ph.D. diss., Tulane University, 1985); Schafer, *Slavery, the Civil Law, and the Supreme Court of
Louisiana* (Baton Rouge, 1994); Schafer, "The Long Arm of Law: Slave Criminals and the Supreme
Court in Antebellum Louisiana," *Tulane Law Review* 60 (1986): 1247–68; Schafer, "Guaranteed
Against the Vices and Maladies Prescribed by Law: Consumer Protection, the Law of Slave Sales,
and the Supreme Court in Antebellum Louisiana," *American Journal of Legal History* 31 (1987):
90–105; Schafer, "'Open and Notorious Concubinage': The Emancipation of Slave Mistresses by
Will and the Supreme Court in Antebellum Louisiana," *Louisiana History* 28 (1987): 165–82;
Richard Holcombe Kilbourne, Jr., *Louisiana's Commercial Law: The Antebellum Period* (Baton
Rouge, 1980); Kilbourne, *History of the Louisiana Civil Code*; Kilbourne, *Debt, Investment, Slaves:
Credit Relations in East Feliciana Parish, Louisiana, 1825–1885* (Tuscaloosa, 1995); James Étienne
Viator, "Louisiana Tort Law, 1809–1860: A Test Case for the Horwitz Thesis," paper presented to
the Louisiana Historical Association, March 1992; Joseph W. McKnight, "Lawbooks on the
Hispanic Frontier," *Journal of the West* (July 1988), 74–84.

vital new insight into the way in which the economic history of the reconstructed South is considered.

Kilbourne's *History of the Louisiana Civil Code* should also put to rest once and for all debates about the civilian origins of Louisiana law that invested the clash of cultures school with its vitality. More importantly, he, like other practitioners of the New Louisiana Legal History, makes jurisprudence and practical application of legal principles an integral part of his analysis. He also considers his evidence in light of the vast body of research on legislative positivism that informs present-day American legal, constitutional, and intellectual history. Thus, Kilbourne with his attention to basic questions of the establishment of the legal system, utilization of judicial records, and consideration of practical applications and wider historical trends conforms closely with Billings's suggestions in the "Needs and Opportunities" essay. What distinguishes him from other New Louisiana Legal historians, though, is his reluctance to compare the legal order in the Bayou State with those of other southern jurisdictions.

Judith Kelleher Schafer, Elizabeth F. Gaspard, Warren M. Billings, Sheridan E. Young, and Mark F. Fernandez, however, have focused closely on those very similarities. Schafer, first in her doctoral dissertation and then in her *Slavery, the Civil Law, and the Supreme Court of Louisiana,* has suggested that the law of slavery and the treatment of slave cases by the high court followed distinctively southern and American patterns. Gaspard's prosopographical study of the legal profession concluded that only 13 percent of antebellum attorneys hailed from the *ancienne population,* meaning that the community of lawyers was overwhelmingly dominated by Americans. Billings's treatment of legal education and criminal law sheds light on the distinctively Anglo-American origins of those important aspects of the legal system. Young's examination of the Court of Errors and Appeals suggests how that bench was patterned closely after other American criminal tribunals. Not unexpectedly, her enquiry also details how the substance and the application of the law were also distinctively American. Billings, in his exposition of court rules, reaches similar conclusions, as does Fernandez in his comparison of procedures and forms in the appellate courts of Virginia and Louisiana. In a word, all these findings portray Louisiana's high courts, manned by a thoroughly

Americanized judiciary, as deeply steeped in Anglo-American traditions. That judiciary became an agent for the injection of not only Anglo-American practices and procedures, but also for an Americanized interaction of common law with codification that is closely related to a marriage of forms that characterized other antebellum southern courts. This acceptance of a preponderant Anglo-American influence on the courts both challenges and complements the validity of the clash of traditions interpretation.[22]

Collectively, proponents of the New Louisiana Legal History have consistently refused to view law in a vacuum. They opted instead for interpretative schemes that mingle social, political, and intellectual history into modes of analysis that treat things legal as one strand in a complex cultural matrix. For example, a recent anthology edited by Billings and Haas, *In Search of Fundamental Law: Louisiana's Constitutions, 1812–1874,* extended the New Louisiana Legal History to embrace constitutional law.[23] The essays showcase in novel fashion the interplay between the tests of experiences and years that led to repeated casting and recasting of fundamental law as the people of the Bayou State adjusted themselves to shifts in imperatives of the moment that have defined Louisiana ever since 1812. Thus, the genre's practitioners fall squarely into the realm of the ideological, law and society, and law and culture schools. Critical Legal Studies have not come to Louisiana.[24]

The essays in this volume exemplify the present state of the New Louisiana Legal History. Essentially, they illustrate three of the major themes in contemporary legal history. Hence the book's tripartite division. In Part I, Warren M. Billings, Florence M. Jumonville, and Carla

22. Gaspard, "Rise of the Louisiana Bar," 183–93; see chapter 5 in the present volume.

23. Warren M. Billings and Edward F. Haas, eds., *In Search of Fundamental Law: Louisiana's Constitutions, 1812–1874* (Lafayette, La., 1993). The volume resulted from a series of symposia that the Louisiana State Museum and the Louisiana State Library sponsored in 1987 and 1988 as part of the state's commemoration of the bicentennial of the Constitution of the United States. Haas specifically recruited authors who were closely identified with the new research.

24. Even as the New Louisiana History emerged, work of a more traditional nature continued to reach print. E.g., Jerah Johnson, "La Coutume de Paris: Louisiana's First Law," *Louisiana History* 30 (1989): 145–55; Gilbert C. Din, "The Offices and Functions of the New Orleans Cabildo," *Louisiana History* 37 (1996): 5–31, and John E. Harkins, *The New Orleans Cabildo: Colonial Louisiana's First City Government, 1769–1803* (Baton Rouge, 1996).

Downer Pritchett consider the impact of the printed word on the evolution of Louisiana law. Unlike the proponents of the conflict-of-cultures thesis, the three authors probe a wider realm of published authorities by moving past mere analyses of digests and codes to identify the books on which lawyers and judges relied, to gauge their content, and to assess their impression on Louisiana law and its practice. These imaginative approaches not only provide the first works of their kind on Louisiana, but they also serve to bind this aspect of Louisiana's legal heritage both to the New Legal History and to recent scholarship on the history of the book.[25]

Billings posits a subtle relationship between thought and action, showing how it applied to legal education in Louisiana. He draws notice to an 1840 rule of the Supreme Court of Louisiana that created a reading list for all prospective candidates for the bar. That "course of legal studies," he demonstrates, remained the very basis of legal learning in the state for nearly eight decades. Then he considers the content and context of those works, concluding that the syllabus fostered a mixed jurisdiction, that it reflected national legal reforms, and that law books form the core of Louisiana's legal heritage. Billings's essay therefore combines intellectual history with the history of the book as it explores the origins, nature, content, and application of the primary texts that defined the state's legal discourse.

Florence M. Jumonville casts her piece along similar lines. In it, she assesses the economic and civic implications of legal publishing during the territorial and antebellum periods. The discussion of government and in-

---

25. Warren M. Billings, "Edward Douglass White: Louisiana's Chief Justice and the American Legal Tradition," *Louisiana Bar Journal* 85 (1991): 74–80; Billings, "The Supreme Court of Louisiana and the Administration of Justice, 1813–1995," *Louisiana History* 35 (1996): 389–405; Billings, "A Neglected Treatise: Lewis Kerr's *Exposition* and the Making of Criminal Law in Louisiana," *Louisiana History* 36 (1997): 452–72; Jeannine Douglas, "Steamboats and Slaves: Issues of Liability in Louisiana, 1831–1861" (M.A. thesis, University of New Orleans, 1991); Robert Feikema Karachuk, "A Lawyer's Tools: The Law Library of Henry Adams Bullard," *American Journal of Legal History* 52 (1998), 160–89; Mark F. Fernandez, "The Rules of the Courts of the Territory of Orleans," *Louisiana History* 37 (1997): 63–86; Judith Kelleher Schafer, "'Details Are of the Most Revolting Character': Cruelty to Slaves as Seen in Appeals to the Supreme Court of Louisiana," *Chicago-Kent Review* 68 (1993): 1283–1340; Schafer, "Roman Roots of Louisiana's Law of Slavery: Emancipation in Louisiana, 1803–1857," *Louisiana Law Review* (forthcoming); Schafer, "'Under the Present Mode of Trial, Improper Verdicts Are Very Often Given': Criminal Procedure in the Trials of Slaves in Antebellum Louisiana," *Cardozo Law Review* (forthcoming).

dependent printers offers an important look into the mechanics of legal publishing in a southern metropolis. Her conclusion that the productions of New Orleans printeries constituted indispensable elements of democracy available to the bench, bar, and the public affords instruction about the very nature of the interpretation of American democracy in the nineteenth century. Jumonville likewise traces the printers' role in the "slow but deliberate" goal of instituting American jurisprudence in Louisiana. Thus, her essay represents an outstanding illustration of the techniques of the New Louisiana Legal History and its intellectual ties to the history of the book.

Carla Downer Pritchett complements Jumonville's work by drawing notice to important but heretofore neglected legal publishers, the state's reporters of court decisions. Pritchett looks at the backgrounds and activities of these individuals and presents them as an independent, professional lot who strove for accuracy and thoroughness in their reportage. She ties their efforts to a growing professionalism of the bench and bar that was characteristic not only of antebellum Louisiana but of the South and the nation as a whole. Her essay concludes with an assessment of how the reporters shaped the state's legal development.

In Part II, essays by Mark F. Fernandez, Sheridan E. Young, and Thomas W. Helis assess how judges and courts fashioned the legal order. Fernandez's "Local Justice in the Territory of Orleans: W. C. C. Claiborne's Courts, Judges, and Justices of the Peace" analyzes Claiborne's role in the making of the courts, the types of courts created, and the social origins of the men who sat on the respective benches. Fernandez concludes that the creation of the judiciary in the territorial period represented a concerted and successful effort by President Thomas Jefferson and Governor Claiborne to mold Louisiana along American lines. Although Fernandez acknowledges creole influence and civilian heritage, he contends that the so-called Creole-American conflict actually had little impact on the formation of the territorial judiciary because American lawyers, judges, and lay magistrates dominated legal and political offices. He thus exemplifies both the New Louisiana Legal History's innate revisionism and its relationship to wider contemporary historiographical trends. That essay joins previously published articles by Young and Helis on the Court of Errors and Appeals, which existed briefly during the 1840s, and the military courts in Union-occupied New Orleans.

Finally, in Part III, the influence of the social history on Louisiana's legal scholars becomes evident in the essays by Judith Kelleher Schafer, Kathryn Page, and Ellen Holmes Pearson. In those essays the use of legal documents to study the history of slavery and race is readily apparent. Thus, all three essays illustrate the part that the New Louisiana Legal Historians are playing in recasting the social history of antebellum Louisiana. For example, in "'Forever Free from the Bonds of Slavery': Emancipation in New Orleans, 1855–1857," Schafer investigates the causes and consequences of the flurry of emancipation cases in the New Orleans district courts during a two-year period just before the Civil War. Using heretofore neglected district court case files, she describes in detail how over a two-year period slaves in the Crescent City sued for their liberty and invariably won freedom in what seemed a pro forma hearing where the outcome was never in doubt. The legislature abruptly closed this extraordinary avenue to freedom and even went so far as to pass a law allowing free individuals to put themselves back into bondage. The essay invites comparisons with other parishes in Louisiana and the rest of the South as well.

Kathryn Page's "Defiant Women and the Supreme Court of Louisiana in the Nineteenth Century" showcases Antoinette Boullard, Fannie Roos, and Josephine Decuir—Louisianians who used the courts to attack society's conventions and nineteenth-century attitudes toward gender. The essay not only rescues three remarkable individuals from historical obscurity, but it also is suggestive of the many opportunities for investigating legal issues pertinent to the place of women in Louisiana society that cry out for examination.

Last, but by no means least, Ellen Holmes Pearson addresses the important question of the legal status of free people of color in antebellum New Orleans. She draws on the manuscript records of the Supreme Court of Louisiana to modify a traditional interpretation. No "slaves without masters," Pearson's free people inhabited an extraordinary "middle ground." Lodged somewhere between full freedom and abject slavery, they maintained legal rights to property and many liberties, which gained them a measure of personal and financial independence, including, curiously, the right to enslave themselves. Such privileges, of course, vanished with the onset of the Civil War, and this third class came to be lumped with former slaves.

These essays mark a coming of age for the New Louisiana Legal History. Several years ago historian Kermit L. Hall, at a meeting of the Society for Historians of the Early American Republic, raised the issue of where to go next. Hall rightly observed that the new enquiry was still in a "descriptive phase." Hall meant that the New Louisiana Legal Historians were as yet tackling merely some of the most basic questions. What was the bar like? What were the courts like? What was the jurisdiction of the courts? The substantive law? At the time, Hall urged a continuation of these endeavors. Now that much of that work is accomplished, it is again time to consider wider and more ambitious projects.

The first step should be an internal criticism of the New Louisiana Legal History. How well have its proponents risen to Billings's challenge? In developing new methods and using neglected sources, the response has been rather impressive. In tying the discipline into the rest of southern and American history, the focus on the similarities between Louisiana and the rest of the country have been profound. In integrating Louisiana legal history into the mainstream of American legal historiography, however, there has been only modest success. Schafer's and Fernandez's treatments of slavery and local courts point in that direction. So do Billings's, Jumonville's and McKnight's studies of legal texts. Viator's as yet unpublished work on torts has questioned the famous Horwitz transformation thesis that argues that American law underwent a profound transformation between the American Revolution and the Civil War, a transformation from a legal system that favored agrarian interests to one that facilitated capitalism. In tort law, this shift represented a movement from strict liability to negligence as the standard. Viator concluded that in nineteenth-century Louisiana, tort actions generally focused on fault as a deciding factor, thus precluding a Horwitz-style transformation. Insofar as tort law is concerned, then, Louisiana's law meshes with that of other southern states, and Viator's findings with those of other legal scholars who have attacked the Horwitz thesis. Consequently, these studies have not broken down the barriers that have made Louisiana appear too colloquial to outside scholars. That said, it is high time that historians move on from the attempt to make Louisiana seem "normal" to outside scholars and to consider glaring needs in certain crucial areas of research.[26]

Greater consideration needs to be given to the interplay between issues of personality and social organization. Study of the Louisiana bar has all but been abandoned, and it is therefore imperative that someone pick up where Elizabeth Gaspard left off. The social, cultural, economic, and political connections of the bench and bar also beg for careful scrutiny. How did the state's lawyers and judges interact with political cabals, family dynasties, and public and private boosters? To which charitable organizations did they belong? How did they respond to state, regional, and national issues of the past two centuries?

Moreover, Louisiana needs to be compared against other jurisdictions. Its southwestern heritage deserves serious attention. And the connections between pre– and post–Civil War legal developments require more careful exploration.

There must be a widening of the definition of "legal history"—akin to what Schafer, Page, and Pearson have done in the area of social history— one that applies legal history methods to enquiries of politics, culture, ideas, race, and ethnicity. In this regard, the study of legal institutions other than courts is surely vital. The legislature, its committees, and its leadership all await rigorous investigation. So do the various bar associations that have existed from the 1840s to the present. Independent regulatory bodies that sprang up in response to Progressive Era reforms and the rise of the administrative state also merit close consideration. Indeed, twentieth-century legal developments of every sort remain terra incognita.

Louisiana legal historians must also eye opportunities to engage the public at large, but that is no easy undertaking, given the technical complexities of their subject. The first task is to gain a wider audience by rendering the New Louisiana Legal History more accessible to general audiences. Natural opportunities for doing just that will present themselves over the next several decades. In the coming decade, Louisianians will mark the bicentenary of the Purchase, whereas in 2013, the courts will celebrate the two-hundredth anniversary of their creation. It is crucial to

26. Morton J. Horwitz, *The Transformation of American Law, 1780–1860* (Cambridge, Mass., 1977); Viator, "Tort Law in Early Louisiana."

capitalize on these commemorations in order to make the people of the state more aware of these events and how history shaped Louisiana's uncommon legal heritage.

In the end, New Louisiana Legal Historians must remain lively. We must recruit new members to our ranks. We must build on the solid work that we have commenced here and elsewhere. We must keep step with methodological advances in our fields. We must maintain high levels of integrity and activity. And most of all, we must join with our fellow historians elsewhere in the abiding quest for a usable past that makes our common endeavor a model example of liberal learning at its best.

Part I

BOOKS AND THE LAW

As the volume professes to be a guide, it like [the lawyer's] dictionary, or any other vade mecum, should constantly be on his table—not only for occasional consultation during the progress of his studies, but that many portions of it may be carefully read, in advance of his studies; so that by frequent reference, and deliberate reading, the entire volume may become, in time perfectly familiar to him.

> David Hoffman, *A Course of Legal Study, Addressed to Students and the Profession Generally* (Baltimore, 1836), 1: xiii

The crime of "Murder" therefore presents itself first to our consideration. But that the reader may be better enabled to understand the precise nature of this offense, contra-distinguished from others of a like nature which fall short of it, it seems necessary to premise with a short elucidation of Homicide in general.

> Lewis Kerr, comp., *An Exposition of the Criminal Laws of the Territory of Orleans* (New Orleans, 1805), 10

At all events, a knowledge of the decisions of the court will tend to the introduction of more order and regularity in practice, and uniformity in determinations.

> François-Xavier Martin, comp., *Orleans Term Reports, of Cases Argued and Determined in the Superior Court of the Territory of Orleans* (New Orleans, 1811), viii.

Law is a book-specific discipline. That is to say, books of one form or another were the means by which to organize and find legal knowledge from the dawn of the written word to the advent of the electronic information revolution. The perfection of moveable type and printing presses in the fifteenth century soon made law books staple fare as printers and booksellers struggled to keep pace with rising demand. Law books were among the many items that European settlers had shipped to the colonies, and the content of those volumes abetted the rise of legal institutions throughout the Americas. The ideas regarding the constitution of polities, the rights of individuals, and the nature of sovereignty inspired certain British colonists to rebel and to create the United States. Severing the bonds between England and the upstart nation set judges, lawyers, legislators, and literate citizens off in search of ways to separate American law from its English antecedent. From the Revolution to the Civil War, their quest for legal independence generated an immense variety of legal texts, the dissemination of which was abetted by improvements in printing presses, more abundant raw materials for book-making, and expanding national markets. This proliferation, with its reliance on technological innovation and its impression on legal thought and practice, has yet to be appreciated in the fullness of its proportions or the magnitude of its significance. The three essays that ensue highlight the formative impact of books on Louisiana law even as they intimate lines of enquiry that may fruitfully be followed elsewhere.

I   *Warren M. Billings*

A COURSE OF LEGAL STUDIES

Books That Shaped
Louisiana Law

Relationships between thoughts and actions make lively topics of historical conversation. No one denies the existence of connections between specific ideas and particular acts, but pinpointing them is often difficult because the links are seldom clear-cut. Occasionally, however, a tie may be
fixed with clarity and precision. Such is the case with books that shaped
the legal culture of antebellum Louisiana.[1]

In 1840 the Supreme Court of Louisiana issued a rule that set new
standards for all who aspired to the practice of law in the state. "The
Court," according to the rule,

> will not be satisfied with the qualification of a Candidate in point of
> legal learning unless it shall appear by Examination that he is well
> read in the following Course of Studies at least—Vattel's law of
> Nations, the Louisiana Code, The Code of Practice, The Statutes of
> the State, of a general nature, The Institutes of Justinian, Domat's

1. E.g., H. Trevor Colbourn, *The Lamp of Experience: Whig History and the Intellectual Origins of
the American Revolution* (Chapel Hill, 1965); Charles M. Cook, *The American Codification Movement*
(Westport, Conn., 1981), 3–69.

Civil laws, Pothier's Treatise on Obligations, Blackstone's Commentaries, Kent's Commentaries, Chitty or Bayley on bills, Starkie
or Phillips on evidence, Russell on Crimes, and the Jurisprudence of
Louisiana as settled by decisions of the Supreme Court.

Therefore, unless a prospective lawyer could demonstrate his mastery of
these works, he could neither pass the bar examination nor be licensed to
practice. The required texts thus influenced the way attorneys and judges
in Louisiana thought about law as they met the social, political, and economic issues of their time. In that way, then, the volumes contributed directly to fashioning the state's legal order in its formative period. The reasons that moved the court to select these particular works, their content,
and their impact are the subjects of this essay.[2]

Antebellum Americans were an unruly people. Nevertheless, they admired things legal. Their law ordained rules of civilized conduct, but it sig-
nified more to them than the mere definition of social behavior. It expressed
fundamental human liberties that their forebears had won so dearly at the
birth of the republic and protected so ingeniously with the greatest of legal
documents, the federal Constitution. Belief in the rule of law was their constant affirmation of their republican virtue. Alexis de Tocqueville, that
acute observer of the United States, caught the importance of values such as
these when he commented on the American affection for law. "The language of the law," he noted, "[became] . . . a vulgar tongue; its spirit . . . [de-
scended] to the lowest classes, so that at the last the whole people [con-
tracted] the habits and the tastes of the judicial magistrate."[3]

Lawyers and judges therefore stood high in the esteem of their contemporaries, so much so that Tocqueville styled the bench and bar the
"American aristocracy." Aristocratic or not, the legal profession drew
thousands of ambitious individuals irrespective of their social origins, in
part because the credentials demanded of a would-be attorney were modest. Attractive too were the political and financial rewards of a legal career, which were quite considerable and singularly opportune in frontier
regions such as Louisiana. George Strawbridge, a Marylander whose

2. Warren M. Billings, ed., *The Historic Rules of the Supreme Court of Louisiana, 1813–1879*
(Lafayette, La., 1985), 9–11, 39.

3. Alexis de Tocqueville, *Democracy in America,* trans. Henry Reeve, 2 vols. (New York, 1954), 1: 290.

failed business caused him to emigrate south soon after the War of 1812, explained the lure of the Pelican State for his kind. "I was," he wrote in his memoirs, "utterly bankrupt. I saw but one resource for my bread, that was the Law which required no capital, and I was determined it should be on new ground." New ground certainly proved rewarding for Strawbridge. He parlayed his "one resource" into a lucrative career as one of the first railroad attorneys in New Orleans and a seat on the supreme court. In short, lawyering in Louisiana, as elsewhere, was among the most accessible and the most desirable of callings in a society whose members prized it because of its abundant opportunities for upward mobility.[4]

Despite their admiration for law and lawyers, antebellum Americans were not uncritical of either. They castigated the one as hopelessly complicated, if not greatly inappropriate to the requirements of a republic, while they censured the others for their lack of learning and for their cunning. On their part, republican lawyers acknowledged the weaknesses in legal education, just as they recognized the law's lack of rational organizing principles akin to those espoused by Jeremy Bentham or those inhering in civil law systems. They likewise decried the English influences on the content of American law, even as they debated their continued indebtedness to British common law. Besides these issues, Louisianians disputed the extent to which their civilian legal customs must meld with the American ways that came with the Purchase and statehood, a discourse that simmered until the 1840s.[5]

4. Ibid., 1: 288; Billings, ed., *Historic Rules,* 1–2; George Strawbridge, "Memoirs of George Strawbridge (1784–1859): Of the Class of 1802 in Princeton University," typescript, 57, Manuscripts Department, Firestone Library, Princeton University, Princeton, N.J. The political rewards of a legal career were considerable. See Donald R. Mathews, "United States Senators and the Class Structure," *Public Opinion Quarterly* 17 (1954): 5–22. Mathews showed that 95 percent of senators in the 1840s had legal training. Gary Nash presented similar findings for Philadelphia ("The Philadelphia Bench and Bar, 1800–1861," *Comparative Studies in Society and History* 7 [1964–65]: 203–20). No comparable studies exist at present for Louisiana.

5. John William Ward, *Andrew Jackson: Symbol for an Age* (New York, 1955), 46–78; Cook, *American Codification Movement,* 69–95; Charles E. Fenner, "The Civil Code of Louisiana as a Democratic Institution," in *Proceedings of the Louisiana Bar Association, 1904* (New Orleans, 1904), 10–3; George Dargo, *Jefferson's Louisiana: Politics and the Clash of Legal Traditions* (Cambridge, Mass., 1975), passim; Richard Holcombe Kilbourne, Jr., *A History of the Louisiana Civil Code, The Formative Years, 1803–1839* (Baton Rouge, 1987), passim; Warren M. Billings, "Confessions of a Court Historian," *Louisiana History* 35 (1994): 261–71.

An obvious solution, all agreed, lay in a refashioning of American law and practice. The quest for remedies became part and parcel of the era of reform that swept the nation in the decades before the Civil War, a search to which the Supreme Court of Louisiana was no stranger. Indeed, the re-formulation of state law commenced the very day the judges first opened their doors to business in 1813. To them fell not only the task of improving the education of the state's lawyers but also the far thornier matter of combining American, French, Spanish, and English legal customs into a workable jurisprudence. Their rule of 1840 was a milestone along the route to the resolution of both problems.[6]

During the first quarter century of its existence, the supreme court consisted of but three members. They tried appeals in New Orleans and rode circuit throughout the remainder of the state, which comprised a western appellate district. Control of admissions to the Louisiana bar, a charge mandated by both the Constitution of 1812 and the Judiciary Act of 1813, was also theirs. These were large responsibilities that got larger as the years passed, but the judges could count on no staff for help in dis-charging them. Law clerks, who now assist in research and opinion draft-ing, were an as yet unheard-of luxury, as were the staff attorneys and ad-ministrators who now move the court's business along in a timely fashion. Instead, there was merely a clerk of court, his deputy, and several scriveners whose primary purpose was to keep the court's dockets and to maintain its records as law and custom then required.[7]

François-Xavier Martin and Henry Adams Bullard, of all the antebel-lum high court judges, left the most visible mark on the state's emerging legal culture. A Frenchman transplanted to Louisiana by way of Mar-tinique and North Carolina, Martin joined the court in 1815 and stayed for thirty-five years. He came to his judicial duties with a solid reputation

6. I refer to members of the court as "judges" rather than "justices" throughout this essay because the latter designation did not come into use until after 1845. The Constitution of 1845 created the of-fices of chief justice and associate justice (Judith Kelleher Schafer, "Reform or Experiment: The Constitution of 1845," in Warren M. Billings and Edward F. Haas, eds., *In Search of Fundamental Law: Louisiana's Constitutions, 1812–1974* [Lafayette, La., 1993], 32–3).

7. Constitution of 1812, art. 4, secs. 1–3; "An Act to Organize the Supreme Court of the State of Louisiana, and to Establish Inferior Courts of Jurisdiction," 1812 La. Acts 18–34. The assignment of the responsibility of admitting lawyers to state supreme courts traced its origins to the eighteenth cen-tury when British colonial governors and their councils of state controlled admissions to the bar (e.g., Frank Dewey, *Thomas Jefferson, Lawyer* [Charlottesville, Va., 1986], chapter 1).

as someone skilled in both civil and common law, in printing, in historical enquiry, and in legal scholarship. Bullard, by contrast, was a Massachusetts native. He studied at Harvard and practiced law in Philadelphia before settling in Natchitoches and starting his legal career anew. A vacancy caused by the resignation of Judge Alexander Porter in 1834 led to his appointment to the court. Temperamentally, both men inclined toward the task of improving the training of lawyers. Martin compiled the first series of the state's law reports and an early digest of the statutes. Bullard actually taught students, which eventually led him to a law professorship at the University of Louisiana—the forerunner of Tulane Law School.[8]

In background and reputation, Bullard and Martin also typified their colleagues on the court. All were immigrant lawyers, some of whom came to Louisiana already well-versed in American, British, and civil law. They were alert to the changing needs of their calling, and they were generally men of broad learning and superior intellect. In those respects they differed markedly from other frontier jurists whose backgrounds came closer to that of their contemporary Justice Thomas C. Browne of Illinois, whom a tart-tongued wag depicted as lacking in "legal education or training which could fit him to be a judge of the Supreme Court." Although the remark may not have applied equally to all western high court jurists of that era, the acerbic barb did not miss Browne by much because the Illinoisan never once wrote an opinion in his entire thirty-one-year tenure as a justice.[9]

8. For a list of the members of the court, see Billings, ed., *Historic Rules,* Appendix I. On the origins of law schools in Louisiana, see Lamar C. Quintero, "The Law School of the Tulane University of Louisiana," *Green Bag* 2 (1890): 116–24; Paul Brosman, "The First Hundred Years," *Tulane Law Review* 22 (1947): 543–6. Neither Martin nor Bullard has a modern biographer. For Martin, see Henry Adams Bullard, *A Discourse on the Life and Character of the Hon. François-Xavier Martin* (New Orleans, 1847); William Wirt Howe, introduction to François-Xavier Martin, *The History of Louisiana from the Earliest Period,* ed. James Gresham (New Orleans, 1882), vii–xxxviii; R. Don Higginbotham, "François-Xavier Martin's History of North Carolina," in Lawrence H. Leder, ed., *The Colonial Legacy* (New York, 1973), 4: 265–82; Warren M. Billings, "A Judicial Legacy: The Last Will and Testament of François-Xavier Martin," *Louisiana History* 25 (1984): 277–89; Michael Chiorazzi, "François-Xavier Martin: Printer, Lawyer, Jurist," *Law Library Journal* 80 (1988): 63–95. For Bullard, see Dora J. Bonquois, "The Career of Henry Adams Bullard," *Louisiana Historical Quarterly* 22 (1940): 999–1106; and Robert Feikema Karachuk, "A Workman's Tools: The Law Library of Henry Adams Bullard" (M.A. thesis, University of New Orleans, 1996), 1–23.

9. Henry J. Leovy, "The Ante-bellum Bench and Bar," in *Proceedings of the Louisiana Bar Association, 1899–1900* (New Orleans, 1900), 10–27; Willard L. King, "A Pioneer Court of Last Resort," *Illinois Review* 20 (1925–26): 573–83.

Background aside, Browne and his Louisiana counterparts shared at least one common attribute. Their control of bar admissions entailed on them a responsibility for establishing the educational requirements for prospective practitioners. Down to 1840, a good name; an apprenticeship in a law office; a college diploma, or a license from another state; fluency in English; and a satisfactory performance on an oral examination sufficed as qualifications for a lawyer's license in Louisiana. Those were not especially stringent expectations, even when measured by the lax standards of the times, but academic rigor was not among the primary concerns of the judges who drew them up in 1813. The requirements were intended first to ease the passage to statehood by certifying lawyers who had been admitted to practice in the territorial courts, and then to assure a regular supply of attorneys thereafter.[10]

Consequently, the number of candidates passed by the court grew rapidly after Louisiana became a state. More aspirants to the bar soon added to the judges' workload, which increased each year between 1813 and 1840. To be sure, the rise in volume resulted from the greater quantity of litigation that was an inevitable consequence of Louisiana's growth, but it was also directly related to the court's structure and to how the judges quizzed the applicants. Nothing in the court's regulations governed the scheduling of examinations, and so candidates took them whenever the court sat. Testing followed no set regime, apart from being oral. There were no means of screening out the unprepared. Neither was there method to the questions or the responses, and like oral arguments of the day, both tended to spin out until someone tired of the exchange. All of which meant that the judges had to balance their time to accommodate litigants and would-be attorneys alike.

Increasingly, that feat became difficult to manage. As of the 1830s, the three-judge court had fallen so far behind in its work that it could scarcely

10. Henry Toulmin, comp., *Digest of the Laws of Alabama* (Cahawaba, Ala., 1832), 26; S. B. Rose, "The Supreme Court of Arkansas," *Green Bag* 4 (1892): 417–31; Walter B. Hill, "The Supreme Court of Georgia," *Green Bag* 4 (1892): 18–31, 65–79; L.C. Krauthoff, "The Supreme Court of Missouri," *Green Bag* 3 (1891): 166; *Revised Code of Mississippi* (Natchez, 1824), 244; "Report of the Committee on Legal Education," in *Report of the Fourteenth Annual Meeting of the American Bar Association* (Boston, 1891), 301–60; Billings, ed., *Historic Rules,* 1–2, 4–5; Warren M. Billings, "The Supreme Court and the Education of Louisiana Lawyers," *Louisiana Bar Journal* 33 (1985): 74–80; Elizabeth Gaspard, "The Rise of the Louisiana Bar: The Early Years," *Louisiana History* 28 (1987): 2.

keep its dockets current. The legislature tried to ease the situation in 1839, when it created two additional judgeships, but even that reform failed to stem the tide. During the first nine months of 1840, for example, the expanded court admitted fifty-eight new attorneys in New Orleans, plus an undetermined number for the western appellate circuit. Confronted with a problem of such awkward dimensions, and led by Martin and Bullard, the court took matters in hand when it revised its control of the bar. The change was embodied in the rule of 1840, which contained the "Course of Studies" as its most significant part.[11]

If there were a single influence that informed the thinking of Martin and Bullard, as they and their colleagues drafted the course, it was the writing of David Hoffman (1784–1854). Now his name is no longer even a scant memory, but in his day his contemporaries esteemed Hoffman for his contributions to law reform and legal education. A Baltimorean, he attended St. John's College in Annapolis before studying civil law at the University of Göttingen and becoming the first professor of law at the University of Maryland. His exposure to civilian legal doctrines influenced his lectures as well as his published writings, which enjoyed wide currency in professional circles across America.[12]

Hoffman's principal work, *A Course of Legal Study, Addressed to Students and the Profession Generally,* first published at Baltimore in 1817, was designed to "produce a learned and accomplished lawyer; and, perhaps, we may say to aid the researches of the Counsellor, the Judge, and the Statesman." Toward those ends, Hoffman divided the course into thirteen parts, each of which he commented on at length, and to which he appended an extensive syllabus of appropriate readings. Together, Hoffman's commentary and the recommended books covered the entirety of

11. "An Act to Increase the Number of Judges of the Supreme Court of Louisiana," 1839 La. Acts 1. In making the addition, the legislature merely followed a constitutional mandate that permitted the court as many as five members. The number of bar admissions comes from the court minute books that are among the archives on deposit with the Department of Manuscripts and Special Collections in the Earl K. Long Library at the University of New Orleans. That is a deceptive figure because it accounts for only the successful applicants. Clerks did not tally those who failed the test. Because the records from the sessions of the western appellate circuit are lost, it is impossible to identify the attorneys admitted outside of New Orleans.

12. *Dictionary of American Biography,* s.v. "Hoffman, David." Anton-Herman Chroust was among the few late-twentieth-century scholars who recognized Hoffman's contributions: Chroust, *The Rise of the Legal Profession in America* (Norman, Okla., 1965), 2: 31–2, 55–6, 202–5.

the substantive law. He supplemented his "titles," as he styled them, with nine practical "auxiliary subjects," which ranged from American history to oratory to professional deportment. In toto, Hoffman envisioned a rounded curriculum that required up to seven years to complete. The book drew high praise from Justice Joseph Story, who lauded it as "a work which enables young men to see the paths of legal science, and points out so many excellent instructions to guide them on their journey."[13]

Quite clearly, in the instance of Louisiana *A Course of Legal Study* also "guided" the supreme court. The judges acquired a copy of the second edition some time after its publication in 1836 and then used it as the model for their reforms to legal education.[14] Both the title of their course and its scheme represented their adaptations of the plan of instruction Hoffman had set forth in his treatise.[15]

Common opinions attracted Martin and Bullard to Hoffman; Martin had a personal acquaintance as well. All three were legal polytheists. That is, they envisioned law as a diverse collection of precepts and regulations, the whole of which governed all human conduct. The product of multiple sources, law could be arrayed into a logical system that gave an ordered meaning to life in Louisiana. Those views coincided with the ideas of Hoffman, who conceived of law as the highest expression of the wisdom of the ages and the very epitome of reason itself. Coeval with the origins of civilization, law, he taught, derived from more than the unique inspirations of one people, or one place, or one epic moment in history. It gathered from the sum of human experience; it changed slowly, and when modifications occurred the inexorable direction was toward greater opportunity and more freedom for the individual. Its manifestation in the United States exemplified the expression of general legal principles in peculiarly American settings. Common law and civil law did not rival one another. To Hoff-

---

13. David Hoffman, *A Course of Legal Study: Addressed to Students and the Profession Generally,* 2d ed. (Baltimore, 1836), 1: 45–6, 2: 826–43; Joseph Story, "Hoffman's Course of Legal Study," *North American Review* 7 (1817): 77; "Hoffman's Course of Legal Studies," *American Jurist* 15 (1836): 341–2. Hoffman dedicated the second edition to Judge Story.

14. That copy is still in the Law Library of Louisiana, which is housed at the supreme court building in New Orleans. I am indebted to the director, Carol D. Billings, who first drew my attention to the fact that the book was in the library collection.

15. Hoffman, *Course of Legal Study,* Table of Contents.

man, as to Bullard and Martin, they were complementary facets of a prized legal gemstone, each to be cherished with equal reverence.[16]

Learning the jewel's intricacies demanded knowledge that was broad and deep. With such understanding would come a sounder cadre of attorneys, better control of the state bar, and more settled legal institutions. Without it the question of what was law in Louisiana would continue to vex, while lawyers would remain ofttimes knavish fools and sometimes mindless pettifoggers who did more ill than good. In framing their curriculum, then, Martin and Bullard intended a remedy that strengthened the training of lawyers even as it furthered the rationalization of Anglo-American and continental legal customs into a distinctly mixed jurisdiction. Their prescription consisted of a syllabus of books that drew equal measures of inspiration from English, American, and continental European sources, much as Hoffman had done. Taken together the readings provided students with what the judges regarded as a comprehensive view of state law.

An introduction to the fundamental axioms of Louisiana law was based on assignments in Sir William Blackstone's *Commentaries on the Laws of England,*[17] Chancellor James Kent's *Commentaries on American Law,*[18] Robert Pothier's *Treatise on Obligations Considered from a Moral and Legal View,*[19] Jean Domat's *Civil Law in Its Natural Order,*[20] and Thomas

16. Ibid., 1: 55–6. The disappearance of Martin's, Bullard's, and Hoffman's papers precludes the establishment of direct personal links between the three men. Clearly, they knew one another by reputation. Hoffman, for instance, cited Martin's translation of Robert Pothier's work on obligations, noting that it was the first English rendition (ibid., 2: 540n). That the court owned Hoffman's treatise argues unequivocally that Martin and Bullard certainly knew about the Marylander. On Martin's relationship to Story, see Martin to Josiah Quincy, 18 December 1841, College Papers, 2d Ser, X (1838–42), Harvard University Archives, Cambridge, Mass. I am indebted to Alan Diefenbach of the Harvard Law Library for his assistance in tracking down the latter item.

17. Sir William Blackstone, *Commentaries on the Laws of England.* The court's copy, a first edition, is in the rare book collection of the Law Library of Louisiana.

18. James Kent, *Commentaries on American Law.* Four volumes, first edition, 1826–30, and many thereafter. The court's copy is missing.

19. Robert Pothier, *A Treatise on Obligations Considered from a Moral and Legal View.* First published in Paris in 1722; first American edition printed at New Bern, N.C., in 1802 by François-Xavier Martin. The Martin edition is now rare, but a copy is in the Law Library of Louisiana.

20. Jean Domat, *The Civil Law in Its Natural Order.* First English edition, translated by William Strahan and published in folio at London in 1722. The Strahan translation, albeit in later editions,

Cooper's English rendition of *The Institutes of Justinian.*[21] Although long dead by 1840, Blackstone was still esteemed as the premier "modern" authority on the sources of English law, which made the *Commentaries on the Laws of England* a basic text. First published at Oxford in 1765, the book went through numerous editions on both sides of the Atlantic, and by 1840 lawyers in Louisiana, as elsewhere in the United States, relied primarily on those printings that incorporated American practices.

Kent's contemporaries hailed the chancellor as America's Blackstone. Born in New York in 1763, he had a noteworthy career as a lawyer and jurist. An enforced retirement provided the opportunity to write, and the result was his *Commentaries.*[22] Kent's exposition, like Sir William's, exhibited a sure-handed mastery of its subject. Although the New Yorker lacked the Englishman's gift of phrase, his prose was nonetheless clear and commonsensible in its approach. He exhibited a pragmatic shrewdness and an aversion to slavish dependence on English precedents that appealed to readers of his generation.[23]

Civilians deemed the writings of Pothier, Domat, and Justinian as crucial to any understanding of their ways. Justinian was the great codifier, who gave method, arrangement, and ornament to the ancient Roman precepts on which all subsequent civil law systems rested. Indeed, the *Institutes* was, and remains, one of the signal documents of the Western legal tradition. The Cooper rendition had an especial appeal in America. Not only was its translator, Dr. Cooper, a Charlestonian, but he incorporated American precedents into the copious notes that accompanied the text.[24] Requiring Domat's work acknowledged Louisiana's indebtedness to French legal influences, but its inclusion also spoke to an Anglo-American interest in civilian methodology that reached back to the 1720s, when William Strahan brought out the first, and best, English translation

---

was almost universally used in Louisiana and elsewhere. A copy, published by Little-Brown & Co. (Boston, 1850) that belonged to Chief Justice George Eustis is now in the rare book collection of the Law Library of Louisiana.

21. Thomas Cooper, *The Institutes of Justinian,* 2d ed. (New York, 1841). First edition, Philadelphia, 1812, and subsequent printings. A copy of the first edition is in the Law Library of Louisiana.

22. Kent served as chancellor of New York for ten years. State law required judges to retire from the bench once they reached the age of sixty, which Kent did in 1823, and he therefore left the bench.

23. *Dictionary of American Biography*, s.v. "Kent, James."

24. Cooper, *Institutes of Justinian,* passim.

of Domat.[25] Pothier's volume was recognized as the premier enquiry into the ethical bases of contractual obligations. Furthermore, the preferred English version was the edition Judge Martin had translated, published, and sold during his days as a printer in New Bern, North Carolina.[26]

Students next had to master specific branches of law. Of these none was greater in importance than the governance of persons and things, for it was in these twin realms of private law that Louisianians departed from the rest of the nation. Private law was grounded in French and Spanish customs, and here was where the mark of civilian traditions pressed deepest. Territorial redactors had gathered up those customs and published them in 1808 as *A Digest of the Civil Laws of the Territory of Orleans, with Alterations and Amendments to Its Present System of Government.*[27] The state legislature gave them fuller point after 1825, when it enacted the *Civil Code of the State of Louisiana*[28] and its concomitant *Code of Practice in Civil Cases for the State of Louisiana.*[29] Thus, while students were expected to know the relevant portions of Blackstone, Kent, Justinian, Domat, and

25. For example, the General Court of Virginia acquired a set of Strahan's Domat in 1730, which is now in the rare book collection of the Virginia Historical Society. Then, too, civil law formed the basis of English ecclesiastical law and equity, as well as parts of admiralty law, and the subject was taught at the universities in Britain.

26. I edited a modern reprint in facsimile that the Law Book Exchange published at Union, N.J., in 1999.

27. Much confusion has arisen about the nature of this volume. Although the title clearly says that it was a digest—that is, a summary—of the laws believed to be in force at the time of publication, modern lawyers, judges, scholars, and others persist in referring to it as a "code," "the old civil code," or "the first civil code." Part of the misunderstanding stems from nineteenth-century usage. Lawyers and judges rather loosely employed the words "digest" and "code" interchangeably, which led later practitioners to the same habit. Beyond that, the insistence on styling the *Digest* as a code is intertwined with the cultural mythology of the origins of Louisiana law. Many Louisianians, and others, persevere in saying that the Bayou State is the only civil law jurisdiction in the country. See, for example, a recent and rather muddled rehearsal of the claim in Carol Flake, *New Orleans: Behind the Masks of America's Most Exotic City* (New York, 1994). Contrary to Flake's assertion, Texans, Californians, New Mexicans, and others in the western United States would be rather bemused to learn that they were without a civil law heritage.

28. *Civil Code of the State of Louisiana.* Published at New Orleans. A copy is in the Law Library of Louisiana.

29. *Code of Practice in Civil Cases for the State of Louisiana.* First published in 1830, the *Code of Practice* went through many editions. One that enjoyed wide usage was the 1839 edition compiled by the New Orleans attorney Wheelock S. Upton. Upton dedicated it to Judge Bullard "as a testimony of respect for his talents and an acknowledgment of the obligation which his friendship and his professional instructions have conferred on his pupil and friend."

Pothier, the major emphasis in this part of the course was the development of proficiency in branches of law that were peculiar to Louisiana. Therefore, the civil code and the code of practice were must readings.

Next came the law of crime and punishment. Its basic provisions dated to the territorial period, when, in 1805, the Legislative Council adopted *An Act for the Punishment of Crimes and Misdemeanors.* Included among the statute's many definitions of misconduct and rules of procedure was the statement that "all crimes . . . shall be taken, intended, and construed according to the . . . common law of England." Subsequent legislatures embellished on these structural principles, even to the point of attempting a codification of statutes and practices, but in the main, development of the criminal law did not keep pace with those in other areas. Moreover, the supreme court refused as early as 1813 to construe its authority so as to permit it to hear criminal appeals. Attempts at reformulating conceptions of the rights of defendants were already on foot by 1840, and there was a burgeoning literature to instruct prospective lawyers in matters such as detection and theories of criminal behavior.[30]

Given these considerations, the court's syllabus contained readings in criminal law that were quite modest. Students were expected to digest Blackstone's general treatment in the fourth volume of the *Commentaries,* plus Thomas Starkie's *Practical Treatise on the Law of Evidence and Digest in Civil and Criminal Proceedings* and William Oldnall Russell's *Treatise on Crimes and Misdemeanors.* The requirement of Blackstone was predictable enough because Louisiana penal statutes were grounded specifically on the British model. On the other hand, Starkie and Russell were more modern English authorities, whose writings provided up-to-date instruction in criminal practice and procedure.[31]

Curiously, Martin, Bullard, and their colleagues overlooked a volume,

---

30. *Acts Passed at the First Session of the Legislative Council of the Territory of Orleans* (New Orleans, 1805), 416–54, 440; Warren M. Billings, "Origins of Criminal Law in Louisiana," *Louisiana History* 32 (1991): 63–77; *Laverty* v. *Duplessis,* 3 Mart. (o.s.) 52 (La. 1813); Hoffman, *Course of Legal Study,* 1: 423–4, 428–32.

31. Starkie's work first appeared in print in London in 1824, whereas Russell's came to print in 1819 (Thomas Starkie, *A Practical Treatise on the Law of Evidence, and Digest of Proofs, in Criminal Proceedings* [London, 1824]; William Oldnall Russell, *A Treatise on Crimes and Indictable Misdemeanors* [London, 1819]). The court permitted students to substitute Samuel March Phillipps, *A Treatise on the Law of Evidence* (London, 1814) for Starkie. All three volumes went through numerous American editions. The court's copies are no longer in the Law Library of Louisiana.

which from this distance seems to have had singular relevance to the education of Louisiana criminal lawyers—Lewis Kerr's *Exposition of the Criminal Laws of the Territory of Orleans: The Practice of Criminal Jurisdiction, the Duties of their Officers, With a Collection of Forms for the Use of Magistrates and Others.* Published in 1805, the *Exposition* was a commentary on the territorial crimes act, which served to acquaint Louisianians with the new statute and its underlying principles. It was the analog of the *Digest of the Civil Laws,* and in 1840 it remained the only printed treatment of its subject. The explanation for the court's ignoring the *Exposition* may lie in the fact that the judges themselves regarded criminal law lightly because they had so little background in it. Or perhaps they attached less importance to the law of crimes because the supreme court did not yet have criminal jurisdiction. They obviously expected would-be lawyers to know about the subject, so they turned to Hoffman for guidance and merely followed his dictates.[32]

Given the importance of trade and commerce to human existence in general, and to Louisiana in particular, Martin and Bullard required study of commercial and international law. Accordingly, they assigned the quintessential contemporary text on foreign relations, *The Law of Nations; or, The Principles of the Law of Nature, Applied to the Conduct and Affairs of Nations and Sovereigns,* written by the eighteenth-century Swiss scholar Emmerich Vattel. For an introduction to commercial law, they picked Joseph Chitty's *Practical Treatise on Bills of Exchange, Checks on Banks, Promissory Notes, Bankers Cash Notes and Bank Notes,* which was prized for its direct approach to its subject.[33]

Instruction in statutory and constitutional law rounded off the syllabus. Here Bullard and Martin demanded readings from state and fed-

32. Lewis Kerr, comp., *An Exposition of the Criminal Laws of the Territory of Orleans: The Practice of Criminal Jurisdiction, the Duties of their Officers, With a Collection of Forms for the Use of Magistrates and Others* (1805; reprint, Holmes Beach, Fla.: Wm. W. Gaunt & Sons, 1986). On Kerr and his work, see Warren M. Billings, "A Neglected Treatise: Lewis Kerr's *Exposition* and the Making of Criminal Law in Louisiana" *Louisiana History* 38 (1997): 261–87. The *Exposition* is now an extraordinarily rare item, and its rarity perhaps explains why modern students have neglected to consider its place in Louisiana legal history.

33. Emmerich Vattel, *The Law of Nations; or, The Principles of the Law of Nature, Applied to the Conduct and Affairs of Nations and Sovereigns* (London, 1793). This is the second English edition, which I own and use. The first English edition was done in London in 1753. The original French edition was printed at Geneva in 1753. The first American printing of the *Practical Treatise* occurred in Philadelphia in 1809. Neither volume is in the court library.

eral statutes, Joseph Story's monumental *Commentaries on the Constitution of the United States,* and "the Jurisprudence of Louisiana as Settled by the decisions of the Supreme Court." Familiarity with the statutes obviously made for better lawyers, just as it revealed how the people's representatives tailored first principles to fit the specific needs of Louisiana or to mark boundaries between national and state authority. Louisiana law was also one part of a constitutional system that permitted, indeed encouraged, a diversity of jurisdictions of varied traditions. Order through heterogeneity was, after all, the presumed singular genius of American judicial institutions.[34]

Apart from an immediate impact on the regularization of legal education in the state, the supreme court's course of study had the intended result of contributing to the goal of a mixed jurisprudence. Lawyers, whether immigrant or native, had to accept the blend as a reality no longer to be disputed. Once the rule of 1840 went into effect, as it did immediately on promulgation, barristers' livelihoods depended on their mastery of the contents of the syllabus. The readings were modified in later years, but the basic scheme for the course remained intact into the twentieth century.[35]

To what extent was the course a reflection of national or regional trends in the antebellum era? At the moment an answer to the question remains tentative, owing to the absence of enquiries comparable to this one. A spot check of the practice in Virginia, Mississippi, Indiana, Michigan, and Illinois suggests that what the Louisiana judges did was unusual for its time. Nothing in the supreme court mandates from any of those states equates with the Louisiana rule. However, the course of study brought Louisiana's legal order nearer to the goals of reformers than was possible elsewhere along the existing frontier or in the long-settled regions of the country.[36]

34. Joseph Story, *Commentaries on the Constitution of the United States* (Boston, 1833). Story published his commentaries in four volumes between 1831 and 1845; Billings, ed., *Historic Rules,* 11. The Law Library of Louisiana owns a partial set of Story in a late-nineteenth-century edition.

35. Billings, ed., *Historic Rules,* 30–1; Rule XIV, 31 La. Ann. viii (1879); Rule XIV, 51 La. Ann. xxxvi (1899); Rule XVII, 136 La. xiii–xiv (1916).

36. In the case of Virginia, a rule like that in Louisiana would have been superfluous. The College of William and Mary established a chair in law as early as 1779, which Nathaniel Beverley Tucker held in 1840. Moreover, the University of Virginia and various proprietary law schools provided for-

A reason for the latter conclusion is linked to characteristics that Louisianians shared with few others of their contemporaries in 1840. No other territory began its progress toward statehood with a vibrant, century-old city already in its midst. Situated at the bottom of the great Mississippi watershed, New Orleans, with its port, its banks, its railroads, its steamboats, and its commerce, offered legal opportunities unparalleled anywhere in the frontier West. That being so, Louisiana became as a magnet for a disproportionate share of bright legal talents. Then, too, legislators in the older states could only dream of codification as the goal of law reform and could achieve its institution piecemeal, if at all. Louisianians, by contrast, had their civilian traditions, the roots of which wound back to a Franco-Hispanic rather than an English colonial past. The juxtaposition of talented individuals, differing customs, and matchless opportunities led to legal habits at once American and yet markedly Louisianian. Those habits also originated in books.

---

mal legal instruction throughout the antebellum period (W. Hamilton Bryson, *Legal Education in Virginia, 1779–1979: A Biographical Approach* [Charlottesville, 1982], 1–41). See also Benjamin Watkins Leigh to Thomas R. Johnston, 9 March 1836, ALS, Library of Virginia [formerly the Virginia State Library and Archives], Richmond; Bryson, "The Transmission of English Law to the Frontier of America," *South Atlantic Quarterly* 45 (1968): 243–62; Michael H. Harris, "The Frontier Lawyer's Library: Southern Indiana, 1800–1850, as a Test Case" *American Journal of Legal History* 16 (1972): 259–81; Elizabeth Gaspar Brown, "The Bar on a Frontier: Wayne County, Michigan," *American Journal of Legal History* 14 (1970): 136–56; Kate Wallach, "The Publication of Legal Treatises in America from 1800 to 1830," *Law Library Journal* 45 (1942): 136–48.

"THE PEOPLE'S FRIEND—THE TYRANT'S FOE"

Law-Related New Orleans
Imprints, 1803–1860

Talented individuals who contributed to the creation of Louisiana's legal culture relied on New Orleans printers to produce the law books and related materials without which neither the government nor the legal profession could have functioned. From the beginning of the territorial period, legislators realized that in a republic, disseminating information concerning government and the law was of vital importance to an informed citizenry, one which, as its knowledge and awareness increased, would be better able to make intelligent political decisions. This necessity was especially important in Louisiana, where a populace predominantly of French ancestry had little experience with self-government. The printed word, described in a motto of the New Orleans Typographical Association as "the people's friend—the tyrant's foe," was not only the best, but also virtually the only, means of reaching most of the citizenry and of expediently recording information for future reference by lawyers and courts.[1]

Government-sanctioned printing in New Orleans dated from 1764,

1. The New Orleans Typographical Association was founded in 1835 and had adopted this as one of its two mottos by 1839. The other described printing as "the art preservative of all arts." *New-Orleans Directory for 1842* (New Orleans, 1842), [92]–[93].

when Denis Braud, a merchant to whom the king of France had granted exclusive printing and bookselling privileges in Louisiana, imported the colony's first printing press. Local officials exercised complete control over Braud's output and that of his colonial successors. As Francis Baily, a visitor to Louisiana, observed in 1797,

> there is but one printing-press in this place, and that is made use of by the government only. The Spanish government is too jealous to suffer the inhabitants to have the free exercise of it; . . . you cannot even stick a paper against the wall (either to recover anything lost, or to advertise anything for sale) without its first having the signature of the governor or his secretary attached to it: and on all those little bills which are stuck up at the corners of the streets you see the word "Permitted" written by the governor or his agent.[2]

Under these conditions, printing flourished intermittently during the Spanish period, but not until the French interregnum did the press, and more than one printer, operate freely. When Thomas Jefferson bought the Louisiana Territory from France, enterprising Americans, drawn by the promise of opportunity, poured into the newly acquired territory. Numerous lawyers were among them. Arriving also were printers who, taking advantage of the abolition of the old restrictions, hastened to set up their presses.

To these pioneer printers and their colleagues fell the responsibility of providing a citizenry unaccustomed to representative government with the information necessary to make intelligent political decisions. John Mowry, who established the *Louisiana Gazette* during the summer of 1804, was aware of the importance of his role. In an early issue he wrote:

> [T]he Editor of the Louisiana Gazette, in offering to the citizens of New Orleans and Louisiana, a new vehicle of public intelligence, is not insensible of the hazard and responsibility which he incurs. . . . Where the press is free, it may, like every other benefit, become a blessing or a curse according to the use or abuse of it. In the hands of integrity, sense, patriotism, and intelligence, it may diffuse good

2. Douglas C. McMurtrie, *Early Printing in New Orleans, 1764–1810* (New Orleans, 1929), 22–4; Francis Baily, *Journal of a Tour in Unsettled Parts of North America in 1796 & 1797* (London, 1856), 313.

principles, sound morals, respect for the duties of public and private life[,] . . . instruct the Merchant, the Cultivator, and the Mechanic, inform the industrious and usefully amuse the idle. . . . In the hands of ignorance, folly, malice, or party spirit, it may poison the principles of morality and happiness, pervert the judgment and corrupt the heart, mislead by false information, and give wings to error to fly beyond the sink of her birth, deduce the affections of the Citizen from the principles of his government, misrepresent its Administration, blacken innocence, disturb the peace of private families, and make society a chaos of sedition, calumny, and malignant passions. It may, like Pandora's box, be the source of a thousand plagues.[3]

Citizens of New Orleans were fortunate that the printers of their city avoided inflicting these perils on them.

The influx of Americans resulted in political conflicts between the Orleannais and the new residents and contributed to the area's rapid cultural and economic development. These conditions, combined with the establishment of the new government and the work it would commission, sparked an increase in the quantity of business available for local printers, precisely when more men were pursuing such employment. For the first time there was competition, and enough work to sustain it.

Between the Louisiana Purchase and the Civil War, more than 150 printers set up shops in New Orleans. Twenty of them, individually or in

3. "To the Public," *Louisiana Gazette,* August 7, 1804, p. 1, col. 1; James M. Bradford, 1805 and 1826; Bradford & (Thomas) Anderson, 1806–1808; (Jean Baptiste Simon) Thierry & (John) Dacqueny, 1810; Thierry, 1811–1812 (Joseph Bartholomew) Baird & (Peter K.) Wagner, 1813; Wagner, 1814–1816 and 1824; J(oseph) C(harles) de St. Romes, 1817–1823, 1839, and 1842; M(anuel) Cruzat, 1825; John Gibson, 1827–1829 and 1831; Charles W. Duhy, 1830 (Thomas) Stroud & (T. J.) Pew, 1832; Jerome Bayon, 1833–1838 and 1848 (Alexander C.) Bullitt (John) Magne & Co., 1840; A. C. Bullitt, 1841 and 1843–1844; Magne & Weisse, 1845; W(atson) Van Benthuysen & P. Besançon, Jr., 1846; W. Van Benthuysen, 1847; G. F. Weisse, 1850–1852; Emile La Sere, 1853–1855; John Claiborne, 1856–1857, Louisiana Acts, 1805–1858, passim; art. 112, Constitution of 1845; 1846 La. Acts 4; *Louisiana Acts,* 1850–1858, passim; Florence M. Jumonville, *Bibliography of New Orleans Imprints, 1764–1864* (New Orleans, 1989); McMurtrie, *Early Printing;* McMurtrie, *Louisiana Imprints, 1768–1810* (Hattiesburg, Miss., 1942); Louisiana State Library, *The Louisiana Union Catalog* (Baton Rouge, 1982, microfiche); Lucy B. Foote, comp., *Bibliography of the Official Publications of Louisiana, 1803–1934* (Baton Rouge, 1942); John Tebbel, *A History of Book Publishing in the United States* (New York, 1972), 1: 51. Although the variation between the quantity of known nineteenth-century imprints and the number actually produced undoubtedly is smaller, an untold quantity of items remain to be located.

partnership with one another, served as state printer before the legislature began in 1858 to elect official printers domiciled in Baton Rouge. Others of their number who never held the state contract also produced law books; for a few, such materials constituted a major part of their output. All of them duplicated monographs on other subjects, ranging in quantity from one item to several score. As a group, they facilitated the dissemination of information on Louisiana law and expedited the labors of the state's legislators, lawyers, and justices.[4]

One of the first dilemmas faced by lawmakers intent on bringing republicanism to Louisiana was to decide in which language to publish announcements and laws, for, as American governor William C. C. Claiborne commented, "The sudden introduction of our Languages into Louisiana has indeed subjected the citizens to considerable Inconvenience and given rise to much discontent." Early attempts to alleviate the situation, at least as far as concerned the judiciary, included keeping the records of the Court of Pleas in both the English and the French languages and appointing bilingual justices. The members of the first Legislative Council for the Territory of Orleans took a cue from these compromises, authorizing the governor to designate a public printer in whose newspaper would appear in French and English all proclamations, orders of the court, and other official announcements. Further, the council required the governor promptly to arrange for two newspapers in the territory to publish French and English texts of any law or resolution of the legislature. Implicit in this act was the requirement that the official printer publish a newspaper; otherwise he could not possibly meet the demands

4. With the exception of bibliographer Douglas C. McMurtrie, few persons have studied the history of printing in New Orleans, but see Samuel J. Marino, "The French-Refugee Newspapers and Periodicals in the United States, 1789–1825" (Ph.D. diss., University of Michigan, 1962); Elrie Robinson, *Biographical Sketches of James M. Bradford, Pioneer Printer* (St. Francisville, La., 1938); Bertram Wallace Korn, *Benjamin Levy: New Orleans Printer and Publisher* (Portland, Me., 1961); John H. Baron, "Paul Emile Johns of New Orleans: Tycoon, Musician, and Friend of Chopin," in International Musicological Society, *Report of the Eleventh Congress, Copenhagen, 1972,* Henrik Glahn, Soren Sorensen, and Peter Ryom, eds. (Copenhagen, 1972), 246–50. For information about colonial printing, which consisted almost entirely of law-related materials, see Florence M. Jumonville, "Frenchmen at Heart: New Orleans Printers and Their Imprints, 1764–1803," *Louisiana History* 32 (1991): 279–310; William C. C. Claiborne to Thomas Jefferson, 10 January 1805, in Clarence Edwin Carter, ed., *The Territorial Papers of the United States* (Washington, 1940) 9: 366–7; Orleans Territorial Acts (1805), 88–93.

of his job. Therefore, the field of candidates for Governor Claiborne's appointment was limited to four, the number of New Orleans printing firms then issuing gazettes.[5]

The governor first filled the position with James M. Bradford.[6] Lured from Kentucky in 1804 by the prospect of political appointment in the new territory, Bradford typified the ambitious American newcomer. He aspired as high as territorial secretary but lost the position to the better connected James Brown, whose brother John was a United States senator. Bradford did, however, possess a skill on which to fall back: printing. In the Bluegrass State, his family had controlled the public printing for a generation, and James had learned the trade from his father. Certainly his experience gave him firsthand knowledge of a state printer's duties. With the official printing for the Orleans Territory in mind, he purchased from James Lyon a year-old newspaper, *The Union, or New Orleans Advertiser & Price Current,* giving it a new format and a new name, *The Orleans Gazette and Commercial Advertiser.*[7]

Publishing announcements and new laws in his paper was only one of the responsibilities of the public printer. The legislative council provided that at the end of the session a compilation of the laws would be printed in a bilingual edition of at least five hundred copies and distributed to judges, council members, and every other federal or territorial official in

5. They were *Le Télégraphe, et le Commercial Advertiser,* a thrice-weekly that was the only bilingual newspaper, published by Claudius Beleurgey; *Louisiana Gazette,* a semiweekly issued by John Mowry; *The Orleans Gazette, and Commercial Advertiser* of James M. Bradford, a thrice-weekly that became semiweekly in June 1805; and the weekly *Moniteur de la Louisiane,* published by J. B. L. S. Fontaine, which still survived from the colonial period. McMurtrie, *Early Printing,* 120–1; T. N. McMullan, ed., *Louisiana Newspapers, 1794–1961: A Union List of Louisiana Newspaper Files Available in Public, College and University Libraries in Louisiana* (Baton Rouge, 1965), 107–201.

6. Although no appointment prior to Bradford's is to be found in legislative records, James Lyon preceded him as official printer. It is likely, however, that his assignment involved printing federal laws rather than those of the territorial council. Lyon, an itinerant printer who arrived in late 1803, had worked in Fairhaven, Vermont; Richmond, Virginia; the District of Columbia; and Savannah, Georgia, where he probably returned when he left New Orleans in 1804. During his sojourn in the Crescent City, he printed one monograph, *Ordinance Establishing the Louisiana Bank* (1804), claiming in its imprint to be "printer to the Government" (McMurtrie, *Early Printing,* 66–8).

7. George Dargo, *Jefferson's Louisiana: Politics and the Clash of Legal Traditions* (Cambridge, Mass., 1975), 38–9; McMurtrie, *Early Printing,* 71–2; John S. Kendall, "Early New Orleans Newspapers," *Louisiana Historical Quarterly* 10 (July 1927): 399. For biographical information on Bradford, see also Robinson, *James M. Bradford.*

Louisiana, with the remainder to be dispensed by the governor. That compilation, issued in 1805, bore Bradford's first imprint as official "printer to the territory" and was the premier volume in a series of session laws that still continues today. Its title page bore the phrase "by authority," meaning that it had been commissioned by the legislature. The same imprimatur appeared on all volumes of session laws and on most other government-authorized publications.[8]

Claiborne, proceeding gradually to introduce the American system of jurisprudence, wrote to President Thomas Jefferson, "The Council have already determined that the Laws should be printed in french & *English;* In the *latter* however, the Laws are to be passed, but official translations thereof are to be made, & this I presume will be satisfactory." Following the council's directive to provide both versions in a single book, Bradford employed a format first used in New Orleans by James Lyon in which the laws in English were printed on the verso of each leaf and the French text on the recto of the following leaf, paged continuously. Except that beginning in the 1847 annual, rectos and versos were paged separately, this format became the standard and existed until 1868, when the official use of French, and with it the bilingual printing of Louisiana session laws and journals of the legislature, ceased.[9]

Amendments in 1806 and 1809 provided for the appointment of two printers, one to handle the printing in French and the other in English, and reinforced the governor's right to make the selection. Furthermore, James Madison, then secretary of state, had left to Claiborne's discretion the selection of a journal to publish federal laws just passed by Congress. Perhaps this strengthening of his authority impelled the governor, in November 1808, finally to take a step that he had no doubt been contemplating for some time: withdrawing the public patronage from Bradford and his partner, Thomas Anderson. For three years the pair had been

---

8. Orleans Territorial Acts (1805), 88–95; Claiborne to Jefferson, 10 January 1805, Carter, *Territorial Papers,* 9: 367.

9. 1847 La. Acts 65; 1868 La. Acts 10; 1806 La. Acts 56–63; 1809 La. Acts 12–15; Claiborne to Madison, 29 January 1809, in Dunbar S. Rowland, ed., *Official Letter Books of W. C. C. Claiborne, 1801–1816* (Jackson, Miss., 1917), 4: 311; Marino, "French-Refugee Newspapers," 260; Claiborne to Madison, 29 January 1809, Rowland, *Letter Books,* 4 : 311–2. Bradford followed the example of James Lyon, who seems to have begun typesetting texts in different languages on facing pages in 1804. He subsequently partnered with Thomas Anderson to form the firm of Bradford & Anderson.

publishing anonymous articles abusing Claiborne and characterizing him as weak, inept, and given to excessive use of power. On January 29, 1809, the governor complained to Madison, "The Orleans Gazette printed by Bradford & Anderson has heretofore experienced all the support which the public printing could give it. The Editors profess to be friendly to the General Administration; But for some time past, their paper has given no evidence of such disposition. . . . [The Courier] is the only one of eight [newspapers] in this City, that gives support to the Government." Realizing finally that he could use to his advantage the patronage that he had the prerogative to bestow, Claiborne awarded the lucrative printing contract—his single most important spoil—to the proprietors of the thrice-weekly bilingual *Louisiana Courier,* J. B. S. Thierry and John Dacqueny.[10]

In addition to publishing the ongoing criticism that stung Claiborne so deeply, Bradford & Anderson had opposed him on major issues, notably Burr's conspiracy and the batture controversy. Although they allowed proponents of the city's position regarding the batture to express themselves in the pages of the *Orleans Gazette,* the pair remained sympathetic to Edward Livingston, the attorney who represented the other side and who had a history of opposing Claiborne at every turn. The governor no doubt had this trio in mind when he complained to James Madison, "The Lawyers and the Printers are the most restless, turbulent members of this Society." Thierry, conversely, remained the governor's ally; indeed, the *Louisiana Courier* was born of the batture controversy, for Thierry had founded it in 1807 as a forum for communicating the public's views. The paper defended vigorously the citizens' right to use the batture, thus endorsing the administration's position. Claiborne named Thierry public printer as a reward for his support, and while he retained the patronage the *Courier* functioned as the official organ of government.[11]

Although Bradford spoke derisively of the post of official printer, he refused to forfeit it without protest and threatened to publish his version of the ongoing quarrel with the governor, thus laying the matter before the public. Claiborne responded, "Publish what you please, you may . . .

10. Orleans Territorial Acts (1809), 12–14; Marino, "French-Refugee Newspapers," 255; Thomas P. Abernethy, *The Burr Conspiracy* (New York, 1954); Dargo, *Jefferson's Louisiana;* Carter, *Territorial Papers,* 9: 754; Dargo, *Jefferson's Louisiana,* 71.

11. Dargo, *Jefferson's Louisiana,* 79.

be assured of receiving no reply, for I deem it improper to enter into a controversy with any Individual touching my official acts. As relates to yourself, Mr. Bradford, I am only conscious of having committed one error, and that was, not having dismissed you as a Public Printer at a much earlier period."[12]

The belligerent printer sold his business interests and moved to St. Francisville, Louisiana. There he founded another newspaper, the *Time Piece,* and resumed criticizing the government, this time directing his attacks toward Congress. Bradford worked also as deputy clerk of the Seventh Superior District Court in Feliciana, and in 1812 he was admitted to the bar. Once again his path crossed that of his former opponent when his name was one of two submitted for Claiborne's consideration for the post of parish judge of Feliciana. The governor twice passed over both would-be judges, first naming John Rhea, who declined the appointment, and then John Hampton. Although he ignored Bradford, Claiborne may have found that the passage of time had softened his attitude toward his erstwhile adversary, for he wrote to Rhea that he found it impossible to feel unfriendly toward either of the unsuccessful candidates. No record exists of further contact between the two; by 1826, when Bradford returned briefly to New Orleans to publish the *Louisiana State Gazette* and again to serve as public printer, Claiborne had been dead for nearly a decade.[13]

In 1813, the first state legislature withdrew from the governor the privilege of naming the official printer. Lawmakers assumed this function themselves and provided for election of the printer by ballot of both senate and house, meeting in joint session soon after the legislature convened. Henceforth there would be only one printer, it being hoped that "a considerable saving to the state will be the result of having the whole of the printing in both languages done by the same person." In compensation for his services, the printer elected during 1813 would receive twenty-five hundred dollars, half to be paid on March 31 and the remainder, pending faithful performance of his job, the following January 25. He was required, before commencing his duties, to post a bond equal in value to his salary.[14]

12. Carter, *Territorial Papers,* 9: 375; Claiborne to Bradford, 29 May 1809, Rowland, *Letter Books,* 4: 372–3.

13. McMurtrie, *Early Printing,* 76; Robinson, *James M. Bradford,* 17–8, [43]; 1813 La. Acts 118.

14. 1813 La. Acts 120, 118.

Those duties included printing, or causing to be printed, "in a work-manlike manner, and with a good type all bills ordered to be printed by either house of the legislature . . . , all the printing necessary to be done for the use of the executive and treasury departments, and all forms for the use of the adjutant general's office of this state." For the first time, the printer was required to publish in his newspaper and in pamphlet form the journals of each house of the legislature, thus making public the law-makers' debates and deliberations as well as total votes on issues of the day. As before, all official printing would be bilingual. The journals of each house, however, were produced in separate volumes, one in French and the other in English, possibly because it was anticipated that bilingual editions would be too thick to be used conveniently. Just three hundred copies of each version were authorized, half the number of copies of session laws.[15]

Within a year the legislature increased the official printer's wages to three thousand dollars, imposed more specific deadlines for the delivery of his work, and required him to prepare an alphabetical index to each future volume of session laws. Subsequent legislatures amended and supplemented this act, lowering and raising bonds and salaries and for a time paying according to the amount of work commissioned instead of a flat annual rate; varying the number of copies of journals and session laws; and adding and deleting categories of persons entitled to receive official publications. 1847 a comprehensive act specified such details of format as the number of lines per page and the width of margins, and increased the duration of the printer's contract to two years.[16]

An immediate need after the Louisiana Purchase was to inform Orleanians of federal laws, especially those that most closely affected them. The first compilation of such legislation, issued less than a year after the

15. Ibid., 118–21. Journals approximate the length of volumes of session laws; see Foote, *Official Publications,* to compare pagination; 1814 La. Acts 10–13 .

16. *Louisiana Acts,* 1814–1857, especially 1st legis., 3d sess., 1814, 10–13; 2d legis., 1st sess., 1815, 6–9; 10th legis., 1st sess., 1831, 76–9; 12th legis., 1st sess., 1835, 54; 12th legis., 2d sess., 1836, 8–9; 13th legis., 2d sess., 1838, 23–4; 1st legis., 2d sess., 1847, 65–8; 2d legis., 2d sess., 1855, 115–6, 293–7; 3d legis., 1st sess., 1856, 76–7; *Lois Décrétées par le Congrès des Etats-Unis d'Amérique, pour le Gouvernement, pro tempore, de la Province de la Louisiane* (New Orleans, 1804). The latter was printed by Beleurgey & Renard, who are not known to have served as territorial printers. After they severed their partnership, however, the city of New Orleans appointed Jean Renard its official printer.

Purchase, set forth laws for the temporary government of Louisiana. In 1806, legislators authorized the publication of a volume summarizing federal laws pertaining to land claims in the Orleans Territory and another containing the Constitution, the Bill of Rights, and certain laws and documents that pertained specifically to the Orleans Territory. Bradford & Anderson, as official printers, produced the English-language portions of both publications; they farmed out to Jean Renard the job of printing the French-language texts, with the result that each side of each leaf was printed on a different press. Four years later the legislature authorized Thierry & Dacqueny to reissue the latter collection in both English- and French-language volumes, adding the Declaration of Independence to the English version.[17]

Many acts of the legislature dealt with matters of enduring importance, establishing as they did either the government and its agencies or commercial and civic institutions. Such laws often appeared as separates by order of the legislature because of their widespread and continuing significance. Those issued by authority included instructions for dividing the Orleans Territory into counties and for establishing courts in the territory and, later, in the state of Louisiana. Other governments also commissioned reprints of legislative acts. In 1818, for example, J. C. de St. Romes, official printer of New Orleans, reproduced *An Act to Incorporate the City of New-Orleans, with Several Acts Relative to Said City* at the city council's direction.[18]

17. *Acts of the Congress of the United States, Relative to the Ascertaining & Adjusting of Land Claims in the Territory of Orleans and District of Louisiana* (New Orleans, 1806); *A Compilation in Which Is Comprised the Constitution of the United States, with the Amendments to the Same; the Treaty by Which Louisiana was Ceded to the United States; the Laws and Ordinance of Congress for the Government of the Territory of Orleans; Together with Two Ordinances of the Governor General & Intendant of Louisiana* (New Orleans, 1806); *Collection, Containing the Declaration of Independence, the Constitution of the United States and Its Amendments, the Treaty of Cession between the United States and the French Republic, As Also the Laws and Ordinances of Congress for the Government of the Territory of Orleans and Two Ordinances of the Governor and Intendant of Louisiana* (New Orleans, 1810); *Recueil dans Lequel Sont Contenus la Constitution des Etats-Unis Avec Ses Amendements, le Traité par Lequel la Louisiane a Etre Cedée aux Etats-Unis, les Lois et Ordonnances du Congrès pour le Gouvernement du Territoire d'Orléans, Ainsi Que Deux Ordonnances du Gouverneur et Intendant de la Louisiane* (New Orleans, 1810).

18. *An Act for Dividing the Territory of Orleans into Counties, and Establishing Courts of Inferior Jurisdiction Therein* (1805), the printing of which John Mowry accomplished for government printer James M. Bradford; *An Act to Organize the Supreme Court of the State of Louisiana, and to Establish Courts of Inferior Jurisdiction* (1813), duplicated by state printers Baird and Wagner.

Businessmen and members of various organizations engaged local printers to reproduce copies of acts that were especially significant to them so that they might distribute the reprints to customers or colleagues. The earliest such publication was *Ordinance Establishing the Louisiana Bank* (1804), printed by James Lyon in his capacity as printer to the Bank of Louisiana as well as to the government. Similar issues detailed the formation of the Planters' Bank (1811), the City Bank of New Orleans (1832), the Commercial Bank of New Orleans (1833), and others. Railroads, hotels, benevolent societies, and organizations of all kinds also distributed copies of their acts of incorporation.[19]

Between Louisiana's admission to the Union in 1812 and her secession nearly a half century later, the state promulgated three constitutions, the first concurrent with statehood and the others in 1845 and 1852. Early in its proceedings, each constitutional convention elected one or two official "printers to the convention" who would accomplish any printing that the delegates might require, such as reference copies of the constitution undergoing revision and, ultimately, the new document the convention created. Proprietors of local printeries submitted proposals for such jobs just as they did for the annual state contract. In addition, the constitutional conventions of 1844–1845 and 1852 published the journals of their debates.[20]

Many pages of the journal of the 1844–1845 constitutional convention were devoted to the selection of the official printer, a decision that had

19. *An Act Incorporating the Planters' Bank, in the City of New Orleans* (New Orleans, 1811), which states in lieu of printer's imprint that it was printed for the Planters' Bank; *An Act to Incorporate the City Bank of New-Orleans* (New Orleans, 1832), printed by Gaston Bruslé; *An Act to Incorporate the Commercial Bank of New-Orleans* (New Orleans, 1833), with separate editions printed by Emile Johns and by Benjamin Levy; e.g., *Act of Incorporation of the Jefferson and Lake Pontchartrain Railway Company* (New Orleans, 1840), printed by order of the board of directors by F. Cook & A. Levy; *An Act to Incorporate the St. Charles Hotel Company* (New Orleans, 1844), duplicated at the Tropic Office; *An Act to Incorporate the Celeste Society, for the Relief of Destitute Widows and Orphans, and for Other Purposes* (New Orleans, 1835), printed by Bayon & Sollée; *An Act to Incorporate the Subscribers to the Consolidated Association of the Planters of Louisiana* (New Orleans, 1827), printed by Buisson & Boimare.

20. See Foote, *Official Publications,* 58–9, for a list of publications of the constitutional conventions of 1844–1845 and 1852. The only item printed at the direction of the convention of 1812 while it remained in session was a broadside that memorialized Congress for the annexation of Florida to the Orleans Territory, of which the sole known copy survives in the Library of Congress. It is dated January 1812 in manuscript.

proven to be uncommonly troublesome. Debates of the issue reveal the convention's heavy reliance on printed copies of their deliberations and the speed with which they required the printer to produce them. The latter consideration impelled delegates to the convention to elect James A. Kelly, despite the protests of rival printer Jerome Bayon that he could do the job for less than the two thousand dollars allowed Kelly. At first the convention met in Jackson, and Kelly had set up shop there; Bayon's business was located in New Orleans, and delegates feared loss of time in sending work to and fro. After much discussion, Bayon withdrew his proposal and Kelly retained the commission.[21]

By the beginning of 1845 the meeting had moved to New Orleans and Kelly had fallen two weeks behind in his work, leaving the convention no alternative but to replace him. This time delegates chose two firms, Jerome Bayon for the French-language portion and Besançon, Ferguson & Co. for the English. The new arrangement proved to be more costly than the convention's original agreement with Kelly. As the proceedings neared a close, delegates voted to pay Bayon three thousand dollars, a sum that covered his costs and left him with a profit of four hundred dollars. Because the debates in English were more voluminous than those in French, Besançon, Ferguson & Co. were allowed five hundred dollars extra.[22]

As the body of laws grew and the population of lawyers climbed, a need developed for digests to assemble all legislation in force at the time and eliminate the need to review each volume of session laws. The legislature authorized one of the earliest such compilations of Louisiana law in 1805 when, as part of An Act for the Punishment of Crimes and Misdemeanors, it directed the governor to "cause to be drawn up and printed and promulgated, in the English and French languages, an explanation of each and every of the crimes and misdemeanors herein before mentioned." Lewis Kerr, a local counselor at law, undertook the project. Following Claiborne's instructions that the work "may be concise, and the Style as plain as the nature of the case will admit, and that it may be ready for the Press as speedily as possible," the next year he completed *An Expo-*

21. Robert J. Ker, reporter, *Proceedings and Debates of the Convention of Louisiana* (New Orleans, 1845), 21–4.

22. Ibid., 101–3, 933–4; Orleans Territorial Acts (1805), 450–1.

sition of the Criminal Laws of the Territory of Orleans. Bradford & Anderson, then serving as "printers to the Territory of Orleans," printed the English-language portion. Once again they farmed out to Jean Renard the job of printing the French translation.[23]

Similar works followed. In 1806 the legislative council commissioned New Orleans lawyers James Brown and Louis Moreau Lislet to prepare a single volume of civil laws based on those then in force, which would serve as a guide for courts and juries. The council sought to create such a work because the change to the American system of government had plunged the civil laws into confusion, rendering some of them invalid because they contradicted federal legislation; others, written in foreign languages, resulted in litigation stemming from different interpretations. Two years later the jurisconsults submitted, and the council promulgated, their digest of the civil laws in force. Legislators ordered the governor to solicit bids on the job of printing six hundred copies in French and English, to engage the lowest bidder, and to distribute copies to courts of justice and recipients of the session laws. Governor Claiborne employed Bradford & Anderson, then serving as official printers, to print the 1808 *Digest.*[24]

In 1816 the legislature authorized the first comprehensive compilation when it resolved to appoint "a person learned in law" to assemble "a general Digest of all the governor's ordinances issued during the first degree of the government of this State and the acts of the Legislative Council, and of the several Legislatures of this State, that are now in force." The compiler was charged also with preserving the phraseology of the laws and with grouping them by subject. Specified public documents crucial to the state's history, including the state and federal constitutions, would precede the laws. The legislature directed the governor to arrange for the printing of one thousand copies. Judge François-Xavier Martin took on

23. Claiborne to Kerr, 14 August 1805, in Rowland, *Letter Books,* 3: 166; Lewis Kerr, *An Exposition of the Criminal Laws of the Territory of Orleans; The Practice of the Courts of Criminal Jurisdiction, the Duties of Their Officers, with a Collection of Forms for the Use of Magistrates and Others* (New Orleans, 1806); Warren M. Billings, "A Neglected Treatise: Lewis Kerr's *Exposition* and the Making of Criminal Law in Louisiana," *Louisiana History* 38 (1997): 261–87; Orleans Territorial Acts (1806), [214]–19; Orleans Territorial Acts (1808), 120–9.

24. James Brown and Louis Moreau Lislet, comps., *A Digest of the Civil Laws Now in Force in the Territory of Orleans, with Alterations and Amendments Adapted to Its Present System of Government* (New Orleans, 1808); 1816 La. Acts [2].

the assignment and, progressing rapidly, put together a three-volume work within the year. As the enactments of each successive legislature increased the body of Louisiana law, these publications fast became outdated. During the antebellum period other prominent New Orleans attorneys produced another half-dozen general digests, each in its turn authorized by the legislature and issued in New Orleans.[25]

Publishing these works was not one of the state printer's duties, and holding the public patronage neither guaranteed nor precluded winning an assignment. Jobs such as this could be, and often were, granted to capable printers who could not qualify for the state contract or chose not to compete for it. Such work supplemented commissions from individuals and businesses and was very lucrative; for example, the legislature authorized an expenditure of up to twelve thousand dollars for printing and binding English- and French-language editions of the 1828 *General Digest.*[26]

With a workable civil code and general digest already available, in 1821 lawmakers turned their attention to the system of criminal law. Declaring it to be defective, the legislature resolved to appoint a lawyer who would prepare a bilingual penal code listing criminal offenses and their punishments, setting forth the rules of evidence, and enumerating the duties of judicial and executive officers. The next legislative session authorized Edward Livingston, a local barrister who became well known for his involvement in the batture controversy, to compile such a code and instructed the governor to have two thousand copies printed, half in French and half in English. Lawmakers also provided for election of three lawyers who would revise the civil code and compile commercial laws and rules of practice.[27]

Livingston had a hand in preparing all of these. He teamed with fellow lawyers Louis Moreau Lislet and Pierre Derbigny to produce the revised civil code and the code of practice, both of which appeared in 1825, and, working alone, drafted codes of commercial and criminal law. These editions of the *Civil Code* and the *Code of Practice* formed part of the

---

25. François-Xavier Martin, comp., *A General Digest of the Acts of the Legislature of the Late Territory of Orleans and of the State of Louisiana, and the Ordinances of the Governor under the Territorial Government* (3 vols.; New Orleans, 1816). Others appeared in 1828, 1841, 1842, 1852, 1855, and 1856. For a complete list, see Foote, *Official Publications,* 179–80.

26. 1828 La. Acts 132–3.

27. Ibid., 1821, 30–3 and 1822, 108–11.

"course of studies" that the state supreme court prescribed in 1840 for study by aspirants to the practice of law in Louisiana.[28]

Although the legislature never approved the criminal code, it directed Livingston to have his work printed. He distributed copies, one part at a time, to legislators for their consideration and to colleagues for their comments. For the job of printing the code, Livingston chose Benjamin Levy. Levy, an experienced bookbinder, came to New Orleans from New York in 1811 and opened a book and stationery store, advertising also that he bound books neatly and promptly. Eleven years later he added a printery and soon came to specialize in law books, which he also sold in his shop. Although he never held the designation of official state printer, Levy won several commissions to print government-supported law books, including the *General Digest* of 1828. In addition, Livingston engaged him to produce the commercial and penal codes, the latter in twenty-two sections issued during a period of five years.[29]

Other members of the bar arranged for the occasional publication of law books. In 1818, for example, Louis Moreau Lislet and Henry Carleton, translators of *Las Siete Partidas,* issued the section on contracts and obligations, purchase, and exchange, two years before their translation appeared in its entirety. Another contributor to his profession's literature was Samuel Livermore, a Harvard-educated lawyer who had practiced in Boston and Baltimore before moving permanently to New Orleans about 1820. His *Dissertations on the Questions which Arise from the Contrariety of the Positive Laws of Different States and Nations,* which he commissioned Benjamin Levy to print in 1828, was noteworthy as the first American work on the conflict of laws, one which influenced

28. Edward Livingston, Louis Moreau Lislet, and Pierre Derbigny, comps., *Civil Code of the State of Louisiana* (New Orleans, 1825), printed by J. C. de St. Romes, a former state printer, and *Code of Practice, in Civil Cases* (New Orleans, 1825); Edward Livingston, *Commercial Code for the State of Louisiana* (New Orleans, 1825), *System of Penal Law* (New Orleans, 1824), and the other sections of the criminal code, all printed by Benjamin Levy; Warren M. Billings, "A 'Course of Studies': Books That Shaped Louisiana Law," see chapter 1 in the present volume.

29. Korn, *Benjamin Levy,* 11–3, 27–9, passim. Almost two-thirds of Levy's known output of 132 books and pamphlets—84 items—pertains to law. Florence M. Jumonville, *New Orleans Imprints; A Translation of the Titles on Promises and Obligations, Sale and Purchase, and Exchange; From the Spanish Laws of Las Siete Partidas* (New Orleans, 1818), printed by the Roche Brothers; *The Laws of Las Siete Partidas, Which Are Still in Force in the State of Louisiana,* 2 vols. (New Orleans, 1820), printed by James M'Karaher.

later legal scholars by focusing their attention on the works of early authors.[30]

Other attorneys, publicizing their views on sundry law-related matters, issued monographs of less enduring significance on a variety of subjects. Among the first was *Esquisse de la Situation Politique et Civile de la Louisiane* (1804), written anonymously but attributed to Pierre Derbigny, the official interpreter and later a Louisiana governor. The unnamed author criticized the Claiborne administration, complaining about the American system of jurisprudence and the lawyers, of whom some spoke French and the others English, recently arrived from the United States. Similarly, Allan B. Magruder of Opelousas held forth on the subject of *Land Claims* (1811), and in 1825 Seth Lewis, judge of the Fifth District Court, commented on Edward Livingston's criminal code.[31]

The legislature promulgated the law, but to the judiciary fell the responsibility for administering it justly and uniformly. Litigation gave rise to the publication of lawyers' briefs and to opinions and decisions of the court. From the time of its establishment in 1813, the Supreme Court of Louisiana had required "the gentlemen of the bar" to furnish it with briefs. In 1846 the court elaborated on this requirement, announcing, "No cause shall be heard by the Court, until the parties shall have furnished to each of the Judges, a printed or fairly written brief or abstract of the Cause Containing the substance of all the material pleadings, facts, and documents on which the parties rely, and the points of Law and fact intended to be presented at the argument with a Complete reference of the authorities." Attorneys, perhaps anticipating that the justices would find the legibility of their penmanship wanting, immediately sought the services of local printers, and the quantity of printed briefs skyrocketed.

As a result of this increased need, more printers began to specialize in

30. *Dictionary of American Biography*, s.v. "Livermore, Samuel"; *Esquisse de la Situation Politique et Civile de la Louisiane, Depuis le 30 Novembre 1803, Jusqu'au 1er. Octobre 1804* (New Orleans, 1804). Claiborne responded to the charges contained therein in a letter to James Madison, October 16, 1804, in James Alexander Robinson, ed., *Louisiana under the Rule of Spain, France, and the United States, 1785–1807* (Cleveland, Ohio, 1911), 2: 268–78.

31. Allan B. Magruder, *Land Claims: Miscellaneous Remarks on Various Kinds of Land Titles, within the Territory of Orleans* (New Orleans, 1811), printed by Thomas Anderson; Seth Lewis, *Strictures on Dr. Livingston's System of Penal Laws, Prepared for the State of Louisiana* (New Orleans, 1825); Warren M. Billings, ed., *The Historic Rules of the Supreme Court of Louisiana, 1813–1879* (Lafayette, La., 1986), 1, 18.

the production of briefs. Some printed briefs had appeared as early as the 1820s, when James Workman, Isaac T. Preston, Samuel Livermore, and other advocates employed local printers—chiefly Benjamin Levy—to print their arguments of selected cases. After 1846, commissions of this kind became the mainstay of Alexander Levy's struggling firm, the successor to the business formerly headed by Levy's father Benjamin.[32] Other printeries, notably those of J. L. Sollée and Louis Dillard, supplemented their other publications with attorneys' briefs, and two more, Edward G. Stewart and Samuel M. Stewart, printed such items almost exclusively.[33]

Decisions were particularly important because they constituted precedents to which lawyers and judges would continue to refer. Judge Martin

32. To provide handwritten or printed briefs remained the attorney's choice until 1877, when the court required lawyers to file with the clerk 10 copies of a printed brief, 1 copy for opposing counsel and the remaining 9 for the court's use; Billings, ed., *Historic Rules,* 34. Jumonville, *New Orleans Imprints,* lists, for example, 2 printed briefs issued in 1844; 4 published in 1845; 25 dating from 1846, of which at least 11 appeared after the legislature enacted the new law on November 24; 68 in 1847; and 102 in 1848. Copies of most of these briefs are included in the Archives of the Supreme Court of Louisiana, on deposit in the Archives/Special Collections Division, Earl K. Long Library, University of New Orleans. Additional items that have not been recorded may exist in this and other collections. E.g., James Workman, *Brief of the Case of Caricaburu, Arieta & Company, Merchants of Havanna* (New Orleans, 1820); Workman, *Defence of the Orleans Navigation Company, Before the Supreme Court* (New Orleans, 1822); Isaac T. Preston, *The Argument of Isaac T. Preston, Esq., Before the Supreme Court, in the Case of the State of Louisiana against the Orleans Navigation Company* (New Orleans, 1822); Samuel Livermore, *An Argument, in a Case Depending before the Supreme Court of Louisiana, between the Bank of the United States, the Bank of Louisiana, the Bank of Orleans and Others* (New Orleans, 1827); Étienne Mazureau, *In the Matter of William Kenner & Co. and of Richard Clague and John Oldham, Versus Their Creditors* ([New Orleans, *ca.* 1828]). All of these except the first were printed by Benjamin Levy. They shared another common characteristic: wordiness. Even the shortest exceeded sixty pages. Five Alexander Levy imprints issued before 1849 are known to survive; all are attorneys' briefs. During the next three years (1849–1851) he printed at least forty-one items, of which thirty-two are briefs. See Jumonville, *New Orleans Imprints,* and unrecorded briefs in the archives of the Supreme Court of Louisiana. Benjamin Levy's bankruptcy in 1843 resulted from the accumulation of injudicious real estate investments, unpaid bank loans, and bad notes he had endorsed, rather than from the inefficacy of his printery and bookstore. Alexander, previously in partnership with Francis Cook, led the successor firm in name only; Benjamin remained the responsible head. Korn, *Benjamin Levy,* 31–6; Jumonville, *New Orleans Imprints;* "Additional Benjamin and Alexander Levy Imprints," *Papers of the Bibliographical Society of America* 62 (1968): 245.

33. In 1847 and 1848 Sollée printed at least twenty works, of which one-fourth were briefs; during the same period Dillard produced a minimum of four publications, of which half were briefs. Such works comprised 100 percent of Edward G. Stewart's output of thirty-nine items, of which thirty bore no imprint except his address (50 Camp Street), and fourteen of fifteen issues of Samuel M. Stewart. See Jumonville, *New Orleans Imprints.*

began early in Louisiana's history to record judgments of the state supreme court. His "old" and "new" series of *Orleans Term Reports,* pertaining to the territorial period, and *Louisiana Term Reports,* commencing
with admission to the union, ran some thirty volumes; continuations by
Branch W. Miller, Thomas Curry, Merritt M. Robinson, and other local
attorneys more than doubled their number. The legislature did not commission the *Reports,* but it recognized the value of this series and was
among the best customers for it. Session laws contain frequent authoriza-
tion of quantity purchases for use by the courts.[34]

By these means, then, did territorial and antebellum legislatures and
lawyers make available to the Louisiana bench and bar, and to the public,
information they viewed as indispensable for the administration of a democratic government. Cognizant of colonial precedents, they moved
slowly but deliberately to institute American jurisprudence. If this goal
were to be achieved, it was necessary to apply laws and court decisions
promptly and consistently, and therefore to provide copies of them for
consultation wherever they might be needed. To prepare those volumes,
legislators and attorneys turned to New Orleans printers, who became
behind-the-scenes contributors to the perpetuation of Louisiana's distinct
legal heritage.

34. E.g., 1816 La. Acts 8–11; and 1818 La. Acts 24–5. Foote, *Official Publications,* 508–10, provides
a list of editions.

CASE LAW REPORTERS IN NINETEENTH-CENTURY LOUISIANA

Case reports—printed opinions of appellate judges—are as essential to the practice of law as grain is to the making of bread. They originated in England, though the first American reports date only to the early national period, as law and practice in the new republic increasingly diverged from that of Great Britain. In Louisiana, for example, case reporting commenced in 1811, and over the ensuing nine decades, a succession of determined men pioneered collecting and publishing decisions of the Superior Court for the Territory of Orleans and the Supreme Court of Louisiana that shaped law in the Bayou State.[1]

Their collective oeuvre falls into three categories: official reports, "unreported cases," and digests. Official reports were the most voluminous, and they were prepared at the behest of the courts or the state legislature. Hence their designation. On the other hand, compilations of so-called un-

---

1. John William Wallace, comp., *The Reporters, Arranged with Incidental Remarks . . .* , 4th ed. (Boston, 1882); John D. Cowley, comp., introduction to *A Bibliography of Abridgments, Digests, Dictionaries, and Indexes of English Law to 1800* (London, 1932); Anton-Hermann Chroust, *The Rise of the Legal Profession in America* (Norman, Okla., 1965), 2: 76–9; Erwin C. Surrency, *The History of American Law Publishing* (Dobbs Ferry, N.Y., 1990), passim.

reported cases recapitulated decisions that official reporters excluded from their publications for one reason or another. Digests, as the name implies, consisted of printed abstracts of opinions rehearsed more fully elsewhere. All three equipped Louisiana lawyers and judges with the very authorities that informed their arguments and opinions. Likewise, case reports provide legal historians, and by extension the New Louisiana Legal History, with valuable published primary sources. For that reason, the story of early Louisiana case reports and the men who rendered them into print deserves close attention.[2]

Seventeen men served as reporters down to 1900. As a group, they were an enterprising lot, at once dedicated to the dissemination of legal information, law reform, and personal profit. They emigrated mainly from the upper South, the mid-Atlantic states, New England, or Europe, so in background they mirrored the demographic attributes of their brethren on the bench and at the bar. Like other attorneys, most also settled in New Orleans because the bulk of the state's legal business originated there.[3]

Arguably the most notable of them was François-Xavier Martin, whose *Orleans Term Reports, or Cases Argued and Determined in the Superior Court of the Territory of Orleans* marked the beginning of case reporting in Louisiana. Martin (1762–1846) was admirably matched to the task, given his background and his scholarly proclivities. Born into a mercantile family of Marseilles, he left France as a youth to pursue a business opportunity in Martinique. That chance proved unpromising, so he next settled in North Carolina, where he fought with the state militia in the waning days of the War for Independence. A self-taught typesetter, he ran a print shop in New Bern and issued a variety of legal treatises, including his own translation of the French civilian commentator Robert Pothier's *Treatise on Obligations Considered from a Moral and Legal View.* Printing law books

---

2. Kate Wallach, *Research in Louisiana Law* (Baton Rouge, 1958), 71–91, summarizes the development of case reporting in Louisiana and provides a chronological listing of the various editions of reports and digests. See also John H. Tucker, Jr., "Source Books of Louisiana Law," *Tulane Law Review* 8 (1933–34): 396–405, and 9 (1934–35): 244–67.

3. T. C. W. Ellis, "The Louisiana Bar, 1813–1913, " 133 La. lxvi–lxxx (1913); Warren M. Billings, ed., *Historic Rules of the Supreme Court of Louisiana, 1813–1879* (Lafayette, La., 1985), 43–50; Elizabeth Gaspard, "The Rise of the Louisiana Bar: The Early Years," *Louisiana History* 28 (1987): 183–97.

inspired him to read law. He eventually won admission to the North Carolina bar as well as renown for his advocacy and erudition. Because Martin was a Jeffersonian, President James Madison appointed him to a judgeship in the Mississippi territory before translating him to a seat on the Superior Court for the Territory of Orleans. The latter nomination compelled him to grapple with how to fashion American and civil law into a system that met the needs of his fellow Louisianians.[4]

Soon after Martin took his seat, he grew vexed by what he styled a "dearth of correct information, in regard to the decisions of the Superior Court," and he began to devise a remedy for the situation. He kept notes on every case that came before him, and he collected copies of opinions from the minute books and files of cases decided before he joined the bench. Next, he enlisted the aid of his colleague Joshua Lewis, who lent his own notes and supplied him with briefs, which enabled Martin to consult the written arguments of counsel. The fruit of these endeavors was volume 1 of the *Reports*. In the preface, Martin articulated as his goal the reduction of "the scattered principles of our jurisprudence into a connected system." Buoyed by the favorable reception of his handiwork, he started compiling a second installment. By the time it came to print in 1813, Louisiana was a state and Martin was its first attorney general. He returned to his reportage soon after Governor William C. C. Claiborne named him a supreme court judge in 1815, and over the next decade and a half he compiled another seventeen volumes of reports amidst preparing opinions, statutory digests, and histories of North Carolina and Louisiana.[5]

A tight-fisted, disciplined man of spare personal habits, who never

4. Martin has no modern biographer. Details of his life and career are to be found in Henry Adams Bullard, *Discourse on the Life and Character of the Hon. François-Xavier Martin, Later Judge of The Supreme Court of the State of Louisiana, Pronounced at the Request of the Bar of New-Orleans* (New Orleans, 1847); William Wirt Howe, "Memoir of François-Xavier Martin," in François-Xavier Martin, *The History of Louisiana from the Earliest Period,* ed. John A. Gresham (New Orleans, 1882), 1: i–xxxvii; R. Don Higginbotham, "François-Xavier Martin's History of North Carolina," in Lawrence H. Leder, ed., *The Colonial Legacy* (New York, 1973), 4: 265–82; Warren M. Billings, "A Judicial Legacy: The Last Will and Testament of François-Xavier Martin," *Louisiana History* 25 (1984): 277–88; Michael Chiorazzi, "François-Xavier Martin: Printer, Lawyer, Jurist," *Law Library Journal* 80 (1988): 79–97; Martin brought out his translation in 1802.

5. François-Xavier Martin, *Orleans Term Reports; or, Cases Argued and Determined in the Superior Court of the Territory of Orleans,* 1: iii, viii; Chiorazzi, "François-Xavier Martin," 85–97 lists all of Martin's publications from his days as a printer to his death.

tasted alcohol until his sixtieth year, Martin died unmarried and a rich man. Such was his gift for augmenting his wealth that he even succeeded in persuading the legislature to mandate the sale of his reports and digests to the courts and other state agencies. His ruling passion, apart from acquiring land and cash, was the law, which accounts for why he threw himself so wholeheartedly into reporting and made the time to do it. However, the demands of his judicial duties, his scholarly labors, and his physical infirmity exacted a toll that gradually wore him down.[6]

Martin suffered from weak eyesight from birth. Diminished vision and heavy workloads finally forced him to give up case reporting in 1830. Complete blindness overtook him once he succeeded George Mathews as chief judge of the supreme court six years later. Subsequently, he went to Paris for an operation to restore his vision, but he returned without success. He refused to yield to his affliction though it greatly hindered him as he tried to keep pace with an expanding docket of cases. Things reached crisis proportions during an interval when he was the court's sole member. They eased momentarily after two energetic young lawyers, George Eustis and Pierre Adolphe Rost-Denis, joined the court, only to worsen after they resigned in disgust at the irascible Martin's opposition to their attempts at streamlining the court's business. The addition of Edward Simon, Alonzo Morphy, Henry Adams Bullard, and Rice Garland in 1840 brought a degree of stability, but Martin's intransigence, and mounting appeals caused by the aftereffects of the Panic of 1837, slowed the court once more. Little progress, it seemed, was possible without a top-to-bottom court reorganization. Demands for such a revamping fueled the clamor for a convention that produced the Constitution of 1845, and with that document came a new structure for the state's entire judiciary. On 18 March 1846, one day after Martin's eighty-fourth birthday, the new court convened, and after a thirty-one-year tenure, the old judge retired. He

---

6. "An Act to Provide for the Distribution of the Digest of the Laws of this State," 1818 La. Acts 24, 36, 38; "An Act to Authorize the Governor of the State to Purchase, for the Use of the State, Thirty Copies of Martin's Reports of the Decisions of the Supreme Court of the State," 1817 La. Acts 8, 10; Mark F. Fernandez, "From Chaos to Continuity: Early Reforms of the Supreme Court of Louisiana, 1845–1852," *Louisiana History* 27 (1987): 19–29; Judith Kelleher Schafer, "Reform or Experiment? The Constitution of 1845," in Warren M. Billings and Edward F. Haas, eds., *In Search of Fundamental Law: Louisiana's Constitutions, 1812–1974* (Lafayette, La., 1993), 21–37.

died eleven months later, much admired and deeply revered for his contributions to Louisiana jurisprudence.[7]

His *Reports,* in particular, contributed mightily to the process of blending English, American, French, Spanish, and Roman precepts into a workable mix of law that addressed the imperatives of a rapidly developing state. They provided judges, barristers, and plain citizens alike a definitive rendition of the most weighty Louisiana jurisprudence. Therefore, in the opinion of his friend and colleague Henry Adams Bullard, Martin had more than surpassed his fondest hope of reducing his beloved law into "a connected system."[8]

Martin the reporter was nothing if not thorough. No appeal escaped his notice, and all found space in the *Reports.* Typically, he summarized the issues, he specified arguments of counsel, and he recorded the opinion of the court in full. At first, such thoroughness seemed both desirable and manageable, especially after statehood, when appeals were limited solely to civil matters and then only to those that involved sums greater than three hundred dollars. As the state enlarged following its admission to the Union, so did the volume of litigation. Not only that, but the supreme court judges began issuing individual opinions after an act of the legislature required them to prepare "separate and distinct opinions," which also increased the reporter's burden. Nevertheless, Martin continued his habit of reporting every case.[9]

Branch C. Miller succeeded Martin, but unlike the judge, he actually held a gubernatorial appointment as the official reporter of decisions. The terms and conditions of his employment were set forth in legislation that became law in 1830. In return for an annual salary of twelve hundred dollars, Miller received either the originals or transcripts of all appeals. These

---

7. (New Orleans) *Daily Delta,* 11 December 1846; Bullard, *François-Xavier Martin,* 33–5; Howe, "Memoir," xxvi, xxviii–ix.

8. Bullard, *François-Xavier Martin,* 12.

9. "An Act to Organize the Supreme Court of the State of Louisiana, and to Establish Courts of Inferior Jurisdiction," 1813 La. Acts 26; *Laverty* v. *Duplessis,* 3 Mart. (o.s.) 52ff (La. 1813); "An Act Relative to the Supreme Court," 1821 La. Acts 96. The latter statute required each judge to deliver his opinion seriatim according to seniority. That requirement did not meet with the court's favor, and it was hurriedly repealed in 1822 ("An Act for the Amendment of Several Acts Regulating the Practice in the Supreme Court," 1822 La. Acts 24–6). Even so, the judges continued to write concurring opinions whenever they felt the inclination.

he was to reduce to "1st, a brief but clear statement of the facts of the case, taken from the record. 2d: The points made by the counsel and authorities, cited in support of them in all cases in which they shall be furnished. 3d. The opinion of the court in the case: and 4th. Lucid marginal notes in the cases, and a copious index to each volume." Once printed, seventy-five copies, "well bound," were to be delivered to the secretary of state for distribution to the courts and state officials. Other copies could be sold to the public for a price "not to exceed ten dollars a volume."[10]

Miller followed Martin's example and strove for complete coverage out of his belief that "judicial reports . . . are the highlights of the law and . . . the evidence of things not seen. . . . A correct publication of them, therefore, becomes of primary interest with the people." That lofty aim achieved a limited result. Miller compiled a mere five volumes before death overtook him in 1833.[11]

Thomas Curry, who was no stranger to legal publishing, succeeded Miller. Among his projects was a digest of state statutes that he and Henry Adams Bullard jointly drafted. He served as reporter of decisions for nine years, during which he edited thirteen volumes, the last five of which he brought out in just fourteen months' time. Despite his efficiency, the number of opinions increased annually, so much so that printing them all in a timely and cost-efficient manner became ever more difficult for him. Part of the trouble stemmed from his mode of reporting, for he strove "to give a full and faithful statement and view of each case, with all the points and principles decided, carefully extracted and prefixed to it in notes." Exhausted by his labors, he finally quit his post in 1841.[12]

That year the legislature favored a petition from Merritt M. Robin-

10. "An Act to Provide for the Publication of the Reports of the Decisions of the Supreme Court of the State of Louisiana," 1830 La. Acts 24–6, which also declared "null and void" all acts or parts of acts, in relation to the reports of decisions of the supreme court (ibid., section 8); 1 La. v–vi (1831).

11. Miller (?–1833) was one of the more obscure early reporters. He settled in New Orleans sometime before 1822, the year he was admitted to practice law, but why Governor Jacques Dupré named him reporter is unclear (Supreme Court of Louisiana Minute Book #2, 1818–23, 276, Supreme Court Archives, Department of Archives, Manuscripts, and Special Collections, Earl K. Long Library, University of New Orleans; "In Memoriam Henry Carleton Miller," 51 La. Ann. v (1899).

12. Henry A. Bullard and Thomas Curry, comps., *A New Digest of the Statute Laws of the State of Louisiana, from the Change of Government to the Year 1841, Inclusive* (New Orleans, 1842); Robert Feikema Karachuk, "A Workman's Tools: The Law Library of Henry Adams Bullard" (M.A. thesis, University of New Orleans, 1996); 8 La. v (1831).

son,[13] a New Orleans attorney, and Emile Johns, a leading city printer of legal materials, when it awarded them a contract to publish the reports. The terms of the agreement were similar to those that had applied to Curry and Miller, though there were several significant modifications. First, the contract ran for three years, but it was renewable for as long as Robinson and Johns performed satisfactorily. Second, Robinson agreed to record the "decisions of the court at length." Third, he was required to compose "concise notes at the head of each case, of the points decided." Fourth, he promised to include a "list of all cases determined within the period embraced by [a] volume, but not reported, with the reasons therefore." The latter stipulation represented a first attempt at streamlining the reporter's duties by reducing the number of cases for inclusion. Unfortunately, the determination of which ones to leave out rested with the judges and the litigants, who balked at excluding anything.[14]

Robinson complained from the start about printing all decisions and the labor he invested in readying them for publication. In his view, the important rulings got buried in a "mass of unprofitable matters," which rendered individual volumes "at once more expensive to be purchased and more inconvenient for use when obtained." He went so far as to write the court, requesting that he be allowed to exclude some decisions, as the law allowed. The judges rebuffed the request, which later led legal historian Henry Plauché Dart to conclude that Robinson took his revenge by publishing "twelve portly volumes covering not quite four years of the court." The ultimate solution, as Robinson conceived it, was for the legislature to follow the example of other states and allow reporters to omit cases "such as [were] mere repetitions of well settled principles of law, established by previous and repeated decisions." Such a remedy remained an impossibility while Martin was chief judge, and for that reason, among

13. A Virginian by birth, Robinson (fl. 1830s–1840s) settled in New Orleans by 1839, the year the supreme court admitted him to practice (Supreme Court Minute Book #5, 1834–39, 533). Like his more renowned kinsman and founder of the Virginia Historical Society, Conway Robinson, Merritt produced various works of law. In addition to the series of reports that he edited, he also published *A Digest of the Penal Law of the State of Louisiana, Analytically Arranged* (New Orleans, 1841).

14. See chapter 2 in the present volume; "An Act to Provide for the Publication of the Decisions of the Supreme Court," 1842 La. Acts 526–32.

others, Robinson supported the move for reforming the court that culminated in the Constitution of 1845.[15]

In 1846, therefore, the legislature drew up specifications for a new series called *Louisiana Annual Reports,* which would commence the following year at "the expiration of the contract with the present Reporter." The enabling law tracked the earlier statute, but it empowered the reporter at his discretion to "report the several cases, more or less, at large, according to their relative importance so as not to increase unnecessarily the size of the volume." Thus, the *Louisiana Annual Reports* became the first selective edition of supreme court decisions. Robinson, who won renewal of his contract, published volumes one through four of the new series, covering cases decided from 1846 to 1849.[16]

William Woodson King (1813–1881) took over from Robinson in 1850. Georgian by birth, King studied at Transylvania College in Kentucky before receiving his A.B. and A.M. at the University of Alabama and a law degree from the University of Virginia. He moved on to New Orleans in 1835, where with Minor Elmore he founded the law firm of Elmore and King, which specialized in batture litigation. Marriage to Sarah Ann, the daughter of Branch Miller, strengthened his connection to the New Orleans legal community, and one of his grandchildren was the novelist-historian Grace King. King, like his predecessors Martin, Curry, and Robinson, also wrote legal texts. That activity, plus his family ties, explain his appointment as Robinson's successor. He proved rather an indifferent reporter, though, who soon fell behind in his work by some fifteen months and left the job having produced only two volumes.[17]

The supreme court assigned the task of clearing up the backlog to William M. Randolph, whom Henry Plauché Dart described as "a lawyer of the younger set." When Randolph turned out his first volume, he ex-

15. 1 Rob. v–vii (1842); Henry Plauché Dart, "The History of the Supreme Court of Louisiana," 133 La. xliii (1913).

16. 1 Rob. viii (1842); "An Act to Provide for the Publication of the Decisions of the Supreme Court," 1846 La. Acts 89–92.

17. Order appointing King court reporter, 3 June 1850, Supreme Court Minute Book #10, 1848–51, 472; Robert Bush, *Grace King: A Southern Destiny* (Baton Rouge, 1983), 2–5; admission of William Woodson King to practice law in Louisiana, 25 February 1836, Supreme Court Minute Book #5, 1834–39, 172; William Woodson King, comp., *The Consolidation and Revision of the Statutes and Codes of Louisiana* (New Orleans, 1852).

pressed the hope that "the large amount of work" he faced would excuse the delay in getting it out. Tongue in cheek, he went on to explain further how "few persons, not familiar with the drudgery of proof-reading, can form a distinct idea of its annoyances. There can be no doubt, that whatever gifts 'come by nature,' correcting proofs is not one of the number." His difficulties were compounded further when in 1855 the legislature again required publication of all decisions. Nonetheless, he continued for another two years before he was replaced by Abner Nash Ogden.[18]

In 1862, S. F. Glenn superseded Ogden, though he did not publish any decisions until after the Civil War. When New Orleans fell to Union forces, the Confederate supreme court shut down and left town for Alexandria, La., but it never sat again. Glenn had considerable difficulty locating texts of decisions handed down in 1861 and 1862 because "the occupation of the rooms of the Supreme Court . . . by various military tribunals" had caused a loss of case files. Moreover, he noted how the surviving records were "thrown into almost inextricable confusion." Despite the chaos, Glenn insisted on reporting every case he could find. He felt that "decisions which to careless and unskilled persons, appear only to repeat the same sense, will often exhibit to a more accurate examiner diversities of signification." Glenn lasted until 1867, when he gave way to Jacob Hawkins, who stayed until 1872. Hawkins compiled volumes nineteen through twenty-four of the *Louisiana Annual Reports* before Charles E. A. Gayarré came out of retirement to take his place.[19]

Lawyer, politician, author, Gayarré (1805–1895) figured prominently in the life of Louisiana for much of the nineteenth century. Born near New Orleans, he read law in Philadelphia and was admitted to the bar of the Crescent City in 1829. There followed a varied public career, as he was by turns deputy attorney, attorney general, secretary of state, member of the state legislature, and district court judge, though sickness kept him from assuming a seat in the United States Senate, to which he was elected

18. Dart, "History of the Supreme Court," xlv; 7 La. Ann. v (1852); "An Act Relative to a Reporter of the Supreme Court," 1855 La. Acts 300–3. Ogden (?–1875) lived and practiced in New Orleans. He served on the supreme court from 1853 to 1855, which obviously qualified him to take on the duties of reporter of decisions (Billings, *Historic Rules,* 48).

19. 16 La. Ann. iii (1866). Union forces captured much of the supreme court archive and transferred it to the War Department in Washington, D.C., where it remained until its return in the 1880s.

in 1835. A sometime Democrat, Gayarré gravitated to the Know-Nothing Party and turned secessionist before he drifted toward the state Republicans, who secured the reporter's place for him. A prolific writer, perhaps his best-known work was his *History of Louisiana* (1851). However, an article, "New Orleans Bench and Bar in 1823," which he published in *Harper's Magazine* in 1888, formed an important addition to Louisiana's early legal historiography.[20]

Gayarré's five volumes were unexceptional in that they represented no advances in the art of reporting decisions. Nevertheless, the opinions themselves are an important record of how the Supreme Court of Louisiana calibrated state law to the requirements that resulted from the destruction of slavery and from the Constitution of 1868, which assured equal rights to all persons. As for Gayarré, he lost his post when Governor Francis T. Nicholls and the Democratic Party "redeemed" Louisiana from Reconstruction in 1877.

Nicholls's supreme court appointed Percy Roberts the new reporter. He edited volumes 29 to 31 of the *Louisiana Annual Reports* before yielding to Henry Denis in 1880. Denis stayed until 1894 and published another fifteen volumes. His successor, former supreme court justice Walter H. Rogers, reported the decisions until 1898.

Acting under the terms of a provision in the Constitution of 1898, the supreme court named T. H. Thorpe and Charles G. Gill successively to the place of reporter. They were the last named reporters of decisions because the office was eliminated in 1900. Moreover, the legislature empowered the state printer, with the supreme court's consent, to contract the task out to the lowest bidder, providing he was a "competent attorney." At that point, the court ordered the entire series renamed the *Louisiana Reports* and renumbered in sequence, commencing with the initial volume of Martin's *Reports*. Accordingly, volume 52 marked the conclusion

20. Supreme Court Minute Book #3, 1823–29, 488; Henry Plauché Dart, ed., "The Autobiography of Charles Gayarré," *Louisiana Historical Quarterly* 12 (1929): 5–29; W. Darrell Overdyke, "History of the American Party in Louisiana," *Louisiana Historical Quarterly* 16 (1933): 84–92; Grace King, "Charles Gayarré: A Biographical Sketch," *Louisiana Historical Quarterly* 33 (1950): 159–89; *Dictionary of Louisiana Biography* (Lafayette, La., 1988), s.v., "Gayarré, Charles Etienne Arthur"; Joseph G. Tregle, Jr., "Creoles and Americans," in Arnold R. Hirsch and Joseph Logsdon, eds., *Creole New Orleans: Race and Americanization* (Baton Rouge, 1992), 167–85. The *Dictionary of Louisiana Biography* includes an extensive bibliography of Gayarré's writings in its sketch.

of the *Louisiana Annual Reports,* whereas volume 104 of the *Louisiana Reports* began the new series. The publishing contract eventually went to the West Publishing Company of St. Paul, Minnesota, which was already well on its way to becoming the premier provider of legal information across the nation. Indeed, the *Southern Reporter,* which formed part of West's National Reporter System, had rivaled the *Louisiana Annual Reports* ever since 1887. To the court, therefore, West seemed a logical firm with which to contract, and so the company would monopolize the printing of Louisiana decisions for ninety years.[21]

Side by side with these official reports were the complementary works of Thomas Courtland Manning, J. Burton Harrison, Judah P. Benjamin, and Thomas Slidell. Their texts were designed to plug gaps or to render court opinions more accessible to practitioners and the public at large by reducing the official reports to a more manageable size.

A North Carolinian by birth and rearing, Thomas Courtland Manning (1825–1887) taught school in Edenton before taking up law and developing a practice there. He moved to Alexandria, La., in the 1850s, reestablished his law practice, and involved himself in state politics. A defender of southern rights, he sat in the secession convention that took Louisiana out of the Union in 1861 before winning a commission in the rebel army and a later appointment as adjutant general. He resigned from the military to assume a seat on the Confederate supreme court. After the war, he gravitated toward the state Democratic party and an alliance with Francis T. Nicholls, who named him chief justice in 1877. When the court was reorganized under the Constitution of 1879, he left, only to return in 1882, when Governor Samuel D. McEnery reappointed him an associate justice. It was during this final stint on the bench that he published his *Unreported Cases Heard and Determined by the Supreme Court of Louisiana from January 8, 1877 to April 1880.*[22]

---

21. "An Act to Provide for the Editing and Indexing of the Supreme Court Decisions," 1900 La. Acts 135–6; Dart, "History of the Supreme Court," lx. State printer W. C. Chevis wrote to the supreme court on 13 December 1902, setting forth the terms under which West Publishing Company proposed to produce the *Louisiana Reports.* The court considered the proposals on the 15th, and on the 18th, it accepted them. The letter and the order of acceptance are in 109 La. xxvii (1903). On the development of West Publishing Company, see Thomas H. Woxland, "'Forever Associated with the Practice of Law': The Early Years of the West Publishing Company," *Legal Reference Services Quarterly* 5 (1985): 115–24.

22. *Dictionary of Louisiana Biography,* s.v. "Manning, Thomas Courtland."

Appearing in 1884 under the imprint of a St. Louis, Missouri, printer, the collection was the first attempt at recording decisions excluded in the official reports. Its value both to practitioners and to historians was minimal because the coverage was so limited. Apparently, Manning had something broader in mind because he hinted cryptically that necessity had forced him to reduce his original three volumes to one. "I am now satisfied," he wrote in the preface, "that in making brevity and condensation paramount objects I have impaired the usefulness of the book." The fact that he turned to a St. Louis print shop suggests that New Orleans printers felt the work had so little commercial appeal to their customers that they declined to take his manuscript. On the other hand, the St. Louis printer may have believed he could profitably market the work if it focused on cases that arose during the time Manning was chief justice. An exact explanation for why Manning elected to publish the *Unreported Cases* as it appeared remains a mystery owing to the disappearance of his manuscript texts and his personal papers.[23]

The story of J. Burton Harrison (1805–1841) and his contribution to law reporting in Louisiana stands in marked contrast to that of Manning. A Virginia Harrison, and Henry Clay's cousin, Harrison was one in a legion of sons of the Old Dominion who left a large collective mark on Louisiana's legal ways. As a youngster, he was a frequent guest of Thomas Jefferson's at Monticello, where he met such luminaries as Daniel Webster; Marie Joseph Yves Roch Gilbert du Motier, marquis de Lafayette; and James Madison. He attended Harvard's newly established law school and received a bachelor of laws degree in 1825. After leaving Harvard, he studied in Richmond a short time before his admission to the Virginia bar. For the next four years he practiced in Richmond and had "no surfeit of fees."[24]

Deep down, Harrison wanted to be a college professor. Consequently, he sought a chair in French and Spanish, first at the University of North Carolina and then at the University of Virginia, only to be rejected on account of his youthfulness. Disappointed by these rejections, he left Richmond in 1829 to tour Europe and to study German. Along the way, he called on Aaron Burr, whom he referred to as the "old conspirator" and

23. Thomas C. Manning, comp., *Unreported Cases Heard and Determined by the Supreme Court of Louisiana from January 8, 1877 to April 1880,* vii.

24. Fairfax Harrison, *Aris Sonis Focisque* (privately printed, 1910), 103.

from whom he sought letters of introduction. In Paris, he attended Lafayette's evening parties and met many expatriated Americans. He also visited the poet Johann Wolfgang von Goethe and spent time with James Fenimore Cooper.[25]

Harrison returned to Virginia in 1831, where friends advised that New Orleans "offered the greatest Metropolitan prizes to a Southern man." Henry Clay told him, too, that business was good there, fees were high, and the attorneys were not very talented, and so he moved south. He was admitted to the Louisiana bar in 1832. Fluency in French and Spanish helped him establish a successful law practice and a wide network of connections, whereas his marriage to Frances Brand, the niece of supreme court judge Alexander Porter, rooted him more firmly in his profession and New Orleans society. He acted as secretary of the New Orleans bar, he lectured in law, and he was a founder of the Louisiana Historical Society. Yellow fever cut him short before his thirty-sixth birthday, but not before he produced a condensed version of Louisiana reports.[26]

A four-volume set, his *Reports of Cases of the Superior Court of the Territory of Orleans, and in the Supreme Court of Louisiana* was published by Emile Johns between 1839 and 1840. Dedicated to then United States Senator Alexander Porter, "at whose suggestion this work was undertaken," it condensed all twenty volumes of Martin's *Reports.* Harrison explained his editorial rationale as follows. He had

> undertaken this work with a conscientious resolution to comprise in his account of the cases, the genuine spirit of every case, to give those opinions of the court wherein any doctrine of whatever value is thrown out, in the very words of the court;—he decided to venture, however, to condense many simple cases, with the most sententious brevity, but if possible without diminishing or obscuring the sense to allude by a single line to the cases of mere fact, and occasionally to treat very cursorily some even labored cases which, since they were argued, have become the common law of all countries exercising trade.

25. Ibid.
26. Supreme Court Minute Book #4, 1829–34, 296; Harrison, *Aris Sonis Focisque,* 103–4, 107–9, 133–4, 138–9, 142.

He excluded arguments of the attorneys on the grounds that "the body of Martin's reports [were] an honorable and safe repository for them and sufficiently accessible too" because they were available "in public libraries or on the shelves of our elders, whether for doctrine or for eloquence."[27]

Cross references were added to the original Martin citations, though Harrison renounced "all claim to a show of research." At bottom, he merely offered his readers "a faithful collection of the *jurisprudence des arrêts* of Louisiana up to 1830: the notes, therefore, comprise only brief references to the prior or subsequent Louisiana cases, wherein the doctrine in question at any time [was] confirmed, contradicted or extended, together with any changes by legislation; and thus the work may be termed, *the Louisiana* cases compared with themselves."[28]

Thus, Harrison's goal was to reduce Martin's *Reports,* which were scarce, expensive, bulky, and verbose, to a convenient, condensed form, and he succeeded in that. He meant to market the set as a useful tool for practitioners, judges, students, or anyone else with an interest in law. The extent to which his intended customers found his product useful is uncertain, owing to the lack of data on the press run or sales records. That no one attempted a second edition following Harrison's death may indicate a lack of buyers. Still, Harrison's compilation merits notice as an early example of attempts to reduce the bulk of supreme court cases to a more manageable form of legal information.[29]

The same observation is equally true for Judah P. Benjamin and Thomas Slidell's *Digest of the Reported Decisions of the Superior Court of the Late Territory of Orleans and of the Supreme Court of the State of Louisiana.* Benjamin and Slidell approached case reporting in a manner wholly different from that of Harrison. Where he was a condenser, they were digesters. That is to say, they compressed cases to the essentials. More importantly, they eschewed chronological arrangement in favor of one that arrayed subject matter by title in alphabetical order. A table of contents and a table of cases served as added finding aids. The end result was a sin-

27. J. Burton Harrison, comp., *Reports of Cases of the Superior Court of the Territory of Orleans, and in the Supreme Court of Louisiana,* 1: iii, v–vi.

28. Ibid., vii.

29. Harrison noted that his brother-in-law, William F. Brand, assisted in condensing the first twelve volumes of Martin's *Reports* before he abandoned the enterprise to enter the ministry (ibid., vii).

gle, compact octavo volume, amounting to a mere 479 pages in the original edition, which came off the press of New Orleans printer John F. Carter in 1834. Their method, in their own words, was presentation of a

> statement of every point or principle decided in every case [which] is, of course, the most essential in a work of this nature; and we believe, that in this respect, the errors or omissions, if any, are very limited in number. The principle difficulties consist in the arrangement or subdivision of the different titles, and occasionally in determining under what title a particular decision should be embraced. We have endeavored to obviate the latter of these difficulties, by repeating such decisions under each title to which they could be considered as applicable; but in relation to the former, we are only able to say, that we have used every effort to make a Digest a convenient work of reference for the profession.[30]

Evidently, their handiwork enjoyed commercial success, because a second edition was printed in 1840. As the title page indicates, Slidell updated the new *Digest* to incorporate decisions handed down since 1834, and so nearly doubled the size of the original version. Noteworthy, too, was the fact that he and Benjamin contracted with Emile Johns to do the printing and distribution. Lacking sales figures, customer lists, or information on book ownership among Louisiana lawyers, it is difficult to know the extent of the clientele for the new edition.

More certain is what either rendition reveals about the editors. Clearly, they were not only clever lawyers, but also skilled scholars with sharp talents for extracting the kernel of complex opinions and legal reasoning from a vast web of words spun by supreme court judges. That they demonstrated like abilities stemmed from native gifts and similar education.

Slidell (1805–1864) is now overshadowed not only by Benjamin, but also by his elder brother John. Born in New York and educated at Yale College, he studied in Spain before settling in New Orleans at John's urging. Admitted to the Louisiana bar in 1833, Slidell later formed a partnership with Benjamin, dabbled in politics as a Democrat, and won election

30. Judah P. Benjamin and Thomas Slidell, comps., *Digest of the Reported Decisions of the Superior Court of the Late Territory of Orleans and of the Supreme Court of the State of Louisiana,* 1.

to the state senate. Governor Isaac Johnson named him an associate justice of the supreme court in 1846. When the court reorganized under the provisions of the Constitution of 1852, Slidell was elected second chief justice of Louisiana. His portrait depicts a smallish figure of a man, delicately featured, whose frail visage bespeaks weak health. If that picture, painted from life, speaks truthfully, then it explains why its subject abruptly resigned his office in 1855. A further assault on his health came the following year during the turbulent New Orleans elections when he was badly beaten by thugs. Shortly thereafter he removed to Newport, Rhode Island, where he lived out the remainder of his days.[31]

Benjamin (1811–1884) is better known to history as the éminence grise of the Confederacy than he is for his contributions to Louisiana law. Born to Jewish parents on the island of St. Thomas in the British West Indies, he moved with his family to Fayetteville, North Carolina, and then relocated with them to Charleston. A bright young man, he attended Yale College, where he first encountered Slidell. He moved to New Orleans at the age of seventeen. Arriving there with only five dollars in his pocket, he soon apprenticed himself to a commercial house and then clerked for a prominent notary. Studies in law and French followed and, at the age of twenty-one, he was admitted to the bar in New Orleans. Once a lawyer, Benjamin began a practice with Thomas Slidell, though he continued to invest heavily in business ventures. Suffering reverses in the Panic of 1837, he ended his stint as an entrepreneur and returned to the law. With Slidell, and the patronage of Slidell's brother John, Benjamin built one of the most important firms in New Orleans. A specialist in appellate litigation, he was so successful that during the first fifteen years of his career, he argued more appeals in Louisiana than any other lawyer of his time, a feat he later repeated in the Supreme Court of the United States.[32]

31. Supreme Court Minute Book #4, 1829–34, 493; Billings, *Historic Rules,* 49; *Dictionary of Louisiana Biography,* s.v. "Slidell, Thomas"; Wayne Everard, "Louisiana's 'Whig' Constitution Revisited: The Constitution of 1852," in Billings and Haas, eds., *In Search of Fundamental Law,* 47–8. The Slidell portrait now hangs in the reading room of the Law Library of Louisiana in New Orleans.

32. Details of Benjamin's life and career derive from Supreme Court Minute Book #4, 1829–34, 424; Pierce Butler, *Judah P. Benjamin* (Philadelphia, 1907); James H. Winston, *Judah P. Benjamin: Distinguished at the Bars of Two Nations* (Chicago, privately printed, 1930); *The Life of Judah Philip Benjamin* (New Orleans, 1937); Eli N. Evans, *Judah P. Benjamin: The Jewish Confederate* (New York, 1988).

Benjamin gained national notice when he took the case of the brig *Creole* with Slidell. He represented an insurance company being sued for the loss of slaves shipped from Virginia to New Orleans. The slaves had mutinied and forced the crew to sail to a British port in the Caribbean, where they made their escape. Benjamin proved that British authorities had enticed the slaves to run for their freedom. Such an enticement, he argued, was tantamount to a foreign intervention that relieved the insurance company of its obligation to honor its policy.[33]

Like Slidell, Benjamin was drawn to politics, though unlike his partner, he was drawn to public rather than judicial office. He was successively a state legislator, a member of the constitutional conventions of 1845 and 1852, and a presidential elector on the Whig ticket of Zachary Taylor and Millard Fillmore. In 1853 he was elected as a Whig to the Senate of the United States and reelected as a Democrat six years later. Withdrawing after Louisiana seceded from the Union, he threw in with the Confederacy and sought preferment in the rebel government. Jefferson Davis first appointed him attorney general, then secretary of war, and finally secretary of state. When the Confederacy fell, Benjamin escaped through Florida to England, where he lived out his remaining days. The loss of nearly all of his papers, which he destroyed shortly before his death, casts much of his political career into the shadows and him as an enigmatic presence of indeterminable influence.

Although most of the state's case reporters paled in comparison to Benjamin, their contributions to Louisiana law were no less profound. Consider their achievements. They summarized the facts and the arguments of counsel, they checked citations for accuracy, they prepared headnotes, they compiled indexes, and they sometimes improved on the opinions themselves. The end result was a steady production of vital legal information presented in an accessible printed format. Without the reporters, in short, the business of law in Louisiana would have been all the more difficult to pursue.

The nature of reporting changed, and as it did, less editorial work was required of the reporters. By this century, according to Henry Budd,

33. Benjamin's representation is discussed at length in William Joseph Poole, "The *Creole* Case" (M.A. thesis, University of New Orleans [formerly Louisiana State University in New Orleans], 1970).

judges had long since gotten "in the habit of stating the facts in their opinions," which enabled them to "cover any possible failure on their part to pass upon questions which would fairly arise under the *real* facts of the case." Once that custom took hold, opinions only needed to be collected and, "largely aided by scissors and paste," bound into printed volumes, which made them mechanical, less interesting, and less instructive.[34]

Then, too, the mechanics and economics of reporting changed over time. Reporters such as Martin, Robinson, Benjamin, or Slidell were attracted to reporting not only because of their affinity for legal scholarship but also because of the potential commercial value of their handiwork. Sales of their reports represented a significant addition to their incomes. Moreover, their political connections enabled them to secure monopoly rights, which increased their profit margins. Although the Supreme Court of the United States held as early as 1834 that a reporter could copyright his published decisions, the effect of the ruling in Louisiana, or elsewhere, was not fully felt until after the Civil War, when large publishing companies began to enter the market. Now independent reporters and printers had to compete with the likes of John West, whose National Reporter System rationalized the dissemination of decisions and whose economies of scale drove competitors from the field. Thus, the assignment of reporting supreme court opinions to West Publishing Company in 1903 closed a chapter in the history of Louisiana law.[35]

34. Henry Budd, "Reports and Some Reporters," *American Law Review* 31 (1913): 514–5 (emphasis added), 516; Surrency, *History of American Law Publishing,* 579.

35. *Wheaton and Donaldson* v. *Peters and Grigg,* 26 U.S. 33 (1834): 591ff; Woxland, "'Forever Associated,'" 120–2.

Part II

JUDGES AND COURTS

In the name and by the authority of the State of Louisiana, Know ye
that reposing special trust and confidence in the Patriotism, Integrity
and abilities of Dominick Augustin Hall, I [William C. C. Clai-
borne] have nominated, and by and with the consent of the Senate,
do appoint him a Judge of the Supreme Court of the State of
Louisiana, and do authorize and empower him to execute and fulfil
the duties of the office according to Law; and to have and to hold the
said office with all powers, privileges and emoluments to the same of
right appertaining, during good behaviour.

> Sybil A. Boudreaux, ed., "The First Minute Book of the Su-
> preme Court of Louisiana, March 1813 to May 1818: Anno-
> tated Edition" (M.A. thesis, University of New Orleans 1983),
> 13–5.

From the territorial period onward, Louisiana courts drew to their
benches thinkers, dolts, rapscallions, and good gray journeymen.
Character and temperament, wit and erudition, conviction and commitment, together determined how judges honored their solemn oaths to uphold the law and to do justice. At the workaday level of routine court sessions, personal qualifications also dictated the approach to tasks and the
intellectual undergirders of rulings. Examples of well-led judicial lives

stood, moreover, as they still stand, as worthy models for aspiring attorney and jurist alike.

Courts afford a forum to grapple with the exquisite task of addressing the ever dynamic legal needs of a diverse citizenry. The contests between litigants range from the trivial to the profound, but in their resolutions arise decisions that enliven the flat words of a statute or impart new meaning to old opinions. Louisiana's courts and judges did more, for it was they who blended American and civil law into a mixed jurisprudence that is the hallmark of the state's legal order.

Studies of Louisiana judges, procedure, or the courts as institutions are few and far between. The next three essays cast light in dark corners via means that simultaneously acknowledge orthodox legal history and depart from conventional wisdom. Traditional treatments of judges and courts draw notice to the development of substantive law and the crafting of its interpretation. The authors of these essays do not. They eschew that approach for a plain reason. Substantive law has long fixed itself in the sights of Louisiana scholars, who have written widely and soundly on the subject. Hence, there is little need to rehearse what others have superbly done already.

Mark F. Fernandez

LOCAL JUSTICE IN THE TERRITORY OF ORLEANS

W. C. C. Claiborne's Courts, Judges, and Justices of the Peace

The acquisition of Louisiana by the United States represents one of the most important elements in the intersection of European and American worlds during the early national period. Although the purchase facilitated the Americanization of Louisiana, few historians have vigorously pursued the topic.[1] One area crucial to the understanding of Americanization is the origin and development of the judicial system. In recent years there has been enquiry into the role of Louisiana's highest courts as agents of Americanization, but scholarship pertaining to the state's lower courts and its officers is virtually nonexistent.[2] How Governor William C. C. Claiborne sought to establish local courts and to find suitable judges and

1. Aside from William Lewis Newton's *Americanization of Louisiana: A Study in the Process of Adjustment between the French and Anglo-American Populations of Louisiana, 1803–1860* (New York, 1980 rept.), and recent and ongoing efforts by Light T. Cummins, little thought has been given to this important aspect of Louisiana history.

2. Recent studies by Warren M. Billings, Elizabeth F. Gaspard, Richard Holcombe Kilbourne, Jr., Judith Kelleher Schafer, Sheridan E. Young, and the author have focused on the highest levels of Louisiana's legal system, the appellate courts, the supreme court bar, the 1812 constitution, and the development of criminal law in Louisiana. See Warren M. Billings, "Louisiana's Legal History and Its Sources: Needs, Opportunities, and Approaches," in Edward F. Haas, ed., *Louisiana's Legal Heritage*

justices of the peace for Orleans Territory between 1803 and 1812 offers an important lesson in the early history of Americanization.

After Napoleon Bonaparte ceded Louisiana to the United States on 20 December 1803, President Thomas Jefferson took decisive steps to organize his newly acquired prize. Jefferson's task proved to be one of the most difficult of his administration. He had, in fact, acquired two distinct territories. Upper and Lower Louisiana, as contemporaries termed them, differed dramatically from one another. The northern portion had never figured prominently in the colonial plans of France or Spain, it was sparsely inhabited, and it lacked an entrenched elite that might have resisted American ambitions. Consequently, it resembled the old Northwest, a region that the Americans had successfully organized and administered during the Confederation period. Lower Louisiana (roughly the area comprising the present-day Bayou State), by contrast, presented a more difficult conundrum. It had been populated throughout the eighteenth century by Frenchmen, Spaniards, Germans, Acadians, British colonists who fled the Regulator troubles in North Carolina, and after 1776, growing numbers of United States citizens. These Europeans, of course, intermingled with healthy numbers of Indian tribes and African Americans.[3]

Recognizing the duality of the purchase, Congress quickly split the

---

(Pensacola, Fla., 1983); Billings, ed., *The Historic Rules of the Supreme Court of Louisiana, 1813–1879* (Lafayette, La., 1985); Billings, "A 'Course of Studies': Books That Shaped Louisiana Law," see chapter 1 in the present volume; Billings, "From this Seed the Louisiana Constitution of 1812," in Billings and Edward F. Haas, eds., *In Search of Fundamental Law: Louisiana's Constitutions: 1819–1874* (Lafayette, La., 1993); Billings, "Origins of Criminal Law in Louisiana," *Louisiana History* 31 (1991): 63–76; Elizabeth Gaspard, "Rise of the Louisiana Bar," *Louisiana History* 28 (1987): 181–93; Richard Holcombe Kilbourne, Jr., "An Overview of the Work of the Territorial Court, 1804–1808: A Missing Chapter in the Development of the Louisiana Civil Code," in Haas, ed., *Louisiana's Legal Heritage,* 107–29; Kilbourne, Jr., *A History of the Louisiana Civil Code: The Formative Years, 1803–1839* (Baton Rouge, 1987); Judith Kelleher Schafer, *Slavery, the Civil Law, and the Supreme Court of Louisiana* (Baton Rouge, 1994); Sheridan E. Young, "Louisiana's Court of Errors and Appeals, 1843–1846," see chapter 5 in the present volume; Mark F. Fernandez, "From Chaos to Continuity: Early Reforms of the Supreme Court of Louisiana, 1845–1859," *Louisiana History* 28 (1987): 19–41; Fernandez, "The Appellate Question: A Comparative Analysis of Supreme Courts of Appeal in Virginia and Louisiana, 1776–1840" (Ph.D. diss., The College of William and Mary in Virginia, 1991).

3. Works detailing the history of settlement in colonial Louisiana are legion. Daniel H. Usner, *Indians, Settlers, & Slaves in a Frontier Exchange Economy: The Lower Mississippi before 1783* (Chapel Hill, 1992); and Carl A. Brasseaux, *The Founding of New Acadia: The Beginnings of Acadian Life in Louisiana, 1765–1803* (Baton Rouge, 1987) offer the best treatments of this subject.

ceded lands into two territories, and the southern section became the Territory of Orleans. Orleans, with its long-settled port and ethnic hodgepodge of inhabitants, promised to be the most difficult area to govern. Indeed, the region had a troubled history of resisting administrative changes. Following the Treaty of Fontainebleau in 1762, when France ceded Louisiana to Spain, French Louisianians resisted efforts by the Spanish governor Antonio Ulloa to introduce Spanish methods of law and government. In 1768, they revolted and sent Ulloa packing to Havana. Although they eventually capitulated to Alejandro O'Reilly, their insurrection served as a caution to Jefferson and his American cohorts.[4]

Thus, the president realized that mere separation of Upper and Lower Louisiana would not resolve all of the administrative problems. Judging that the *ancienne population* in Orleans would be just as suspicious of rash innovation and brusque leadership as they had been in the 1760s, Jefferson appointed his trusted friend, cousin, and adviser William C. C. Claiborne (1775–1817) as governor. Together, the two fleshed out a cautious policy for the territory, which resulted in a bumpy, yet successful, administration that culminated in the admission of Louisiana as the eighteenth state in the Union.[5]

President and governor faced unique concerns in organizing Orleans Territory. In Upper Louisiana, Jefferson could rely on the tried and tested measures pioneered in the old Northwest. Thus, he introduced a United States presence, military officials, and territorial officers to organize the northern territory according to American fashion. Introduction of Anglo-American legal practices proved an easy thing, as it had in the Northwest, because of Upper Louisiana's sparse population and its lack of an indigenous elite that could support alternative measures. Indeed, the Northwest Ordinance of 1787 simply built on Britain's Quebec Act of 1763, which had provided for the organization of that frontier area under British rule. Even though the English imposed an alien legal system on the people of Quebec, they faced few challenges. Without an organized, powerful dis-

---

4. John Preston Moore, *Revolt in Louisiana: The Spanish Occupation, 1766–1770* (Baton Rouge, 1976); Carl A. Brasseaux, *Denis Nicolas Foucault and the New Orleans Rebellion of 1768* (Ruston, La., 1987).

5. Fernandez, "Appellate Question," 110–5.

senting faction to lead them, Canadian traders merely adjusted to British changes such as the imposition of the common law. The British also had the wisdom to tolerate the Quebecois penchant for Catholicism. Similarities between the British organization of Quebec and the American organization of the Northwest Territory were profound. The Americans, then, faced few unprecedented challenges in organizing the Northwest and did so with a high degree of efficiency. Upper Louisiana would follow the same track.[6]

In Orleans Territory, on the other hand, Claiborne and Jefferson encountered an entrenched and historically rebellious elite. Congress again posited the provisions of the Northwest Ordinance as the model for organizing Orleans, but the milieu was different and the task ultimately more complex, if not to say bothersome. Possibly the most trying aspect of the project was the creation of an Americanized legal system, and that charge fell to William Charles Cole Claiborne.

Claiborne arrived in Louisiana after a lengthy legal and political apprenticeship. As a teenager, he clerked for the United States House of Representatives. At twenty-one, Claiborne returned home to Sussex County, Virginia, where he read law and entered the bar before moving to Tennessee in search of opportunity. Plying his newfound calling on the Tennessee frontier, he established a thriving criminal practice and soon rose through the ranks of the territory's elite. In 1796 his neighbors elected him a delegate to the Tennessee constitutional convention. That same year, he accepted an appointment to the new state's supreme court. When Andrew Jackson vacated his seat in the United States House of Representatives for one in the Senate, Claiborne replaced him and returned to the chamber where he once served as a clerk. Congressman Claiborne, like many southerners, gravitated to the Democratic-Republican faction. His cousin and Republican visionary, Thomas Jefferson, mentored the young representative, who soon became immersed in attacks on Federalist foreign policy. Like other Jeffersonians, he also became an outspoken critic of the Alien and Sedition Acts. When Jefferson rode the Republican wave into the White House, he chose Claiborne to replace the

6. Clarence E. Carter, "The Office of Commander-in-Chief: A Phase of Imperial Unity on the Eve of the American Revolution," in Richard B. Morris, ed., *The Era of the American Revolution: Studies Inscribed to Evarts Boutell Greene* (New York, 1939), 183.

Federalist governor of Mississippi Territory, Winthrop Sargeant. Claiborne's successful handling of Mississippi's Indian problems led Jefferson to offer his cousin the Louisiana governorship when James Monroe turned it down.[7]

In anticipation of receiving Louisiana, Jefferson ordered Claiborne, along with the military adventurer-cum-intriguer James Wilkinson, to New Orleans as commissioners of the United States government to accept the colony from the French. If the retrocession from Spain to France and the cession of the colony to the United States went smoothly, Claiborne's administrative talents could be put to good use. If a problem developed, Wilkinson's military skills would then be tested. The transfers proceeded without incident; thus Claiborne emerged as the central figure in the American contingent.[8]

His actions as governor of the Territory of Orleans have been the subject of much debate, among both his contemporaries and later historians. He emerges from treatment by the latter as an honest man of moderate abilities. Nineteenth-century historians focused on his lack of French and his apparent distaste for things creole as flaws in both his moral character and his capacity to govern. Some more modern scholars have complimented him for his sober discharge of a daunting task that probably required a man of greater stature and vision. Others see him as a wavering, impotent character who is frequently eclipsed by stellar figures such as Jackson or Wilkinson. One recent assessment denigrates his early administration as stubborn and riddled with doubt, but treats his later years more kindly.[9]

Claiborne's career as a whole is a difficult one to assess. Those who emphasize stubbornness, along with a degree of bumbling and indecision, are no doubt right in their assessments, as are those who credit the gover-

7. Joseph T. Hatfield, *William Claiborne: Jeffersonian Centurion in the American Southwest* (Lafayette, La., 1976), 28–40; *Dictionary of American Biography,* vol. 2, s.v. "Claiborne, William"; Hatfield, *William Claiborne,* 41–95; William C. C. Claiborne to Thomas Jefferson, 5 October 1804, in Clarence E. Carter, comp., *The Territorial Papers of the United States* (Washington, D.C., 1940), 9: 307; Elizabeth Gaspar Brown, "Legal Systems in Conflict: Orleans Territory, 1804–1812," *American Journal of Legal History* 2 (1957): 41–2; Fernandez, "Appellate Question," 113–5.

8. Fernandez, "Appellate Question," 113–7.

9. For a good analysis of conflicting historiographical views of Claiborne, see R. Randall Couch, "William Charles Coles Claiborne: An Historiographical Review," *Louisiana History* 36 (1995): 463–5.

nor with diligence, efficiency, and sincerity. More to the point, Claiborne had a long career, and like most Americans of his generation, he was often confronted with unprecedented situations, and he should be viewed as the sum of his parts rather than judged by a handful of them.

In constructing a judicial system for the Territory of Orleans, Claiborne did a marvelous job, though Secretary of State James Madison and the president deserve some of the credit for its creation. When he dispatched the gubernatorial commission to Claiborne, Madison advised him to use great care in his dealings with the populace. Jefferson also made his motives clear in his instructions to Claiborne: Louisiana was to follow Anglo-American patterns of justice. Even so, Jefferson also understood the tenuous relationship between the *ancienne population* and recently arrived American officials. Reminding the governor how distrust of alien legal principles had incited Louisianians to rebel against Ulloa, Jefferson instructed Claiborne to install an American system of justice in a moderate fashion, incorporating native principles of law and justice whenever possible to dispel the fears of Orleannais. Nonetheless, the overall thrust of the instructions required the imposition of Anglo-American principles and institutions.[10]

Acting under such mandates, and with his own innate sense of caution, Claiborne assumed the intricate task of fusing alien French and Spanish legal customs with Anglo-American precepts of law and justice. Unlike the English in Quebec or his compatriots in the Northwest, Claiborne operated in a busy metropolis surrounded by a suspicious and powerful elite. Moreover, French shenanigans on the eve of the cession further complicated his job.[11]

Pierre Clément de Laussat, whom Napoleon dispatched to Louisiana as prefect, fully expected to revamp the colony into a model of French colonialism. En route to New Orleans, Laussat received revised additional orders instructing him merely to preside over the retrocession of the colony from Spain and then to hand it over to the Americans. During the brief period that the colony actually remained in French hands, Laussat inexplicably proceeded to try to reinvent its administration. He suspended

---

10. Fernandez, "Appellate Question," 113–5.

11. For a brief analysis of Laussat's efforts and its ramifications regarding the territory's court system, see ibid., 111–44.

all vestiges of Spanish rule by closing the Cabildo and voiding all Spanish law. Although he managed to begin his restructuring of the colony's administration by the time he handed the keys to the city over to Wilkinson and Claiborne, he had not reinstituted its laws. Consequently, the Americans inherited a territory devoid of law or judicial institutions. That void theoretically gave Claiborne carte blanche to cast the legal system however he might, but Laussat had done him no service. Realistically, the governor was constrained by his own innate caution, his instructions, and the potentially obstreperous Orleanians.[12]

Therefore, the governor accepted the likelihood that the territory's laws would become a jumble of civilian and common law principles that mingled English and American constitutional mandates with continental doctrines. He had no flexibility, though, regarding the structure of the territorial courts. They would follow American forms, which ensured that thoroughly Americanized courts would, in time, devise a mixed jurisprudence for Louisiana. In 1803, however, no one had tried such an arrangement anywhere else in the United States or its territory, and no one, least of all Claiborne, understood just how one might be accomplished. The quest began once he set about creating local courts and judgeships. It was riven with uncertainty and marked, understandably, by much experimentation.[13]

Claiborne turned first to the immediate problems posed by Laussat's suspension of the Spanish law. To fill the judicial void, he instituted two temporary courts, the governor's court and a court of pleas. The former provided a territory-wide tribunal to consider pending civil and criminal causes, and, at the governor's discretion, appeals from the latter. No records survive from the governor's court, and Claiborne's letters provide no explanation of his rationale, although his enabling ordinance cited a need for "justice."[14]

Governor's courts were not without precedent in the Anglo-American experience. In colonial times, justice usually flowed from the executive division. After the Revolution, Americans slowly separated powers between different branches of government, but such division remained a relatively

12. Ibid.
13. Ibid.
14. Ibid., 116.

new concept in 1803. Claiborne's native Virginia entered the Revolution with its governor and highly placed members of its legislative council sitting as its general court. That bench held original and appellate jurisdiction in both civil and criminal matters. Removal of its royal governor vis-à-vis the Revolution caused Virginians to experiment with a variety of arrangements. Initially, a modified version of the old general court continued into the early national period along with a complicated morass of other tribunals with unique and sometimes overlapping competence. By 1788 the Virginians had learned through experience and trial and error that there was no need to replicate England's entire judicial structure, and they adapted a more streamlined court system. These events occurred during Claiborne's lifetime. As a student and member of the Old Dominion's bar, he became familiar with these examples. Thus, his governor's court made up of the governor and highly placed members of the Legislative Council of the Territory of Orleans reflected judicial arrangements that Claiborne knew and that had served his home commonwealth well.[15]

What is known of the governor's court stems from Claiborne's own description and Edward Livingston's sketchy notes. It quickly turned into an overbearing chore so strenuous that Claiborne plainly could not accommodate to its demands, and he abolished it. Another reason for its closure was his discomfort with the muddled state of territorial law, especially in regard to alien precedents and capital cases. In the end, then, the governor's court existed for only a very short time and did little to inform the early history of Louisiana's judiciary. The court of pleas, however, was another matter.[16]

If the governor's court stemmed from Claiborne's desire to institute a court for all of Louisiana, the court of pleas was organized with New Orleans specifically in mind. As the center of commerce, the Crescent City was a busy place, and in the wake of Laussat's suspension of the judiciary, a rising number of civil suits mounted and their litigants cried out for resolution. Thus, Claiborne conceived the court of pleas to meet a

15. For a detailed comparison of the post-Revolutionary Virginia courts with the territorial arrangements in Orleans, see ibid., 30–216.

16. William C. C. Claiborne, " An ordinance to aid in the Administration of Justice," 30 December 1803, in Dunbar S. Rowland, ed., *Official Letterbooks of W. C. C. Claiborne, 1801–1816* (Jackson, Miss., 1917), 1: 317–9.

pressing municipal legal need. It was comprised of seven members and had jurisdiction in civil matters of three thousand dollars or less. More serious judicial questions would have to await the creation of a superior court system.[17]

Claiborne modeled the court of pleas after the American courts in which he had practiced. If the governor's court loosely resembled Virginia's general court, then the court of pleas mimicked inferior benches elsewhere. Claiborne created nine judgeships for the court; however, he did not expect all nine to sit simultaneously because any seven would make a quorum. In this regard, he imitated the practice at the time in any of a number of municipal courts throughout the nation. For instance, Claiborne's scheme closely resembled the hustings court in Richmond, Virginia, which the governor would have known quite well.[18]

Creating the court was easy; Claiborne merely promulgated an enabling ordinance. Finding judges was difficult; that became a monumental task. Anticipating problems with most territorial appointments, and needing intelligence regarding prospective appointees, Jefferson had asked James Wilkinson to draw up a list of suitable candidates. Wilkinson, in turn, enlisted the aid of Evan Jones—a fellow American who had emigrated to the city in 1786 and become a prosperous local merchant. Jones possessed two qualities of extraordinary value in the early territory: He was an American and he knew the locals. He dutifully compiled his list, which was apparently amended, possibly by one Labigarre, a Frenchman known only by Jefferson's description of him as a man with "a so-so reputation, he married a Livingston, sells Antiseptic gas."[19]

The Jones-Labigarre list provided Claiborne with little real help. Many of the residents were described in frank terms, as Wilkinson had as a high priority identifying potential troublemakers. At times the information was confusing because the compilers sometimes disagreed with each other's analyses. For instance, Jones described Eugène Dorsiere as "well

17. Fernandez, "Appellate Question," 128–92; Fernandez, "The Rules of the Courts of the Territory of Orleans," *Louisiana History* 38 (1997): 63–86.

18. Fernandez, "Practicing the Revolution: Law and Courts in Revolutionary and Post-Revolutionary Virginia" (forthcoming).

19. "Characterization of New Orleans Residents," 1 July 1804, in Carter, ed., *Territorial Papers* 9: 248–58.

informed mild & energetick, possess'd with sound & deliberate mind full of integrity, he is more friendly to the american Government being born in the mountains of Switserland, where in his cradle he imbibed principles of Liberty, he is the friend of Order & much attach'd to the welfare of this province, Upright & virtuous Morals." By contrast, Labigarre depicted Dorsiere as one whose "character is greatly overrated, he was formerly a dancing master in Philadelphia, but He is doubtless a man of good disposition and fair character; tho destitute of influence." Most individuals on the list had some drawback that rendered their fitness as judges questionable, to say the least. Nonetheless, Claiborne had numerous positions to fill; so, he was forced to choose among the less desirable prospects.[20]

His initial appointments to the court of pleas reflect his dilemma. Consider the nine he named: Anthony Argotte, Beverly Chew, Benjamin Morgan, William Kenner, Paul Lanusse, Francis Guerin, Gaspard Dubuys, William Garland, and Eugène Dorsiere. Argotte spoke no English but had a good grasp of Spanish law. He had been alcalde and president of the municipality during the Spanish regime, so he knew something of judicial proceedings. Jones described him as a man of "doubtful morals" and "much addicted to gaming." Labigarre remarked how he was "rather stubborn & self-conceited, & finally unfit to hold any office under the american government." Claiborne, however, found few candidates with better qualifications, so he appointed Argotte both as a judge and as the French clerk. Lanusse, in Jones's estimation, was "unfit for Political or Civil appointments." Guerin was a farmer who favored American rule, which was a point in his favor, but lacked legal training. Labigarre characterized Gaspard Dubuys as an "active magistrate" and friendly to American rule. Jones, by comparison, noted that Dubuys's commission business was of "some what doubtful circumstances" and that his talents were "very moderate . . . his weight in the Society not great." Finally, the dancing master, Dorsiere, rounded out the Orleannais appointments. American émigrés made up the remainder. Chew, Morgan, Kenner, and Garland all stood high in the local merchant community. None of them had any legal training or any other qualifications that

20. Ibid.

suited them for service on the court. But they were Claiborne's country-men, familiar with American justice, and perhaps potentially important political allies.[21]

The basic procedures, forms of writs, and general business of the court accorded with established Anglo-American practices. These practices, set forth in the court's early rules, reflect Claiborne's desire to give American patterns to the mixed jurisdiction. At the court's first session in the Hôtel de Ville on the evening of 10 January 1804, judges adopted fifteen rules of procedure that would have provided a fine starting point for any American court in any jurisdiction. Litigants would initiate cases via writs of summons, capias, and attachment as practiced in virtually every other American local court. Rule four provided for a speedy trial, thus extending important constitutional guarantees. Anglo-American methods for securing bonds, issuing subpoenas, or executing judgments were likewise codified. Because Congress had not yet attended to the fine points of Louisiana's territorial organization, all processes would be issued in the name of the governor.

The significance of these rules was their imposition of a distinctively American structure on the territory's first viable court. Thereby they initiated a habit that would be followed again and again throughout the nineteenth century. Once the legislative council came into being, it would follow the lead of the court of pleas when it adopted the Practice Act of 1805, and in subsequent statutes that erected other inferior courts for the territory.

And so, even before Congress split the Louisiana Purchase in two, Claiborne had provided for a modicum of local justice. His efforts, especially insofar as they installed Americanized patterns of judicature, provided important institutional precursors for Louisiana's judicial system. Establishing some temporary courts and finding suitable judges, however, solved only one of the problems that Laussat had created for the Americans. There remained the problem of what was or what was not law in the territory.

Without laws on the books, Claiborne hypothetically had free rein to effect a legal revolution. The historical response to such innovation in Louisiana, however, was a rebellious one. Thus, Secretary Madison's ad-

---

21. Ibid. For an analysis of the court of pleas, see Fernandez, "Rules of the Courts."

vice to proceed cautiously, especially in regard to constructing laws, seemed prudent. A cautious policy, however, would not fill the legal vacuum. Claiborne and other territorial officials, then, had to devise new laws that provided for a fair and constitutionally acceptable form of justice, allayed local suspicion of American innovations, and provided a viable system of conflict resolution.

In 1806, at Claiborne's behest, the legislative council appointed two jurisconsults, James Brown and Louis Moreau Lislet, to compile a digest of the territory's civil (private) law. Drawing on French conventions, projets for the *Code Napoleon,* Spanish doctrines, and English and American commentaries, Brown and Moreau Lislet produced *A Digest of the Civil Laws Now in Force in the Territory of Orleans, with Alterations and Amendments Adapted to Its Present System of Government* (New Orleans, 1808). Legal scholars and historians have long misinterpreted the meaning and impact of the *Digest,* but recently the picture has become more clear.

Never intended as a comprehensive code, the *Digest* collected important Roman, continental, and Anglo-American doctrines to serve as a guide for Louisiana lawyers and judges. It was used in concert with gubernatorial ordinances and acts of the territorial legislatures. While the *Digest* was in preparation, bench and bar relied on European (especially Spanish) and American customs. Once published, the *Digest* became the single most important guide to territorial private law, but it remained only one of many for determining the laws in force. Of equal importance, the *Digest* closely resembled Claiborne's overall legal policy. It mingled American law with local customs, thereby satisfying the governor's instructions to install an American legal system with caution and respect to local concerns.

Moreover, the way in which territorial judges utilized the *Digest* as a source for judicial interpretation and as a basis for establishing precedent distinguished Louisiana from wholly civilian jurisdictions. French, Spanish, even Roman conventions were prescribed in the *Digest,* but they were never invested with the authority of a civil code. Rather, judges used them in concert with decisions, statutes, ordinances, and other authorities as a basis for adjudications based on precedent the same way that American judges did elsewhere.[22]

22. Fernandez, "Appellate Question," 99–145, 282–91.

Definition of the territory's private law, however, tells only the more well-known side of Claiborne's quest to locate the laws in force. Less appreciated, but perhaps more important to an understanding of Americanization and territorial rule, was the move to specify the criminal (public) law. Without criminal statutes on the books, the territorial government's ability to keep order rested solely with the military. Although Orleanians were accustomed to martial law during the Spanish regime, Claiborne understood that an overly forceful American military presence would hinder his administration. He also had a deep republican distaste for standing armies. So, defining criminal laws was a centerpiece in his scheme to reorganize the legal system.

Jefferson's instructions regarding the common law also figured prominently in Claiborne's thinking, and for that reason, too, few continental practices could be maintained. Under American law, an accused is presumed innocent and protected by certain constitutional guarantees. Protection against unlawful search and seizure, the right of habeas corpus, trial by jury, due process, and a speedy trial, all central to the American conception of liberty, were unknown in colonial Louisiana before 1803. Thereafter, penal law would have to attend to these liberties, which was why Claiborne ignored French and Spanish criminal law. In this crucial sphere, then, true legal revolution occurred in the years following the Purchase.

Revolution, however, is a tricky matter. Rarely does one go according to plan; internecine battles among the leaders, historical accident, or whimsy all thrive in its midst. Louisiana's revolution in criminal law was no exception. It began when Claiborne convened the first session of the legislative council in December 1804, but its early origins are murky owing to the loss of the journals and other working papers. The councillors recognized that the territory's criminal laws had to follow Anglo-American patterns exclusively because of the congressional mandate that the courts "shall have common law jurisdiction." Accordingly, they formed a committee to draft a crimes bill. Dr. John Watkins chaired the committee and solicited help from Claiborne, as well as the members of the New Orleans bar. In January 1805, Watkins reported the committee's recommendations to the council, which assigned a clerk, James Workman, to edit the committee's draft into statutory form. Workman's revision stayed on the table for several months as the council resolved other matters. But the council eventually revised and adopted a final Crimes Act. Claiborne signed the bill, which became law on 4 May 1805.[23]

The Act for the Punishment of Crimes and Misdemeanors contained fifty-two sections covering three basic issues at law: offenses, prosecutions, and punishments. In this regard, the Crimes Act resembled similar statutory provisions that had been adopted throughout the United States. One need only compare it to the revised code of Virginia, for instance, to understand its relationship to other American criminal legislation. (As both Claiborne and Watkins hailed from the Old Dominion, it seems reasonable to assume that their Virginia background colored their thinking.) Over thirty categories of offenses were defined in the Crimes Act. Misdemeanors fell under the jurisdiction of various local courts, whereas felonies came under the purview of the superior court alone. The statute extended the usual American constitutional protections of due process and trial by jury to all suspects, but it also offered innovative privileges such as the right to an attorney, "free access" to counsel, a copy of the indictment, the jury list, and the power to subpoena witnesses. Furthermore, criminal matters were to be "taken, intended and construed according to and in conformity with the common law of England; and the forms of indictment (divested however of unnecessary prolixity), the method of trial, the rules of evidence and all other proceedings whatsoever in the prosecution of the said crimes, offenses and misdemeanors, changing what ought to be changed, shall be, except as is by this act otherwise provided for, according to the said common law." Although various aspects of the bill remained unclear—lawyers and scholars then and now have disagreed about what the council meant by "unnecessary prolixity"—the Crimes Act represented a giant step in Louisiana's revolution in criminal law. It filled the void left by Laussat's suspension of the laws in force, it followed the congressional mandate, and it marked one of Claiborne's major successes in implementing his instruction. Loopholes and imperfections in the act were corrected in July 1805, after Claiborne signed "An Act Supplementary to the act for the Punishment of Crimes and Misdemeanors."[24]

23. Orleans Territorial Acts (1805), 416–64; Billings, "Origins of Criminal Law," 63–77.
24. Orleans Territorial Acts (1805), 63–73.

Mere passage of legislation, however, rarely suffices to define laws in force. To explain the state of the territory's penal laws, the legislative council requested that the governor draw up an exposition of the new criminal law at the same time it appointed the jurisconsults to compile the *Digest of the Civil Laws*. His experience with the governor's court taught Claiborne that his time was too precious for such endeavors, even though he was eminently qualified. So he passed the task on to one of his protégés, an Irishman named Lewis Kerr. Kerr was one of those shadowy figures commonplace in territorial histories. His background and origins are elusive. He appeared in Mississippi Territory in 1802 and established a law practice in Natchez. Soon he entered Claiborne's household, where his legal proficiency proved useful. Claiborne took Kerr with him to New Orleans and provided him with minor sinecures. Eventually, Kerr earned a commission in a militia battalion of free blacks and, with Claiborne's patronage, became sheriff of New Orleans and a United States marshal. Then Claiborne enlisted him to prepare the exposition, which Kerr completed and published in 1806. Although Kerr's fortunes in New Orleans dissipated after he was implicated in the Burr conspiracy, his *Exposition of the Criminal Laws of the Territory of Orleans* remained a popular publication. The *Exposition* also became one of the most successful agents of Americanization in the region.[25]

Written in English and translated into French by Louis Moreau Lislet, the *Exposition* guided at least two generations of lawyers through Louisiana's criminal proceedings. As was standard for legal treatises, Kerr introduced his work with a brief history of the criminal arrangements in the territory, then outlined the contents of the book. He defined the offenses named by the 1805 statutes, then he presented "a succinct detail of criminal proceedings, and the principal rules of evidence." Finally, he concluded the book with a handy appendix of forms of records and procedures that he had adapted for use. In a word, Kerr provided even the uninitiated with a helpful guide to criminal practice. The treatise drew on the territory's statutes as well as English and American conventions. Ever the legal scholar, Kerr took care to point out how territorial arrangements and American practices differed from English conventions. Thereby, users

25. Fernandez, "Appellate Question," 129–34; Billings, "A Neglected Treatise: Lewis Kerr's *Exposition* and the Making of Criminal Law in Louisiana," *Louisiana History* 36 (1997): 452–72.

of the *Exposition* received a crash course in comparative English and American penal justice. English authorities such as Sir Edward Coke, Sir William Blackstone, and Sir Matthew Hale were introduced to Louisiana's criminal practitioners. The Virginian William Waller Hening also received Kerr's close attention. In fact, some of the writs adapted in the appendix seem to be drawn directly from Hening's guide for Virginia's justices of the peace.[26]

Claiborne, the legislative council, and Lewis Kerr revolutionized the penal law on paper. Refinements grew out to its application and practice in the territory's courts that replaced the governor's court and the court of pleas. Taking their cue from Congress, Claiborne and the legislative council created a new judiciary comprised of a superior court of original and appellate jurisdiction and a system of county courts. The latter had original jurisdiction over petty criminal crimes and civil matters involving under fifty dollars in value.[27]

Whereas New Orleans lawyers and businessmen were for Claiborne an ample source of candidates for the court of pleas, there were not enough to go around when it came to picking men for the superior and the county benches. Naming suitable appointees soon became a perennial and most vexing administrative problem for the governor as he had to fill upward of two hundred seats between 1804 and 1812. Claiborne's own criteria for prospective officers, ethnic biases, the novelty of the laws in force, and low salaries shrunk the pool of available magistrates and slowed the hunt to a pace suitable only to gastropods.[28]

In setting qualifications Claiborne tried to be both practical and political. He sought out not only those qualified in terms of legal learning but also those who spoke for the interests of the *ancienne population*. These criteria made the task of finding suitable candidates a near impossibility. A full contingent on the superior court bench was not recruited until spring 1806, even though Claiborne courted the most qualified legal minds across the country. He tempted the likes of Peter Duponçeau of Phila-

26. See the comparison of writs in Fernandez, "Appellate Question," 296–300.

27. "An Act for Dividing the Territory of Orleans into Counties, and Establishing Courts of Inferior Jurisdiction Therein," Orleans Territorial Acts (1805), 144–88.

28. These figures reflect numbers from my database of judges and justices of the peace. Fernandez, "Appellate Question," 118–28.

delphia, Ephraim Kirby of Connecticut, and John Prevost of New York. They seemed naturals to him, given their fluency in foreign tongues, their knowledge of civil law, and their affinity for codification. Low pay, other opportunities, and death kept all but Prevost from accepting Claiborne's offer. Once the bench stabilized, Claiborne kept it filled, though he abandoned his hopes of drawing members from the *ancienne population,* because none qualified as knowledgeable in the law. He turned instead to Americans or thoroughly naturalized residents such as François-Xavier Martin.[29]

Involving members of the *ancienne population* in the county courts was crucial to Claiborne's judicial policy because their presence would deflate suspicions of an Anglo-American court system. But Claiborne found it difficult to interest them in serving. Ironically, Creoles stood to gain the most from these appointments because the county court system brought an end to the volatile continental practice of using military commandants to administer civilian affairs.[30]

One problem that Claiborne faced in attracting local residents was a change in American attitudes toward the idea of magistracy itself. Throughout colonial America, members of local elites vied for positions on the county bench to ensure their social position and to gain hegemony over their communities. By the early national period, as colonies became states and grew more settled, qualities such as wealth and family position overshadowed political officeholding as the source of community status. Time-consuming and low-paying positions such as seats on commissions of the peace actually came to be regarded as burdens—freight that the educated and highborn (and often best qualified) residents could live without. Louisiana was not immune to these trends, and many similarly situated Creoles turned Claiborne a deaf ear.[31]

29. Only Prevost served on the Superior Court for the Territory of Orleans.

30. Codification seemed a lively course given the confused status of Louisiana's laws in force in the early nineteenth century. A comprehensive law code, however, was a long time in coming (Richard Holcombe Kilbourne, Jr., *A History of The Louisiana Civil Code: The Formative Years, 1803–1839* [Baton Rouge, 1987], 96–158); Fernandez, " Appellate Question," 115–7; George Dargo, *Jefferson's Louisiana: Politics and the Clash of Legal Traditions* (Cambridge, Mass., 1975), 106–19.

31. Virginia provides an outstanding laboratory for understanding the role of the local magistracy in the construction of county elites. For glimpses into the role of county judges there, see Gwenda Morgan, *The Hegemony of the Law: Richmond County, Virginia, 1692–1776* (New York,

Another hindrance had purely political origins. At times throughout the territorial period, the *ancienne population,* led by the American Edward Livingston among others, protested Claiborne's government. In addition to raising objections in the legislature and to signing formal memorials to Congress, some locals refused to accept Claiborne's appointments as a subtle form of protest. Even those who accepted territorial positions often resigned their offices when political contests became heated.[32]

Finally, many Creoles shied away from involvement with the legal system merely because they did not understand its alien Anglo-American components. A frustrated Claiborne wrote to Secretary of State Robert Smith in 1811 that such was "the dread of these good People of Courts and Lawyers, that they seem unwilling to come within their vortex, even in the character as Officers."[33]

Claiborne and the legislature's tinkering with the territory's laws and courts thoroughly Americanized its court procedures. Legislative acts prescribed that superior court judges and local justices of the peace follow American practices in all levels of proceeding including the construction and use of summary writs, habeas corpus, trial by jury, and prosecutions by indictment and by information. Few Creole Louisianians cared to master the language and practices dictated by these regulations. The combination of American judicial practices, politics, low compensation, and native fear of the American legal "vortex" forced those who did to resign their positions in short order.[34]

Accordingly, as American residents stepped into the vacancies, a new American contingent of officials dominated local justice in the same fashion as their counterparts on the territory's higher courts, as even the briefest glance at a reconstituted civil list shows. Such a preponderance gave the territorial judicial system an obvious American flavor that influenced antebellum Louisiana's judicial system as well.[35]

1989) and A. G. Roeber, *Faithful Magistrates and Republican Lawyers: Creators of Virginia's Legal Culture, 1680–1810* (Chapel Hill, 1981).

32. Dargo, *Jefferson's Louisiana,* 3–105 contains a useful analysis of political attitudes and their impact on the judicial system in the territorial period.

33. Claiborne to Robert Smith, 18 March 1811, in Rowland, ed., *Official Letterbooks,* 5: 183–4; Claiborne to Thomas Jefferson, 15 July 1806, in Carter, ed., *Territorial Papers,* 9: 675.

34. Claiborne to Jefferson, 15 July 1806, in Carter, ed., *Territorial Papers,* 9: 675.

35. For a characterization of the fears of the Orleanians, see ibid., 674.

Of the nearly forty appointments to county or parish judgeships, only four went to men of Louisiana origins. In April 1809, when territorial officials prepared a copy of the civil list, those four—Peter B. St. Martin of St. Charles Parish, Charles De Latour of Plaquemine, Michel Cantrelle, of St. James, and Charles Fagot of St. Bernard—were on the roster. Others, such as James White and Edward D. Turner hailed from Pennsylvania and Massachusetts, whereas John C. Carr, Peter Dormenon, Louis Moreau Lislet, and Achille Trouard came from England or France. Indeed, the 1809 list provides the most comprehensive description of the territory's twenty county judges. Of that number, three were born in France, one in England, two in Pennsylvania, three in Virginia, two in Connecticut, three in Massachusetts, one in North Carolina, and one in Kentucky.[36]

Those who migrated from other frontier regions tended to have vital links to the elite structure of those communities. For instance, Kentuckian Thomas Lewis was a scion of an influential family and kin to Joshua Lewis of the superior court. Similar patterns can be detected among the scores of Claiborne's justices of the peace. In all, the governor named around two hundred, the majority of whom were Americans, though he was a bit more effective in enticing Louisiana natives to sit on the bench. Still, Jefferson found the task of finding suitable candidates for Orleans to be the most difficult administrative problem in all of the territories.[37]

As agents of Americanization, county judges and justices of the peace presided over the day-to-day application of American judicial practices on the most basic levels of the legal system, the local courts. These inferior courts represented in the territory, as elsewhere in the republic, the one agency of government that most likely touched ordinary citizens in the routine course of their daily lives. Although other avenues for the forging of communal bonds existed, at county court sessions citizens attended to fundamental questions of life, liberty, and property. A majority of the men who dispensed local justice were Americans, as were the courts and the procedures that governed them. Therefore, county courts in the Territory of Orleans translated into more than mere forums for conflict

---

36. "A List of Civil and Military Officers," 21 April 1809, in Carter, ed., *Territorial Papers,* 9: 835. It should be noted here that civil lists from the territorial period are quite incomplete.

37. Carter, ed., *Territorial Papers,* 9: 598–602, 662, 700, 749–51, 796–7, 824; Jefferson to Claiborne, 3 May 1807, ibid., 728.

resolution or the maintenance of social order; they became vital arenas for cultural contact, assimilation, and Americanization.

In the end, fashioning territorial courts cut to Anglo-American patterns represents the most enduring feature of Claiborne's effort to extend American precepts of justice to an alien environment. Likewise, Claiborne set the institutional foundation for the state of Louisiana's judicial structure. Success also opened a way to continued intrusion of common law, as Louisiana men of law grappled with ways to harmonize diverse legal customs into a workable jurisprudence. Clearly, then, the practices, procedures, and Americanizing trends first fleshed out in the territorial period profoundly influenced the complexion of judicial institutions in antebellum Louisiana.

As Old World met New in the Territory of Orleans, Americans and Creoles engaged in a complicated battle for cultural hegemony. Both groups achieved qualified successes in many areas. But on the crucial battlefield of the local courts, the Americans, led by Governor Claiborne, won a decisive victory in the initial stages of the campaign. Ironically, that was not part of Claiborne's design. Although both the governor and his president favored the adaptation of an Anglo-American legal system, Claiborne initially counted on the avid participation of native Louisianians. Their refusal to enter into the "vortex" of the court system "even in the character as Officers," however, paved the way for American control of the judiciary. Once in office, Americans solidified their hegemony over the courts from the local to the highest appellate levels, turning Louisiana's judicial bodies into representative models of American justice.

Creation of the territorial judiciary marked an important stage in the Americanization of Louisiana. By controlling the judiciary, Americans came to dominate one of the most important structures of Louisiana society. The place where conflicts are resolved speaks to the very nature of the community. In antebellum Louisiana, Americans and their traditional practices and procedures defined the instruments of conflict resolution. American voices, American ideas, and American practices informed the character of the judicial system and allowed for the smooth transition of Louisiana from continental province to American state. Local justice played an extraordinary part in that transition.

5   *Sheridan E. Young*

LOUISIANA'S COURT OF ERRORS AND APPEALS, 1843–1846

The written history of Louisiana's legal system has yet to be told in the full measure of its richness and complexity. One topic obviously in need of attention is the development of the state's appellate courts. While scholars are now examining the supreme court in the nineteenth century, no one has considered the court of errors and appeals, Louisiana's first high court for the adjudication of criminal appeals. This essay presents a study of the court's place in its state's legal history.[1]

Whereas most nineteenth-century state supreme courts took both criminal and civil appeals, the Supreme Court of Louisiana read the state constitution of 1812 in such a way as to limit the court's jurisdiction to civil matters. This state of affairs created a need for a court with author-

Reprinted, with permission, from *Louisiana History* 33 (1992): 66–80.

1. Warren M. Billings, "Louisiana's Legal History and Its Sources: Needs, Opportunities, and Approaches," in Edward F. Haas, ed., *Louisiana's Legal Heritage* (Pensacola, Fla., 1983), 189–202; Billings, ed., *The Historic Rules of the Supreme Court of Louisiana* (Lafayette La., 1985), and Mark F. Fernandez, "From Chaos to Continuity: The First Reform of the Supreme Court of Louisiana, 1845–1853" (M.A. thesis, University of New Orleans, 1985).

ity to review criminal trials, a need the legislature met in 1843 when it established the court of errors and appeals.[2]

During the period of its existence, the court of errors and appeals reviewed twenty-three cases and made eighty-five rulings involving criminal law, appellate procedure, and the question of retrials. The court granted two new trials and reversed the judgment of a lower court only once. By ordering four interrupted trials to continue, the high court of appeal may have brought some criminals to justice who otherwise would have gone free, but its main importance lies not in the outcome of the cases it influenced but rather its role in developing criminal law in Louisiana. The court established guidelines for appellate procedure in criminal cases, for the granting of new trials, and for the forms of indictment. As Louisiana's first appellate court in criminal matters, the court of errors and appeals established a series of rulings for the lower courts to follow. It also created a body of case law that guided the state supreme court when it assumed jurisdiction over criminal appeals after 1845. Finally, the court of errors and appeals demonstrated the feasibility of allowing a superior court to hear appeals in criminal matters. The purpose of this essay is to present a history of the court and, through an analysis of its decisions, to establish the court's role in the shaping of Louisiana's legal heritage.[3]

Lacking a written penal code, Louisiana's antebellum criminal law had as its main source a territorial law, the Crimes Act of 1805. Intended to supplant French and Spanish practices, that statute declared crimes be "taken, intended and construed according to and in conformity with the common law of England; and the forms of indictment (divested however of unnecessary prolixity), the method of trial, the rules of evidence and all other proceedings whatsoever in the prosecution of the said crimes, of-

2. Fernandez, "From Chaos to Continuity," 11; *Laverty v. Duplessis,* 3 Mart. (o.s.) 42ff (La. 1813). Section 2 of article IV of the Constitution of 1812 reads, "the supreme court shall have appellate jurisdiction only, which Jurisdiction shall extend to all civil cases when the matter in dispute shall exceed the sum of three hundred dollars."

3. Merritt M. Robinson served as the reporter for the court of errors and appeals. He published the court's rulings in volume eight of his *Reports of Cases Argued and Determined in the Supreme Court of Louisiana.* Original manuscripts for nine of the cases survive, and they are housed with the archives of the Supreme Court of Louisiana on deposit in the Earl K. Long Library, University of New Orleans. Those documents were transferred to the supreme court in 1846 when it assumed jurisdiction for criminal appeals and the court of errors and appeals became defunct. Only one of the nine cases is complete. Robinson did not report two of them.

fenses and misdemeanors, changing what ought to be changed, shall be, except as is by this act otherwise provided for, according to the said common law." Those provisions created nearly as many problems as they resolved. For example, what exactly did the phrase "common law of England" mean? Did it include statutory law? Was the term restricted to the English law as it existed down to 1805? Did it include common law as it had developed in America, and what exactly was referred to by the phrase "changing what ought to be changed"? Concerning the wording of an indictment, what criteria should be employed to detect "unnecessary prolixities?" Governor William C. C. Claiborne considered this Crimes Act sufficiently confusing to order an exposition of it in 1806.[4]

After Louisiana achieved statehood in 1812, the legislature worked to continue judicial practice as it had developed during the territorial period. The Judiciary Act of 1813 retained the territorial statute as the basis of criminal law in the new state. A major change in the legal order came not through legislation but as a result of the supreme court's reading of the new state constitution, which went into effect in 1812. The constitution invested the supreme court with "appellate jurisdiction only, which jurisdiction shall extend to all civil cases when the matter in dispute shall exceed the sum of $300." In one of its earliest decisions, *Laverty* v. *Duplessis* (1813), the supreme court construed that constitutional provision as prohibiting it from receiving criminal appeals, and so there was no mechanism to review convictions until 1843.[5]

The supreme court's unwillingness to take cognizance of criminal cases, combined with the problematic Crimes Act of 1805, added to the confusion of a legal order in transition. Such untidiness did not sit well with the state's judges and criminal lawyers, some of whom filled the pages of *Louisiana Law Journal,* their state's first professional legal periodical, with a chorus of complaints. "We have in Louisiana ten different tri-

4. "An Act for the Punishment of Crimes and Misdemeanors," in *Acts Passed at the First Session of the Legislative Council of the Territory of New Orleans* (New Orleans, 1805), 440. Section 47 of this act limited its application to free whites; during the court of errors and appeals' existence, slaves faced criminal prosecution under an act of 7 June 1806, commonly referred to as the Black Code, *Acts Passed* (1806), 150–90; Lewis Kerr, *An Exposition of the Criminal Laws of the Territory of Orleans: The Practice of the Courts of Criminal Jurisdiction, the Duties of their Officers, with a Collection of Forms for the Use of Magistrates and Others* (New Orleans, 1806).

5. "An Act to Organize the Supreme Court of the State of Louisiana, and to Establish Courts of Inferior Jurisdiction," 1813 La. Acts 16–34; Constitution of 1812, sec. 2, art. IV.

bunals in criminal cases," wrote S. W. Downs, a New Orleans trial lawyer. "Laws are not only differently construed in different parishes, but also at different times in the same parish where, under the circuit system a different judge happens to preside." Downs pointed to examples of criminals escaping punishment merely due to lenient judges.[6]

In an article titled "On the Necessity of a Court of Appeals in Criminal Cases," E. A. Canon termed the lack of a court of appeals in criminal cases an "aweful and dangerous chasm" in his state's judiciary system and called for a "talented, upright and independent" legislator to secure legislation creating such a tribunal. It was a "most flagrant inconsistency," he complained, that in the "chivalrous" state of Louisiana one could appeal to the supreme court in civil matters when the dispute involved a sum above three hundred dollars but could not ask for relief from the outcome of a criminal trial when "honor and life" were at stake.[7]

Responding to need, the legislature hit on the idea of a special court of criminal appeals, which it erected in 1843 when it passed "An Act to Establish a Court of Errors and Appeals in Criminal Matters." Under this statute the new court would sit twice yearly in New Orleans. Three judges, any two of whom made a quorum, comprised the court. A simple majority decided cases, but in the event of ties, the lower court's rulings prevailed. The act authorized the court to review questions of law "arising in the progress of any prosecution for violation of any penal law of the State, where the punishment may be death, or imprisonment at hard labor." It specified that an appeal be grounded in either a writ known as a bill of exception or a writ of error. The bill of exception was an appellant's written statement of an objection or of objections to the rulings or instructions of the trial judge and included the facts and circumstances on which the appellant based his complaint. Such a writ enabled an appellant to introduce matters not already in evidence, thus providing the means by which the appellate court could set aside the judgment of a trial court. The writ of error, on the other hand, was the procedural device for appealing a conviction on the grounds that the trial judge had committed substantial errors during the trial's conduct. "An Act to Establish a Court

6. S. W. Downs, "Notes on Criminal Law," *Louisiana Law Journal* 1 (1842): 31.

7. E. A. Canon, "On the Necessity of a Court of Appeals in Criminal Cases," *Louisiana Law Journal* 1 (1941): 78–84.

of Errors and Appeals in Criminal Matters" further required an appellant to present his exceptions or assignments of error "in manner and form as now provided by law for appeals in civil cases." In noncriminal cases, the counsel for a prospective appellant would present the lower court with a petition setting forth the reasons why his client wished to have the supreme court review his case. The lower court judge would, provided the request conformed to these standards, sign the document, which the appellant could then present to the high court.[8]

The 1843 act called on the state governor to appoint the new tribunal's judges. Alexandre Mouton selected Thomas C. Nicholls, George Rogers King, and Isaac Johnson to man the court. In naming Nicholls, King, and Johnson, the governor selected well-qualified men who, as shown by their careers before and after the demise of the court of errors and appeals, were skilled in criminal law.

Thomas Nicholls, presiding judge during the court's life, came from a prominent family with a long history of activity in the state's judicial system. He took up the study of law at an early age and received a license to practice in 1809 when he was only eighteen. He operated a law office in Opelousas and later moved to Donaldsonville, where he served as district judge, a position he held when he gained his seat on the court of errors and appeals. When the Constitution of 1845 did away with Nicholls's job, the governor sought to appoint him to the supreme court bench. His poor health prevented him from taking the appointment, and he died in 1847. Nicholls's youngest son, Francis T., served as governor of Louisiana and then as chief justice of Louisiana.[9]

George Rogers King, the only court of errors and appeals judge formally trained in common law, was born in St. Landry Parish, Louisiana, in 1807. After graduating from the University of Virginia Law School, he returned to Louisiana, where he established a law practice in Opelousas. He then served in the state house of representatives and as district attorney and district judge, which gave him varied and valuable experience before Mouton named him to the court of errors and appeals. King's

8. "An Act to Establish a Court of Errors and Appeals in Criminal Matters, and for Other Purposes," 1843 La. Acts 58–61; Wheelock S. Upton, comp., *Code of Practice in Civil Cases for the State of Louisiana* (New Orleans, 1839) contained regulations governing procedure in civil cases.

9. "The Nicholls Family in Louisiana," *Louisiana Historical Quarterly* 6 (1923): 5–18.

achievements as judge of the appellate court led to his appointment to the Supreme Court of Louisiana in March of 1846. There he served as associate justice until 1850. He retired to Opelousas, where he died in 1871.[10]

Like Nicholls and King, Isaac Johnson had extensive experience in the legal profession prior to his appointment to the court of errors and appeals. A native of West Feliciana, he was the son of an Englishman who settled in Louisiana while it was a Spanish province. Johnson studied law in his uncle's office, and his election to a two-year term in the House of Representatives in 1833 launched an active career in law and politics. In the legislature, he served on the Judiciary Committee. At home Johnson sat on various committees, including one to maintain a parish patrol for the protection of life and property against robbers and vagrants. He then served as judge of the third district court. Governor Mouton appointed him secretary of state, and on his resignation from this position, the governor named him to the court of errors and appeals. Johnson served as Louisiana's tenth governor before his death in New Orleans in 1853.[11]

Both the enabling act and the general uncertainty of the state's criminal law placed these judges in an unusual position of power. As long as their rulings violated neither their oath of office nor the spirit of known criminal laws, they were free to do as they wished. Although the Crimes Act of 1805 called for the appropriation of English common law in Louisiana, the statute's provision for "changing what ought to be changed" provided seemingly unlimited power to alter that law. The judges therefore felt at liberty to draw on the entire body of English and American law and to alter common law as they saw fit.

Nicholls, King, and Johnson set out to modify English common law to suit the needs of criminal jurisprudence in their state. Their opinions expressed a general belief in reason and progress, a belief common to nineteenth-century lawyers. In *State* v. *Ferguson* (1846), for example, Judge Nicholls described absurdities that had vanished before the "advanc-

10. Henry Plauché Dart, "The Celebration of the Centenary of the Supreme Court of Louisiana," *Louisiana Historical Quarterly* 6 (1921): 117.

11. Judge William D. Boyle took Johnson's position on the appellate court in 1846, at which time the latter resigned to campaign for governor. Admitted to the Louisiana bar in 1836, Boyle was elected to the state legislature in 1838. He composed only one of the court's opinions. Sidney Joseph Aucoin, "The Political Career of Isaac Johnson, Governor of Louisiana, 1846–1850," *Louisiana Historical Quarterly* 31 (1945): 941–87.

ing light of reason and law." The "absurdity" in question was the English judges' past authority to keep juries together until their members could reach a verdict, an authority made necessary, according to Nicholls, by the "exigencies of an age of barbarism." Hand in hand with their general faith in worldwide legal progress, the three judges felt that Americans possessed a special ability to perfect English common law because Americans could view English law objectively. Nicholls, for example, believed that by allowing new trials in capital cases, a thing not permitted in England, the "humanity and good sense" of the respective states had divested the English common law system of a "bloody feature," and the American judicial system, through a "perfection of reason," had restored "the beauty and symmetry of the whole law." Although Nicholls possessed a more idealistic faith in the "perfection of reason" than did his colleagues, a desire to produce practical results, based on the assumption that such results were possible, figured into all of the judges' decisions. They refused to adopt those parts of common law, both English and American, that they deemed useless to the needs of Louisianians, and they interpreted statutory and case law to produce a body of commonsense decisions.[12]

To achieve their desired rulings, Nicholls, Johnson, and King employed their knowledge of Anglo-American precepts in distinctive ways. When faced with a lawyer's citation of a law favorable to his client and not wanting to rule for the appellant, they would simply reject the precedent as inapplicable and opt for one that suited their plans. They also mediated between English and American common law, adapted common-law principles to uniquely American situations, and read statutes to suit their judicial strategy.

Most often and most simply, Nicholls, Johnson, and King generally employed rules that would produce a desired outcome. Exemplifying the judges' use of this judgment-making technique was their decision to allow new trials in capital cases. In *State* v. *Hornsby* (1844), Hornsby, convicted of manslaughter, appealed to the high court, asking for a new trial in which he could present evidence discovered after his first trial. Deeming the request legitimate, the court annulled his conviction and ordered a retrial. English law prohibited new trials for persons convicted of felonies,

12. *State* v. *Ferguson,* 8 Rob.613 (La. 1846); *State* v. *Jones,* ibid., 573ff.

but the court of errors and appeals' judges looked to the common law as it existed in other states to sanction such retrials. Admitting that English law, as adopted into Louisiana by the Crimes Act, did not allow retrials in capital cases, Judge Johnson nevertheless favored them because they accorded with "the great current of American decisions. In England," he wrote,

> there is no doubt, in case of treason or felony, that a new trial cannot be granted when the proceedings have been regular; but if the conviction appears to be unjust to the judge, he may respite the execution to enable the defendant to apply for a pardon, but this court has decided . . . that all judges who are empowered to hear and determine indictments for crime, are invested with a discretionary power to grant new trials in capital cases, as well as in [those of] misdemeanor.

Judge Nicholls termed the granting of new trials in all cases in his state "coeval . . . with the government" and one of the people's safeguards.[13]

The basis for the court's decision permitting new trials in capital cases, like that of a later ruling permitting the state to appeal, was the judges' faith in their ability to achieve the "best" outcome. Judge Nicholls wrote in favor of giving to the state the privilege of appealing against a defendant, although he believed that English common law would not accept such appeals for fear of placing an accused twice in jeopardy. In *Jones,* Isaac Preston, a district attorney, appealed to the court of errors and appeals on behalf of the state. In this case, a grand jury indicted Jones, who then labeled his indictment defective because the grand jury had been illegally constituted. The lower court agreed and quashed the indictment. Preston, however, believed the grand jury to have been legal, and he asked the court of errors and appeals to reinstate the indictment. Judge Nicholls agreed with Preston. Nicholls examined the English doctrine of double jeopardy and concluded it had no application to the Jones case. The defendant, he explained, having had no trial because his indictment had been quashed, had not been placed in jeopardy at all.[14]

13. *State* v. *Hornsby* ibid., 583ff; *State* v. *Charlot,* ibid., 529ff; *Jones,* ibid., 573. Judge Johnson dissented in the latter ruling but did not explain his reasons for so doing.

14. Isaac T. Preston (1793–1852) graduated from Yale College in 1812. He worked as judge of the First District Court of New Orleans and then as the state's attorney general from 1823 to 1829 and

Nicholls based his ruling on a section of the 1843 act that authorized his court to review questions of law. "The court is thereby vested with authority to review . . . all questions of law," he wrote. "By dismissing [this] appeal, the court would not declare, but make the law. Neither has this court or any other court a right to make a distinction where the law has made none." But for all his elaboration on the need to follow the law, the judge's motive for permitting the state appeal in this instance was of a practical, rather than a philosophical, nature. Following two pages of argument in favor of adhering to the 1843 act exactly as written, Nicholls revealed the real reason for his decision. Almost in passing, he sketched a scenario in which a lower court quashed a good indictment "necessarily to be quashed in its turn . . . thereby defeating the ends of justice and insuring impunity to crime."[15]

In order to accept the principles of new trials in capital cases and appeal on behalf of the state, the court's judges ignored the Crimes Act's provision for the adoption of English law, relying instead on the common law as developed in other states in the first instance and the act establishing their court in the second. By adopting those rules that allowed them to achieve desired results and rejecting ones that did not, the judges worked to facilitate the administration of criminal justice in their state.

Periodically called on to reconcile conflicts between the state constitution and statutory law, Nicholls, King, and Johnson honored the principle that enabled them to rule as they pleased. In the Jones case, the First District Court of New Orleans drew a jury in conformity to an 1844 law, but the defendant complained that the statute contravened Louisiana's constitution, which required jurors be drawn from different venues than those specified in the act. The court of errors and appeals decided that the constitution's authors did not expect territorial divisions to remain permanently intact and that the legislature had a "right" to limit or widen the jurisdiction of the district courts as it saw fit. In this case, as in several others, the judges made extensive references to legislative intent. They considered legislators to be sensible men concerned with achieving practical results, and the judges interpreted statutory law accordingly.

---

again from 1842 to 1845. Preston was a member of the constitutional convention of 1844 and sat as a supreme court justice from 1850–1852.

15. *State* v. *Jones,* 8 Rob. 573 (La. 1846).

Believing in the existence of appropriate conclusions to legal disputes, they felt justified in interpreting statutory law to support such satisfactory decisions.[16]

Nicholls, King, and Johnson also found mediation between two opposing rules to be helpful in justifying their opinions. Called on to decide whether the absence of jury sequestration would prove fatal to its verdict, the court of errors and appeals' ruling in *State* v. *Hornsby* (1844) illustrates this use of compromise. In England and the colonies the law had obliged courts to keep these persons together until they reached a verdict. If the court adjourned, it placed a bailiff in charge of the jury and swore him to keep it together. By the nineteenth century, English and American courts had relaxed this rule in some circumstances. Judge Nicholls considered recent decisions on the matter, both in America and in England, to be contradictory. He noted that some adhered to the old English rule of no separation while others did not. Nicholls sought a middle ground between the two principles and maintained that while capital trial juries should not disperse after being sworn in, they might be permitted to do so in instances of less serious felonies. His plan was to "adopt that rule which seems to offer the greatest security to the accused" without interfering with the administration of existing law, and he negotiated between what he viewed as two opposing opinions to reach this goal.[17]

The judges also adjusted English statutes to meet situations specific to Louisiana. Perhaps the clearest illustration of this decision-making technique occurred in the court's finding in a murder case, *State* v. *McCoy* (1844). While in Louisiana, McCoy inflicted on another a wound from which the victim later died in Mississippi. According to English common law, when a person injured someone in one place, and the victim died from the wound in another locale, venue would be established in the parish where the victim died. By this rule, because his victim died in Mississippi, McCoy argued he could not legally stand trial in Louisiana, and thus that his conviction was improper and illegal. But the high court

16. "An Act to Exempt Certain Persons in the Parish of Rapides from Serving on Juries," 1844 La. Acts 9; *State* v. *Jones*, 8 Rob. 573 (La. 1846).

17. *State* v. *Hornsby*, 8 Rob. 545 (La. 1844). In this case a lower court found the accused guilty of manslaughter. Hornsby appealed to the court of errors and appeals on the ground that the lower court had allowed the jury to separate during periods of adjournment.

judges sought to uphold McCoy's conviction. To do so, they looked to another English statute that permitted prosecution of murderers whose vic-
tims died in foreign countries. By equating North American states to foreign countries, the judges made a decision that enabled their state to try
McCoy. This adaptation of an English law to solve a venue problem specific to the United States had the practical outcome of enhancing the
state's ability to bring criminals to justice.[18]

While the court of errors and appeals judges selectively employed individual English and American precepts to suit the needs of their state,
they also interpreted and applied individual statutes to uphold their views
on appellate procedure, new trials, and the wording of indictments. The
judges utilized statutory law to control the flow of appeals and to restrict
the chances of criminals being released from punishment as a result of
procedural flaws. In an effort to enable the court to use its time efficiently,
Nicholls, King, and Johnson required that appeals meet certain specifications. The state's supreme court was unable to keep up with its workload,
and the court of errors and appeals sought to limit requests for trial re-
views to avoid a similar problem. Besides increasing the court's work, allowing defendants and convicts to make frivolous appeals would have led
to the release of criminals, an action the court's judges sought to prevent
whenever possible.[19]

Through statutory interpretation and application the judges aimed to
limit court workloads and to prevent the possible dismissal of guilty persons. Nicholls, King, and Johnson turned to a provision in the 1843 statute
creating their court to qualify the types of appeals they could hear. Section
two gave the court of errors and appeals power "to review questions of
law; which questions shall be presented by bills of exception taken to the
opinions of the judge of lower court, or by the assignment of errors apparent on the face of the record, taken and made in manner and form as now
provided by law for appeals in civil cases." On the basis of this authority,
the court refused to review the case of *State* v. *Major* (1844). Major, convicted of rape in the First Criminal Court of New Orleans, submitted his
case's record together with a bill of exceptions. Johnson refused to review
the case because the bill of exceptions lacked the district judge's signature.

18. *State* v. *McCoy,* 8 Rob. 545 (La. 1844).
19. Henry Plauché Dart, "The History of the Supreme Court of Louisiana," 1913 La. xlii–xliii.

He considered the document "unauthenticated and . . . not in form to authorize us to inquire into its contents."[20]

Refusing to consider improperly taken appeals was one way the court restricted its workload; explaining why such appeals would not be considered in the future was another. In *State v. Brown* (1844) a lower court found an indictment against Brown for perjury and then quashed the indictment; the lower court tried and convicted Brown. He then appealed to the court of errors and appeals claiming that the quashing of the first indictment amounted to an acquittal. Judge Johnson, agreeing to review a case he would have been justified in ignoring, explained that Brown should have voiced his objection to the court of the first instance instead of to the court of errors and appeals. Johnson's ruling set a guide for future disregard of similar appeals.[21]

By adhering strictly to provisions of the 1843 act in some situations but not in others, Johnson and his colleagues reviewed or dismissed cases as they saw fit. In the Major case, Johnson refused to consider an appeal that was technically incorrect. But in the Brown appeal the judge did review an ill-contrived complaint. In both cases, expediency motivated his actions. Johnson ruled to qualify future appeals. He considered *Brown* to explain why the request was not legitimate, and his comments here, like those in the Major case, set a precedent for future refusal to consider similar issues.

In lowering the possibility of frivolous appeals, the judges helped to prevent such requests from interfering with their ability to consider serious ones. Besides refusing to comment on technically incorrect appeals or commenting on them in such a way as to prevent like claims in the future, these men worked to restrict defendants' right of appeal. In the case of *State v. Hornsby* (1844) the court of errors and appeals ordered the tribunal of original jurisdiction, which had convicted Hornsby of manslaughter, to retry the case. During the initial stages of his new trial, Hornsby appealed again to the high court, arguing that its decision to grant him a second trial amounted to an acquittal. The court decided against Hornsby and ruled out the possibility that such appeals would be considered in the future. From then on, wrote Judge Johnson, the right of appeal in criminal

20. "Act to Establish," sec. 2; *State* v. *Major,* 8 Rob. 553ff (La. 1844).
21. *State* v. *Brown,* 8 Rob. 566ff (La. 1844).

cases could arise only after the trial court had rendered its verdict, judgment, and sentence. Limiting the circumstances under which persons convicted of crimes could appeal served to increase the likelihood that appellants would confront Louisiana's courts only with substantial questions concerning lower court trials.[22]

Nicholls, King, and Johnson restricted the situations in which the court could grant second trials on the basis of newly discovered evidence in another move toward reducing unnecessary litigation. Most persons who sought retrial usually pled the discovery of evidence which, had it been known of sooner, would have altered their trials' outcomes. The court forbade retrials in criminal cases on the basis of newly discovered evidence that was irrelevant or of which the accused had been aware before the trial. It employed this rule to deny two appeals, and it extended its underlying principle by requiring an appellant to disclose the name of a witness supposedly discovered after the first trial. These decisions had the effect of discouraging certain types of requests for new trials.[23]

The court discouraged the use of trivial errors as a basis for appeal. A number of technical rules, left over from ancient common-law times when the English legal system included provisions designed to protect the

22. In *State* v. *Hornsby,* ibid., 554ff, the grand jury found an indictment against Hornsby for perjury. During this trial's initial stages, the district attorney, discovering a flaw in the indictment, discontinued further proceedings. Another grand jury then presented a second bill of indictment against the defendant for the same offense. On the basis of this new bill, the lower court tried and convicted Hornsby. He then appealed to the court of errors and appeals claiming that the interrupted first trial amounted to an acquittal. The high court considered this objection as one that the defendant should have presented to the lower court.

23. In *State* v. *Charlot,* 8 Rob. 529ff (La. 1844), a lower court convicted Charlot of cow theft. Charlot appealed to the court of errors and appeals, stating that a witness discovered after his trial could establish two facts: first, that the witness frequently took dinner with Charlot at his abode and second, that the witness on no occasion found "beef on [Charlot's] table nor [perceived] any evidence that a cow had been killed." The appellate court dismissed this evidence as irrelevant because Charlot's indictment charged him with stealing, not with killing a cow. In *State* v. *Clark,* 6 Rob. 533ff (La. 1844), a St. Landry Parish court convicted Clark for larceny of a heifer. Clark appealed to the court of errors and appeals for a new trial on the basis of a newly discovered witness who might prove that Clark resided in Rapides Parish, where he was confined to his home with a foot injury at the time of the theft. The high court considered Clark's appeal and concluded that the evidence did not disprove the jury's finding that Clark "at some time within twelve months anterior to the finding of the indictment, committed larceny of a heifer in the parish of St. Landry." *State* v. *Lennon,* 8 Rob. 5 (La. 1844), found Lennon guilty of inveigling slaves.

accused from serious penalties for relatively minor offenses, applied to the wording of an indictment. The indictment was a key ingredient in criminal procedure, for it set forth with reasonable particularity the crimes alleged against the accused. By common law, a convict could plead the slightest error in the wording or punctuation of his indictment and have his sentence annulled. Thus, if a defendant were named Peter Williams, but an indictment styled him Pete Williams, his attorney could argue that his client was not the man named in the indictment and so by common law should go free, although all knew Peter Williams and Pete Williams to be one and the same.

One of the court's major accomplishments was its use of the Crimes Act to end this anachronism. The statute of 1805 included a provision for "divestment" from indictments of "unnecessary prolixities," and the court, so far as its members could agree on this phrase's definition, vigorously pursued this goal. They thought absurd the possibility of a criminal going free as a result of a meaningless flaw in the wording of an indictment.

Judge Johnson addressed himself to this problem in *State* v. *Sheldon* (1844). Sheldon appealed his conviction for forgery, claiming that his indictment lacked an exact duplicate of the forged instrument, as required by English common law. This indictment misrepresented words that someone had scribbled in the note's margin. Classifying the inaccurately copied words as "surplusage," Judge Johnson seized the opportunity to purge criminal procedure of an "unnecessary prolixity" and ruled it inessential that an indictment for forgery set forth "the ornamental parts" of a bill.[24]

While the Sheldon case demonstrates a desire to divest indictments of their prolixities, the court of errors and appeals tried to ensure the inclusion of certain technical requirements. That desire is evidenced in *State* v. *Kennedy* (1845). Kennedy appealed a murder conviction, claiming substantial defects in the wording of the indictment that brought him to trial. After naming the time and place at which he allegedly injured his victim, the indictment stated that the latter "a few hours after did die" when, or so Kennedy claimed, it should have related that the victim "a few hours

24. *State* v. *Sheldon,* 8 Rob. 540ff (La. 1844).

after did, then and there die." Because the law defined murder as a mortal stroke resulting in subsequent death and because it stipulated that the victim die from the wound within a year and a day, that law also specified that an indictment make the time and place of death clear by explicitly stating these facts at the first mention of the death and referring to them thereafter with the words "then and there." Judges King and Johnson agreed with Kennedy's argument and annulled the lower court's decision. Nicholls, dissenting from this ruling, felt constant repetition of the words "then and there" to be "unnecessarily prolix," and as such, prime candidates for deletion from the standard form of indictment. He argued that the statement in question was clear in meaning according to plain common sense. King and Johnson, on the other side, argued in this instance to restrict the court's power to disregard or alter English law. To King especially, the repetition of time and place of death constituted an "essential averment" by common law that was not to be disregarded in his state.[25]

This dispute underscores the ambiguity of the 1805 Crimes Act. In one sense, the act granted lawmakers extensive authority to rework English common law to suit Louisiana's needs. But the act was silent on post–1805 English law that served to bring outmoded common law into line with present-day circumstances. King admitted that the English Parliament had passed an act providing "remedies for many of the inconveniences of the common law" but wrote that he felt obligated to disregard this act because it had been passed after 1805. He said that he felt himself unauthorized to disregard the Crimes Act. Nicholls, in contrast, felt compelled to change "what ought to be changed" on the basis of the 1805 act.[26]

At this point, one might inquire into what individual role each judge played in making the court's decisions. Would a court of errors and appeals with three Judge Johnsons at its helm have annulled more lower court rulings because of technical errors in indictments?

Judge Nicholls's opinions, as noted earlier, differed from his colleagues' in that Nicholls expressed less faith in English law and more faith in the court of errors and appeals' ability and authority to modify that law. Nicholls viewed English common law as outmoded, and he possessed an

25. *State* v. *Kennedy,* 8 Rob. 590ff (La. 1845).
26. Ibid.

idealistic belief in an American ability to bring the English system into line with American reality.

While all the judges professed respect for British law, Nicholls made statements that, although seemingly deferential, often subtly poked fun at that law. In a discussion of a then-defunct English provision for keeping together indecisive juries until they could reach a verdict, he sarcastically referred to the rule as "a happy invention truely." Nicholls held a lofty view of his duty as a judge and of the judge's role as rule maker. In his objection to Johnson's review of the Kennedy case, Nicholls interpreted the 1805 act as having conferred "great power upon the judges." The idea that "the Legislature could travel through the whole body of the common law, repudiating here, pruning there, re-enacting this provision and repealing that," he wrote, "is too preposterous to be entertained for a moment."[27]

While in the Kennedy case Judges King and Johnson argued in favor of limiting judicial power to modify existing law, in other instances they proved willing to extend their court's authority. In *McCoy,* Judge King extended the court's ability to apply post–1805 English law under certain circumstances. In this instance, King, like Nicholls in most of his decisions, sought to put legislative intent into line with changed circumstances. Explaining that he could not believe that past legislators were "guilty" of the absurdity of enacting laws without providing for the adoption of future changes designed to enforce those laws, King opened the door to the acceptance of English law "as it existed in 1805, modified, explained and perfected by [recent] statutory enactments." Johnson and Nicholls agreed; all three considered it necessary to modify post–1805 English common law and were willing to interpret the Crimes Act accordingly.[28]

King and Johnson differed with Nicholls only in the extent to which they were willing to modify English rules. While King agreed to adopt post–1805 statutes passed by the English Parliament to modify British statutory law made prior to that time, he chose not to place recently passed English statutes relaxing restrictions on the wordings of indictments in this category. To retain indictment specifications he viewed as essential, King wrote in the Kennedy case, "no principle appears to be better settled

27. *State* v. *Ferguson,* 8 Rob. 613ff (1846); *State* v. *Kennedy,* 590.
28. *State* v. *McCoy,* 8 Rob. 545 (La. 1844).

than that, in indictments for high offenses . . . the averment of time and place is to be repeated to every issuable and triable fact." Judge Johnson defended this argument by maintaining that a decision to eliminate the requirement for constant repetition of time and place of death in the indictment might lead to future rejection of any standard for the document to follow. More cautious in their view of judicial ability, King and Johnson, in contrast to the more idealistic Nicholls, considered the possibility that judges might dispense with essential, as well as nonessential, specifications for the indictment. Thus the judges, while in basic agreement about the need to modify law to suit changing conditions, disagreed as to which situations called for such action.

By the end of its final sessions in 1846 the court of errors and appeals had produced a body of case law that established the outlines of a uniform procedure for criminal appeals, rules governing retrials, and a more workable form of indictment. The court's creation was part of a process taking place in other areas of Louisiana's judicial system as well as in the United States in general. In adopting English law, the first Anglo-Americans accepted a legal system that did not anticipate New World needs. As law received from England proved unsuited to circumstances in republican America, the new country's judicial system placed unprecedented demands on its adopted legal structure.

In Louisiana, as in other states, the legal profession took steps to establish and to define a judicial system suited to its needs. Edward Livingston prepared a code of civil procedure for Louisiana, which the legislature adopted in 1825. Although he had written a criminal code, the state rejected it, leaving the courts to rely on the vague Crimes Act of 1805 for guidance in criminal matters. When the state supreme court refused to hear criminal appeals, the system experienced added difficulty.[29]

Initiating a process of standardization in criminal justice, the court achieved its main purpose. It provided lower tribunals and the reformed supreme court with a group of rulings which ensured that these judicial bodies would apply criminal law more consistently than had previously been possible. From 1846, when the new state constitution transferred the court of errors and appeals' authority to a restructured supreme court, to

29. Charles M. Cook, *The American Codification Movement: A Study of Antebellum Legal Reform* (Westport, Conn., 1981); and Fernandez, "From Chaos to Continuity."

the turn of the century, Louisiana supreme court judges cited court of errors and appeals rulings over 150 times.

The fact that the architects of the 1845 constitution provided for the new supreme court to hear appeals in criminal matters attests to a perceived need to continue a proven process. In granting the supreme court power to hear criminal appeals, the lawmakers made their state's appellate system more financially efficient. Investing the supreme court with criminal jurisdiction reduced costs. The constitution's creators probably reasoned that the new supreme court, with its membership increased from three to five judges, would be able to handle the additional work.

King, Johnson, and Nicholls combined their legal experience with their nineteenth-century faith in progress to bring English law into line with American and Louisianian realities. The fact that these judges did not always agree underscored the difficulty of their task.

OF GENERALS AND JURISTS

The Judicial System of New Orleans under Union Occupation, May 1862–April 1865

Reconstruction began in New Orleans on 1 May 1862, when Major General Benjamin F. Butler and twenty-five hundred Union soldiers occupied the city. They had captured the largest of the Confederacy's cities a little more than fifteen months after Louisiana's secession. Butler now faced the difficult chore of restoring order to a rebellious metropolis of 170,000 souls. The greater part of his task involved the creation of a loyal city government, which in turn required Butler to reopen and reconstruct the city's judicial system. In a process stretching over three years, Butler, his successor Major General Nathaniel P. Banks, and their colleague Brigadier General George F. Shepley, the military governor of Louisiana, overhauled the city's courts, eventually returning them to their antebellum status.

Before the Civil War New Orleans was the center of judicial activities in the state. It was the seat of the United States District Court for the Eastern District of Louisiana, the Supreme Court of Louisiana, the state's district courts for the parish of Orleans, and the city's recorders courts. The United States District Court naturally handled all cases in federal law, while the supreme court heard appeals from all the state courts. State law assigned each of the six district courts different jurisdictions. First district court tried all felonies, while second district court dealt primarily with probates and successions. All other civil litigation was divided among the four remaining district courts. The six recorders courts, which were designed to try misdemeanors, heard all petty criminal cases.[1]

By the time Butler entered New Orleans this court system had all but collapsed; indeed, city government had virtually disintegrated in the panic that preceded the city's fall. Such order as existed had been maintained by a militia of foreign residents known as the European Brigade. Food was scarce, as the Union's naval blockade had ruined the economy of this great port. Added to these woes, the citizenry violently opposed the prospect of Union military rule. In these circumstances Butler's first task was to restore law and order.[2]

Butler and his deputy, Shepley, knew well the importance of law to the ordering of society. The forty-four-year-old Butler was a self-made man who became one of Massachusetts's most successful lawyers and politicians. He was not a professional soldier; a staunch Unionist, small "d" democrat, and skillful practitioner of the art of politics, he gained his general's stars through political maneuvers, something not uncommon in the Civil War. Though privately kind and charming, Butler could be tactless, belligerent, and rude when dealing with people who opposed him. He knew well the dangers of the collapse of order and government in a large city, for it was he who had suppressed the civil disorders in pro-Confederate Baltimore in 1861. President Abraham Lincoln gave him command of the land forces in the New Orleans expedition. Having no desire to serve in Virginia, Butler had secured his appointment with the help of an old friend, Secretary of War Edwin M. Stanton. As commander of the Department of the Gulf, his responsibilities included the conduct of military operations along the Gulf Coast west of Pensacola and areas inland.[3]

1. "An Act to Organize District Courts in the Parish and City of New Orleans," 1853 La. Acts 190–3; 1855 La. Acts 315–17.

2. Gerald M. Capers, *Occupied City: New Orleans under the Federals, 1862–1865* (Lexington, Ky., 1965), 79–82; Elizabeth J. Doyle, "Civilian Life in Occupied New Orleans" (Ph.D. diss., Louisiana State University, 1955), 29–30.

3. The best biography of Butler is Richard S. West, *Lincoln's Scapegoat General: A Life of Benjamin F. Butler* (Boston, 1955).

For his second in command Butler selected the forty-three-year-old Shepley, a close personal and political friend. Like Butler, Shepley was a New England lawyer and politician, having long served as United States attorney in Maine. Known to be vehement and impetuous, he was not noted for his intellect, though he had been educated at Harvard and Dartmouth colleges. In June 1862, Lincoln appointed him military governor of Louisiana. According to Stanton, the "great purpose" of his appointment was to "re-establish the authority of the Federal Government in the State of Louisiana, and provide the means of maintaining peace and security to the loyal inhabitants of that State until they shall be able to establish a civil government." With such vague instructions, there was no specific delineation of the relationship between Butler's and Shepley's offices. But as they were close friends they had no problems, and Shepley played a subordinate role to Butler. In practice he supervised civilian government by acting as the state's chief executive officer. When inquiring about local governmental issues, Lincoln generally went to Shepley instead of Butler.[4]

This lack of clarity regarding Shepley's duties reveals one of the outstanding facts of the occupation's history: no overall policy existed concerning the administration of occupied New Orleans. To the Lincoln administration, New Orleans was a military objective, and no one in Washington had considered what to do with it after it was captured. Preoccupied with much more important problems, Lincoln placed all responsibility for handling the occupation on Butler and Shepley, and later Banks. In fact, the government all but refused to provide instructions, even when queried by the local commanders. Lincoln and Stanton tended not to act, but rather react, and then only in serious matters. Thus, the occupation would essentially be the local commanders' responsibility.[5]

Initially, Butler intended to place New Orleans under relatively mild rule. In his proclamation of 1 May, he declared the city was under martial

4. *Dictionary of American Biography*, s.v. "Shepley, George"; United States War Department, *The War of the Rebellion: A Compilation of the Official Records of the Union and Confederate Armies*, 128 vols. (Washington, D.C.,1880–91) [hereinafter cited as *OR*], 3d ser., 2: 141; Roy P. Basler, ed., *The Collected Works of Abraham Lincoln* (New Brunswick, N.J., 1953–55), 5: 504–5.

5. Jessie Ames Marshall, ed., *Private and Official Correspondence of General Benjamin F. Butler during the Period of the Civil War* (Norwood, Mass., 1917), 2: 67, 360–2; *OR*, 1st ser., 6: 506–8; 15: 639–40; Basler, *Collected Works of Lincoln*, 6: 364–5.

law, but he also stated a desire to restore most of the municipal authorities' powers as quickly as possible. Civilian government would have some measure of autonomy; the military authorities would intervene only when their interests were threatened. The courts, both civil and criminal, would remain as they were, excepting "all disorders and disturbances of the peace done by combination and numbers and crimes of an aggravated nature, interfering with the forces of the United States." Such offenses would be tried in a military court.[6]

The employment of military courts to try civilians was not unknown to American martial law. Precedents for this practice derived from the Mexican War, when the army used such courts in occupied Mexican territories. Nor were they exclusive to New Orleans; they had existed wherever Union armies occupied Confederate territory. In practical terms they exercised unlimited powers, which subordinated normal peacetime constitutional rights to the needs of local military authorities.[7]

Butler quickly established two military tribunals, the provost court and the military commission, one to try misdemeanors, the other felonies. As judge of the provost court, Butler appointed Major Joseph M. Bell, a close friend and political colleague. The handsome, clear-eyed Bell was, like Butler, a successful Massachusetts lawyer; he was the son-in-law and law partner of the late Rufus Choate, dean of the Massachusetts bar. Noted for his fairness and great sense of humor, he served without pay as Butler's aide-de-camp. He opened court on 4 May. Originally, its purpose was twofold: to court-martial enlisted personnel for minor breaches of military discipline and to try civilians for petty violations of martial law. The military commission dealt with more serious matters. Butler created the commission on 6 May "for the trial of all high crimes and misdemeanors which by the laws of any state of the Union, or the United States, or the laws Martial, are punishable with death or imprisonment for a long term of years." It consisted of five officers of the rank of captain or above, with Bell as its legal advisor.[8]

---

6. *OR,* 1st ser., 6: 717–20.

7. A. H. Carpenter, "Military Government of Southern Territory," *Annual Report of the American Historical Association for 1900* (Washington, D.C., 1901), 469–70, 484.

8. *OR,* 1st ser., 15: 552; (New Orleans) *Daily Delta,* 28 May; Benjamin F. Butler, *Autobiography and Personal Reminiscences of Major General Benjamin F. Butler; Butler's Book* (Boston, 1892), 521;

In spite of his high hopes, Butler soon discovered that a policy of kindness would not work. Most New Orleanians, he found, still believed in the Confederate cause as passionately as he held to the Union's. From the very first, people resisted the rule of the "Damn Yankees." Shopkeepers defied orders to open, mobs jeered Butler and his headquarters, and Union soldiers were openly threatened and insulted in the streets. The mayor and the city council refused to cooperate. Butler realized that his only option was force. Using the city government's protests over his infamous "Woman Order" as an excuse, on 17 May he arrested the mayor, the chief of police, and several of their associates, and imprisoned them at Fort Jackson near the mouth of the Mississippi. He then appointed Shepley acting mayor, and replaced the police with his own soldiers.[9]

The events of these troubled weeks leading up to mid-May left their mark on the courts in the city. The supreme court was the first casualty. (The United States district court had closed long before on 26 January 1861, the day of Louisiana's secession.) On 24 February the high court adjourned, on apparent agreement of the district court judges to do the same; with invasion imminent the justices felt the closing of the courts would facilitate the reorganization of the state militia under a new state law, and would thus aid the defense of the state. Scheduled to reconvene 5 May, it never did, and four of the five justices fled during the crisis before the Union victory. Their clerk dutifully reported for work on 5 and 6 May, but as none of the justices appeared, under the authority granted him by state law he adjourned the court *sine die.*[10]

The five civil district courts met similar fates; like the supreme court justices, their judges simply quit. None of the judges paid any attention to the supreme court's announcement of 24 February; all stayed open until mid-April, when the Union forces began battering at the city's downriver defenses. Within a week of Butler's arrival the judges of the second and

---

Minutes of the United States District Court for the Eastern District of Louisiana, 25 June 1860–October 6, 1862, 83; minutes of the provost court and the military commission from 4 May to 6 October 1862 are found in this volume; *OR*, 1st ser., 15: 722–3.

9. Capers, *Occupied City*, 60–2, 67–9; Marshall, *Official Correspondence*, 1: 490, 497–501.

10. Minutes, U.S. District Court, 82; Minutes of the Supreme Court of Louisiana 15, 618–9, Department of Special Collections, Earl K. Long Library, University of New Orleans; (New Orleans) *Times*, 6 June 1864.

third district courts made feeble attempts to continue, but soon gave up. Fourth and fifth district courts never reopened. Only Judge Rufus K. Howell's sixth district court managed to continue. A Unionist, Howell held court throughout the summer of 1862, though only intermittently, and judging only the barest handful of cases.[11]

Unlike the civil courts, the courts with criminal jurisdiction closed because of certain actions taken by Butler and Shepley. The recorders courts became casualties in the wake of Butler's crackdown of 17 May. Shepley closed them on 20 May as a general part of the military's assumption of police powers, and transferred their duties to the provost court. First district court shut down three weeks later, but not because of any actions directed specifically against it. In fact, Judge Thomas W. Collins made a highly successful attempt at resuming normal operations. After closing for only a week, he reopened on 9 May and was conducting business as usual by 13 May; he even heard a murder case on 2 June. What caused this court's closure was Butler's General Order #41 of 10 June. As a means to increase Union control and ferret out closet Confederates, the order compelled every individual who performed any legal function, be they judge, sheriff, notary, or attorney, to swear loyalty to the United States or forfeit their office. Collins refused, and his court closed 12 June. Like those of the recorders, his duties went to the provost court.[12]

During the next four months Union army officers would be the sole source of justice in New Orleans. The smaller share of judicial work rested with the military commission. It met infrequently, trying only a small number of cases. Accusations against civilians were "in the form used in Courts Martial," except that detailed descriptions of the accused's personal life were included, such as "whether or not he has been a loyal citizen, his antecedents, character, and acts in that regard." The commission also slightly modified Fifth Amendment rights, relaxing "the Rules

11. Minutes of the Second District Court for the Parish of Orleans, 25: n.p., entries of 12 April–10 May 1862; Minutes of the Third District Court for the Parish of Orleans, 21: n.p., entries of 19 April–9 June 1862; Minutes of the Fourth District Court for the Parish of Orleans, 23: n.p. entry of 19 April 1862; Minutes of the Sixth District Court for the Parish of Orleans, 9: n.p. entries of 23 April–24 September 1862; (New Orleans) *Times,* 6 June, 7 July 1864.

12. (New Orleans) *Daily Picayune,* 21 May 1862; Minutes of the First District Court for the Parish of Orleans, 28 September 1861–5 November 1863, 271–320; *OR,* 1st ser., 15: 483–4; (New Orleans) *Daily Delta,* 13 June 1862; Minutes, First District Court, 326.

of Evidence of the English Common law" so that in trials defendants could be questioned against their will, though they could refuse to answer. In spite of such irregularities, it was still a fair tribunal, and a large percentage of defendants was acquitted. But those found guilty could expect harsh punishment. For threatening to kill a landlord for renting a house to Union officers, the commission sentenced William Bengic to confinement at Fort Jackson at hard labor, "wearing a ball not less than twelve pounds weight, attached to his left leg by a chain not less than four feet long, for the term of his natural life." George Posey received a similar sentence, though for only twenty-one years, for attacking a Union soldier "with murderous intents."[13]

By far the greatest burden fell on the shoulders of Bell in the provost court. At first he had little to do except try soldiers for drunkenness and civilians who insulted soldiers. He turned aside cases of civilians brought before him for offenses outside martial law, because he felt he lacked jurisdiction over such matters. But with the closure of the civilian criminal courts his duties expanded rapidly; by 12 June he possessed all criminal jurisdiction in New Orleans, except for those serious cases dealt with by the military commission. He was also responsible for administering the loyalty oaths. In addition to these tasks, circumstances required him to tackle a more complicated problem: because the sixth largest city in the country could not do without some means of settling civil disputes, Bell assumed the duties of a civil court judge.[14]

The tasks facing the provost court were indeed great. Bell had shouldered an enormous case load, having become virtually the only judge in New Orleans; it was not unusual for him to hear a hundred cases a day. But Bell and his prosecutor, Lieutenant Colonel J. B. Kinsman (who also served as provost judge in Bell's absence), were more than equal to the tasks confronting them. Bell quickly realized that his situation was one in which he had to discard standard legal procedures. Army regulations required the provost judge to decide cases other than those of martial law according to applicable local laws. But Bell disregarded them, because he believed that when Louisiana seceded, "she took her laws with her." Accordingly, he eliminated most legal formalities and complex proce-

---

13. *OR,* 1st ser., 6: 722–3; Minutes, U. S. District Court, 88, 91.
14. Minutes, U. S. District Court, 84–127, passim.

dures, and decided cases on their individual merits, using common sense and wisdom.[15]

Because of this underlying principle, proceedings in the provost court were quite informal. The court generally convened every day except Sundays and holidays, opening at 8 a.m. By far the greater part of Bell's case load involved petty criminal actions. The court generally entertained only oral arguments, and kept the scantiest of records. In a striking departure from the laws of Louisiana, and even most free states, all blacks were allowed to testify against whites. There were no jury trials; Bell delivered both verdict and sentence. Most criminal proceedings lasted but a few minutes, and Bell became quite famous for his speed. "He would," in the words of Butler's biographer James Parton, "dispose of fifteen cases in thirty minutes; an hour was considered a long trial."[16]

In handling civil cases, Bell essentially followed the same procedures. Although he preferred not to hear civil matters, the people of New Orleans brought their disputes to his bench. To keep his options open and prevent his court from being inundated with civil litigation, he refrained from setting any hard and fast rule on whether to hear them. Sometimes he publicly declared that he would hear no civil cases at all, as he lacked jurisdiction in such matters; on other occasions he announced he would take them, but only if the events involved had occurred after 1 May. In spite of his public declarations, the provost court did try civil causes throughout the summer of 1862, though their number was always minuscule in comparison to Bell's criminal docket.[17]

All manner of civil litigation eventually came before the provost bench, including debt collection, probates, divorces, and even manumissions. Perhaps the most important type of civil case tried by Bell arose from Butler's regulations concerning the city's currency. Early on, Butler decreed that Confederate currency was no longer legal tender in New Orleans. Naturally, a problem arose: did loans and bank deposits made in Confederate dollars have to be repaid in United States currency? Bell es-

---

15. (New Orleans) *Daily Picayune,* 25 November 1862; Minutes, U.S. District Court, 113, passim; Carpenter, "Military Government," 470; James Parton, *General Butler in New Orleans* (New York, 1864), 432.

16. Parton, *General Butler,* 432–4; (New Orleans) *Daily Delta,* 3 June 1862.

17. (New Orleans) *Daily Picayune,* 30 May, 12 and 25 June 1862; (New Orleans) *Daily Delta,* 19 June 1862.

tablished the rule in June when Dennis Sullivan Durand sued the Bank of Louisiana for the payment of his account in United States rather than Confederate currency. Bell ruled in favor of Durand. The bank immediately appealed his decision to Butler, claiming the provost court lacked jurisdiction. Butler, playing the role of an appellate judge, upheld Bell. Under his martial law, Butler stated, the provost court held jurisdiction in any matter he said it did.[18]

Cases of great substance like the currency affair were, however, the exception rather than the rule in the provost court. Bell's position was actually one of the most burdensome in the entire military government. Daily he faced a long parade of offenders of both sexes and races, ranging from drunks to petty thieves. Occasionally his patience wore thin, and he lashed out against complainants and arresting officers who failed to appear and civil matters he felt were petty or trifling. But Bell was blessed with a great sense of humor, which, along with his fairness, made him a popular figure in the city. Perhaps he was too popular. His court became a source of entertainment for the local loungers and loafers, whose rowdiness often disrupted the proceedings. During one exceptionally trying session Bell declared that spectators who had no business before the court were not allowed, and those loitering inside the bar would be arrested as vagrants in four minutes; "thereupon there was a stampede of the unwashed that was refreshing to see."[19]

In addition to the provost court, the provost marshal's office also took on some duties normally reserved for civil courts. For example, a problem arose concerning the default of renters. The war depressed the New Orleans economy, and many families, especially the poorer ones, could not pay their rents. The number of such cases grew so large that it was soon impossible for the provost court to hear them all. As a temporary solution the provost marshal opened a special court with the sole purpose of dealing with landlords' and renters' complaints. Its proceedings were similar to those of the provost court.[20]

Occasionally Butler, as commanding general, acted as a criminal

18. Parton, *General Butler,* 432–4, 423, 532; Minutes, U.S. District Court, 113, 121–4, 211, 280, passim; *OR,* 1st ser., 15: 472–3.

19. (New Orleans) *Daily Picayune,* 12 June, 30 August 1862; (New Orleans) *Daily Delta,* 3 and 8 June 1862.

20. (New Orleans) *Daily Picayune,* 26 July 1862; (New Orleans) *Daily Delta,* 8 July 1862.

judge, especially when the accused person was the object of his ire. One such case involved a gang of thieves. Disguising themselves as Union soldiers, they gained entrance to dwellings on the pretext of conducting searches, and then proceeded to rob the occupants. They were apprehended and brought before Butler, who immediately ordered that they be hanged. Particularly offensive acts of civil disobedience also caught his attention, as in the instance where a woman taught her children to spit at Union soldiers, and made fun of a Union officer's funeral procession as well. Butler sentenced her to indefinite solitary confinement at Ship Island. He similarly sentenced an attorney who carried about a small cross he claimed was made from the bone of a Yankee soldier. Butler simply would not tolerate insults to the United States or his soldiers, and he dealt with such offenders as harshly as possible.[21]

The system of ad hoc military justice partially ended in the fall of 1862. Butler and Shepley both recognized the great difficulties the lack of sufficient civil courts caused in this commercial city. As hostility to the occupation had cooled somewhat, they decided to take a first step in restoring some civilian government: they would reopen some of the civil courts. As the state's governor was normally responsible for filling judicial vacancies, Shepley, as military governor, handled this task. His first move was to order that the provost court would no longer hear civil disputes, except those specifically referred to it by Butler.[22]

The next step was the appointment of suitable judges, men who were competent attorneys as well as staunch Unionists. Shepley decided to keep the loyal Rufus K. Howell as judge of the sixth district court. For the second district he chose J. L. Whitaker, and for the third district Ezra Hiestand. The fourth and fifth district courts would remain closed, and Bell kept all his criminal jurisdiction. These three reconstructed courts officially opened in September with the presentation of the judges' commissions. All, even Howell, were commissioned by Shepley; although Howell had never vacated his office, Shepley still gave him a new commission to make it quite clear that Howell, like the other two judges, derived his powers from the military. Within two weeks all were operating normally. On 13 October Shepley announced that these courts were now available to

21. *OR,* 1st ser., 15: 476–8, 510–2.
22. (New Orleans) *Daily Picayune,* 30 August 1862.

handle all civil causes, except those involving the military. The next day he declared that henceforth all rent cases would be heard in these courts. After five months of confusion and ad hoc measures, regular civil justice had returned to New Orleans.[23]

These matters stood until December when decisions taken in Washington brought change and disruption to both the New Orleans high command and the courts. Unknown to Butler, Lincoln had replaced him on 9 November with Major General Nathaniel P. Banks. Butler did not find out until Banks arrived in mid-December. Lincoln's reasons for dismissing Butler grew out of Butler's treatment of New Orleans's foreign residents and their consulates. These foreigners generally sympathized with the Confederate cause, which Butler detested, and instead of being diplomatic, he treated them the same as rebels: brusquely, rudely, and with contempt. Lincoln feared European intervention in the war, and the foreigners' complaints about Butler made him a foreign relations liability, so Lincoln replaced Butler.[24]

A new commanding general meant the departure not only of Butler, but also of most of his staff. Shepley remained as military governor, but Bell decided to return to Massachusetts with his old friend; he resigned shortly after Banks's arrival. During his seven-and-a-half-month tenure as provost judge he had, with the able aid of Kinsman, served with the greatest distinction, giving an admirable performance under adverse and laborious circumstances. Among the many able men who surrounded General Butler, one contemporary commented, "no one labored more assiduously or more effectively in the services of the people of New Orleans than Major Bell." Amid great accolades, a grateful New Orleans legal community presented him with a tribute and a testimonial, which he received with "much tears." Butler, too, deserved praise for his handling of the city's judicial difficulties. During his tenure as commanding general of the Department of the Gulf he had, with the able aid of Shepley and especially Bell, successfully settled the judicial crisis.[25]

23. Minutes, Second District Court, 25: n.p., entries of 22 September–1 October 1862; Minutes, Third District Court, 21: n.p., entry of 30 September 1862; Minutes, Sixth District Court, 21: n.p. entry of 3 October 1862; (New Orleans) *Daily Picayune,* 15 and 16 October 1862.

24. Doyle, "Civilian Life," 23–5; Capers, *Occupied City,* 98–103.

25. Parton, *General Butler,* 434; (New Orleans) *Daily Picayune,* 21 December 1862.

The stability of the New Orleans court system would be badly shaken in 1863, but through no fault of Banks. Like Butler, the forty-four-year-old Banks possessed an extensive legal background and was a successful self-made lawyer; he too was a political general. An important northern politician, he had served as governor of Massachusetts and as speaker of the United States House of Representatives. But the two had completely different personalities. Banks tended to be indecisive, cool, distant, and nowhere near as combative, which partially explains why Lincoln chose him. Presumably, he would not cause trouble the way Butler had; but life for Banks in New Orleans would not be easy. Although he intended to govern New Orleans much more leniently than Butler had, the citizenry saw his kindness as a Union retreat. Also, he and Shepley did not get along, and because of the vague delineation of their authority, their squabbling caused a rift in the command structure.[26]

But the greatest disruptive influence on Butler's reorganized court system was not Banks, but a new judicial body, the United States Provisional Court for the State of Louisiana. Its judge, Charles A. Peabody, a Sewardite politician from New York, also arrived in New Orleans in mid-December. Lincoln, using his presidential war powers, created this court in October by executive order. According to the order, which doubled as Peabody's commission, the provisional court possessed unlimited authority "to hear, try, and determine all causes, civil and criminal, including causes in law, equity and revenue, and admiralty, and particularly all such powers and jurisdiction as belong to the District and Circuit courts of the United States."[27]

In reality the provisional court's nature differed substantially from that of standard federal courts, and seemed to flaunt the Constitution. The order's broad wording gave the court original jurisdiction not only over federal cases, but also over cases arising from state law, a power no federal court possessed. Congress had no influence over the court. Peabody himself never faced senate confirmation, and he and his officers were paid from War Department contingency funds, not general judicial appropriations. Moreover, Peabody was not tenured for life as were all other federal

26. For a biography of Banks see Fred Harvey Harrington, *Fighting Politician: Major General N.P. Banks* (Philadelphia, 1948).

27. Harrington, *Fighting Politician,* 102; *OR,* 1st ser., 15: 582.

judges; he served at the pleasure of the president, and the appointment did not extend "beyond the military occupation of New Orleans or the restoration of civil authority in that city and the State of Louisiana." Lincoln even exempted the court from the appeals process, declaring its judgments would be "final and conclusive." Presumably only Lincoln himself, and not the Supreme Court of the United States, could overturn its decisions.[28]

Lincoln's stated reason for instituting the new court appeared honest enough. Since the rebellion had "swept away the civil institutions of that State, including the judiciary and the judicial authorities of the Union," it was "indispensably necessary that there shall be some judicial tribunal existing there capable of administering justice." It seemed he was merely providing, on a temporary basis, an institution to render justice in Louisiana until regular courts became operational. In fact, his true reasons were quite different. Besides their travails with Butler, New Orleans's foreign residents complained to the State Department that no tribunal existed in the city where they could take their legal disputes, since foreigners could only sue in federal court. Both contemporary analysis and Peabody's own later account agree: Lincoln instituted the provisional court on the advice of the State Department to provide legal relief for New Orleans's foreign residents, and thus improve the Union's foreign relations.[29]

The provisional court indeed solved the foreigners' legal difficulties, but beyond their relief the court turned out to be a great mistake, and ultimately caused more trouble than it was worth. The best way to handle the foreigners would have been to appoint a new United States district judge for New Orleans. In fact, such an appointment would have fit in neatly as a continuation of Butler and Shepley's gradual restoration of the courts. The court's broad powers were bound to cause trouble. Lincoln's executive order, which had not been carefully drawn up, gave Peabody a blank check to conduct any judicial activities he pleased, evidently to ensure that no case involving a foreigner would lay outside his province. In

28. *OR,* 1st ser., 15: 582.

29. Ibid., 581–2; Charles A. Peabody, "United States Provisional Court for the State of Louisiana," *Annual Report of the American Historical Association for 1892* (Washington, D.C., 1893), 199–203; "United States Provisional Court for the State of Louisiana," *American Law Register* 13 (1864–1865): 386.

addition, after this bold intervention the Lincoln administration returned to its policy of benign neglect. From his very first day of operations Peabody went beyond dealing with foreigners and exercised the full powers implicit in his commission. Lincoln had in fact created a legal Frankenstein, a powerful judicial institution beyond Banks's control. The court became, in effect, "the alpha and the omega, the beginning and end of justice in Louisiana." Conflicts and confusion were inevitable.[30]

Relations between Banks and Peabody began cordially enough, with Banks immediately appointing Peabody as the new provost judge. Both Banks and Shepley took the stated purpose of the provisional court at face value. They could do little else; incredibly, neither they nor anyone in the War Department had been informed of the exact nature of the provisional court's mission. Soon after Peabody's arrival Shepley announced the coming opening of the provisional court and promised the military's full cooperation.[31]

The provisional court opened on December 31, with Peabody presenting his credentials and swearing in the attorneys who would practice before the court; by mid-January it was in full operation. Initially, the greater part of his docket involved federal cases. He immediately decided that in addition to new federal suits, he would take up cases that remained on the defunct United States district court's docket, but only on a selective basis, with the burden of proof on why he should not hear a particular case resting with the defendants. Gradually he began to hear more and more civil cases in Louisiana law. He also became the judge of the city's capital crimes, assuming the military commission's jurisdiction over murder.[32]

In spite of its auspicious beginnings, the provisional court soon became a center of legal controversy. No one challenged its federal jurisdiction, but its assumption of authority in state litigation was another matter. The points of contention over state cases concerned the handling of appeals from the three lately reopened district courts and the defunct Supreme

30. "The Authority of the 'Provisional Court' of Louisiana," *American Law Register* 386; Peabody, "Provisional Court," 205, 71.

31. *OR,* 1st ser., 15: 702; (New Orleans) *Daily Picayune,* 30 December 1862.

32. Minutes of the United States Provisional Court for the State of Louisiana, 1: 1–4; (New Orleans) *Daily Picayune,* 13 and 23 January 1863.

Court of Louisiana. Dissatisfied parties naturally wished to appeal unfavorable rulings from these courts. In normal times the appeals would have gone to the supreme court, but it no longer existed. As the provisional court was the only superior tribunal available, appellants brought their cases there, and Peabody decided to hear them. Besides these new appeals, there also existed the question of what to do about cases already docketed, but never decided, in the supreme court. These appellants also demanded relief in the provisional court, and as in the cases of the old federal court, Peabody agreed to hear them.[33]

Virtually the entire legal community of New Orleans rejected Peabody's policy on state appeals. Led by the three district court judges, the opposition declared that the provisional court, being a federal court, had no business hearing state appeals. The three district judges refused to send up records until Peabody issued court orders forcing them to comply. Instead of Peabody trying these cases, opponents argued, it was the responsibility of the chief executive officer of the state, namely Shepley, to appoint a new supreme court so appeals could go to their proper place. Some lawyers even began to assert that the provisional court was in fact unconstitutional, arguing Lincoln had no power to create such a court.[34]

Although only the Supreme Court of the United States could rule on the provisional court's constitutionality, the state supreme court controversy could be handled locally. On March 7 the New Orleans bar formally petitioned Shepley to appoint a new supreme court. Shepley now faced a sensitive dilemma: He understood the problems caused by the lack of a supreme court and the sensibilities of the judges and lawyers concerning Peabody's actions, but he also did not want to offend Peabody by siding against him. So Shepley concocted a curious compromise. In April he appointed three new supreme court justices. As associate justices he chose J. L. Cole, a former supreme court justice, and second district court judge Whitaker. The new chief justice was none other than Charles A. Peabody! Yet despite this effort, the whole idea was stillborn. Appointing a complete outsider to such an important post was unworkable. Though commissioned and paid, with Peabody receiving $3,541.66, the new justices never sat together as a body, and they never heard an argument or

33. Minutes, Provisional Court, 1: 3–5.
34. (New Orleans) *Daily Picayune,* 4, 7, and 28 February 1863.

decided a single case. In the end, the entire dispute was resolved in Peabody's favor. Besides his court, there was no other means of meeting the local need for an appeals court.[35]

As the supreme court controversy simmered, Banks's and Peabody's relationship began to deteriorate. Banks began to have misgivings about the provisional court's jurisdiction. He questioned whether it was a valid tribunal empowered to try any matter it chose. More specifically, he felt that the court was not competent to decide maritime prize cases or actions arising from the seizure of rebel property by virtue of the Confiscation Acts. He even went so far as to suggest to Stanton that the best way to clear up the question would be the appointment of a United States district judge for New Orleans. He proposed Peabody as a satisfactory choice.[36]

Banks's problems with the provisional court quickly changed from personal doubts to an ugly confrontation between the two men. Peabody's attempt fully to enforce the Confiscation Acts became the crux of their conflict. In the spring of 1863 he began large-scale seizures of rebel property, bringing the goods to New Orleans where they were auctioned off. The proceeds then went into the court's coffers. Peabody's officers became unusually zealous in conducting such operations, seizing rebel property wherever Union forces advanced into Louisiana. His men demanded, and sometimes got, army and navy escorts to conduct raids beyond Union lines just to seize property.[37]

By the end of March, Banks found this situation intolerable. He conceded Peabody's right to confiscate, but he could not tolerate the difficulties Peabody created for the army in the conduct of military operations. One of Banks's major concerns was forage. An army on the march lived partially off the land, and he needed the foodstuffs that Peabody had seized. Banks felt, justifiably, that his command prerogatives were being infringed. He knew the ultimate blame lay in Washington, for the failure to set a policy. His complaint to the War Department could not have been more blunt: "In a department under martial law the Army cannot be held

35. Ibid., 8 March 1863; Henry Plauché Dart, "History of the Supreme Court of Louisiana," *Louisiana Historical Quarterly* 6 (1921): 48; Peabody, "Provisional Court," 210; Ben Robertson Miller, *The Louisiana Judiciary* (Baton Rouge, 1932), 36.

36. *OR,* 1st ser., 15: 669.

37. Peabody, "Provisional Court," 205–6.

subordinate to a civil tribunal in matters which clearly affect its existence. The court ought only to adjudicate upon subjects turned over or transferred to it by the military branch of government. . . . The time is rapidly approaching when it will be necessary to define and limit the powers of each."[38]

Banks's harsh words resulted in some action, and the War Department gave him its full support. Henry Halleck, the general-in-chief, quickly replied that though the war department indeed had not been informed of the court's duties, there were some general principles that governed the matter. He reminded Banks that he possessed the highest authority in Louisiana, and "neither the court nor its officers should be permitted to interfere with or embarrass your movements." The court could not seize anything the army needed, and if its officers interfered with his operations, he should "send them back to the city, or, if necessary, out of the department." Banks had "full power," and only needed to exercise it "with discretion and justice."[39]

In addition to this ringing endorsement, Banks soon received something else he wanted: a regular United States district court. On 17 June, with great fanfare and ceremony, Edward H. Durell presented his credentials as United States district judge for the Eastern District of Louisiana, and was duly sworn in by Judge Whitaker. Durell was a bona fide federal judge, appointed by Lincoln and confirmed by the Senate. He officially opened his court on 24 June. Thereafter, Peabody dealt primarily with cases only in Louisiana law.[40]

Yet neither Halleck's backing nor the new federal court solved the conflict between the judicial and military authorities. The proper spheres for each were still not delineated, and Durell, like Peabody, refused to recognize Banks's absolute power. Again, the main issue involved confiscations. Their showdown came in November 1863 over the captured steamer *Alabama*. Banks was converting it for military use, but Durell wanted its ownership adjudicated in court under the Confiscation Acts. Durell had

38. *OR,* 1st ser., 15: 697; 694–5.

39. Ibid., 702.

40. (New Orleans) *Daily Picayune,* 18 and 25 June 1863; Barbara Rust, "Preliminary Inventory of the Records of the United States Court for the Eastern District of Louisiana," RG 21: 61, National Archives and Record Administration Regional Depository, Ft. Worth.

his marshal seize the ship and halt conversion work. But Banks stood up to him, his soldiers retook the ship, and Durell backed down. He soon challenged Banks again, when Banks was in the field, by seizing all the cotton in New Orleans. The city was thrown into such an uproar that Banks's chief of staff felt he might have to arrest Durell, but things soon cooled down. Only a strong policy from Washington could ever resolve the issue.[41]

While all the controversy went on over the provisional court, trouble developed in the provost court as well. Unlike Bell's court, Peabody's provost court was never highly regarded. His appointment was a mistake; the provost judge's duties were heavy enough as it was, and the provisional bench, besides taking up more of his time, was more important to him. The quality of justice in the provost court plummeted. Peabody began to hold shorter hours, in spite of his large case load, so that prisoners would languish in jail awaiting trial, even for minor offenses. To relieve some of the pressure he began to devolve some of his provost court duties on his clerk, August DeB. Hughes, who became quite notorious for his corruption, especially where court fees were involved. Because of these problems and the antipathy between the two men over the provisional court, Banks decided that Peabody's control of the provost court was no longer acceptable.[42]

But how to get rid of him? Peabody did not want to give up his position, and Banks felt it politically inadvisable to attack him directly. Instead, he decided to change Peabody's jurisdiction. On June 2, Banks created a new court styled "the Provost Court of the Department of the Gulf," with Colonel Charles Dwight of New York as judge. This court's stated purpose was to try "all cases of violations of special or general orders, violations of the rules and articles of war, violation of the recognized laws of war, or other offenses arising under the military jurisdiction," where such crimes did not involve the death penalty. Crimes committed by soldiers against civilians, not involving the death penalty or stripping officers of their commissions, would also be heard in this court. Thus, the new provost court's purpose was essentially the same as the old court's was initially. Peabody's provost court continued to operate, but now all crimes

41. *OR,* 1st ser., 1, 26, pt. 1: 793–5, 801–2, 807–9.
42. Doyle, "Civilian Life," 236–7; (New Orleans) *Daily Picayune,* 2 September 1863.

involving the military were out of his hands. Banks then extended the new court's jurisdiction to include capital cases of the same general nature, all death sentences having to be approved by him. Dwight's court was soon in full operation, handling such crimes as smuggling, fake passports, concealed weapons, and the sale of liquor to soldiers. A. A. Attocha, Dwight's prosecutor, replaced him as judge on 13 August, though Banks did not make it official for two months.[43]

Banks soon found a way to get rid of the old provost court. At the beginning of July, Peabody left for the North on a four-month vacation, recessing the provisional court and leaving Hughes in charge of the provost court. With Peabody gone, Banks decided to act, and on 31 August he abolished the old court. The provost marshal seized its records, and its duties were shifted to the new court. As his reasons for taking this action, Banks asserted that the old court had not been established by the military authorities, was not consistent with the proper governance of the army, and was not conducted according to military law. The last two points were flimsy, and the first downright false, but it mattered not; Banks had won his victory.[44]

The end of Hughes and the rise of Attocha was welcome news to the people of New Orleans. Attocha became a quite popular figure, providing "universal satisfaction," but his control of the city's criminal jurisdiction did not last long, as Banks had decided to continue the advance of Reconstruction by reopening the civilian criminal courts. In September Shepley announced the coming reopening of the first district court and two of the recorders courts. The recorders came first, opening on 5 October. As judge of the first district court, Shepley chose third district judge Hiestand, who took up his new duties on 4 November. Attocha's provost court continued to operate, but only with its martial law jurisdiction.[45]

As 1863 drew to a close, the court system had reached a new point of stability. No major changes occurred in 1864, despite the political and military events of that year. In March Michael Hahn was elected governor in

43. *OR,* 1st ser., 26, pt. 1: 533–4, 649; (New Orleans) *Daily Picayune,* 18, 21, and 24 June; 22 July; 14 August 1863; *OR,* 1st ser., 1, 26, pt. 1: 763–4.

44. Minutes, Provisional Court, 1: 147; *OR,* 1st ser., 1, 26, pt. 1: 706–7.

45. (New Orleans) *Daily Picayune,* 11 September 1863; ibid., 10 and 17 September; 6 October 1863; Minutes, First District Court, 327–8.

the state's occupied parishes. Shepley then resigned as military governor, returning the executive powers of state government to civilian hands. A month later, a convention met in New Orleans to draw up a new state constitution. Banks headed for disaster that spring. He marched his army up the Red River Valley toward Shreveport, and retreated after suffering a humiliating defeat. He was replaced in September by Major General S. A. Hurlbut. In the courts the only deviations from the mundane procedures of dispensing justice were personnel changes among the judges; all new commissions were issued by Hahn. The provisional court continued to operate, and Peabody managed to stay out of trouble. In the provost court Attocha lost his virtue and resigned in May under suspicion of corruption. He was replaced by the twenty-one-year-old Colonel Henry Clay Warmoth, a future governor of Louisiana, who held the post until he resigned in October and was replaced by Colonel G. Norman Lieber.[46]

Complete restoration of the judicial system came with the end of the war. In the winter and spring of 1864–1865 a new state legislature met, and among its actions it organized a new state court system. The system devised for New Orleans was practically identical to the antebellum system, except that judges would be appointed by the governor to six-year terms, instead of being elected to four-year terms. Hahn resigned as governor in March 1865 and was succeeded by Lieutenant Governor J. Madison Wells. Under the authority of the new state constitution and acts of the new state legislature, Wells appointed a new supreme court and finally reopened the fourth and fifth district courts. For the new supreme court Wells chose W. B. Hyman to be chief justice, and as associate justices Zenon Lebauve, Robert B. Jones, John N. Iseley, and the ever-loyal Rufus K. Howell. It reopened on 4 April. After a three-year interregnum the (New Orleans) *Daily Picayune* could faithfully report "the judicial organization of Louisiana is now complete in all courts of exclusive, appellate and concurrent jurisdiction."[47]

But some loose ends remained. The provost court continued its mar-

46. Willie Malvin Caskey, *Secession and Restoration of Louisiana* (Baton Rouge, 1938), 107; Harrington, *Fighting Politician,* 146–7; *OR,* 1st ser., 41, pt. 3: 297; Doyle, "Civilian Life," 239–41.

47. "An Act Relative to District Judges within the State," 1865 La. Acts 74; "An Act to Provide for the Removal of All Causes Pending in the Supreme Court of the State, under the Constitution of 1864," ibid., 76; "An Act Relative to District Courts in the Parish and City of New Orleans," ibid., 82–6; (New Orleans) *Daily Picayune,* 5 April 1865.

tial law jurisdiction into the classical period of Reconstruction, as long as occupation troops stayed. Shortly before his death, Lincoln appointed Peabody to be the United States attorney at New Orleans. Peabody continued as provisional judge until he closed the court on July 25, 1865. State cases still pending before his court went, under a new state law, to the proper state court. Congress finally abolished the provisional court in July 1866 and transferred all federal cases on its docket to the appropriate United States district or circuit court. Perhaps the loosest end of all involved the issue of the constitutionality of justice as rendered by the military courts, and the constitutionality of the provisional court itself. Naturally, only the Supreme Court of the United States could have the final say in these matters. Throughout the 1860s and 1870s, litigation involving martial law came before the high court, and it consistently ruled in favor of the actions taken by the military. In the instance of the provisional court, the justices ruled that the president indeed possessed the authority under his war powers to create such a court, and that all its decisions were valid. The high court also declared the New Orleans provost court to be a valid tribunal, and specifically affirmed its decisions over civil cases in Louisiana law. The most succinct summation of the issue was made by the Supreme Court in the case of *United States* v. *Diekelmann,* which also involved the occupation of New Orleans. As stated in the opinion of Chief Justice Morrison Waite, "Martial law is the law of military necessity in the actual presence of war. It is administered by the General of the Army, and is, in fact, his will. Of necessity it is arbitrary but it must be obeyed."[48]

Reconstruction of the judicial system of New Orleans involved chaos, confusion, corruption, strange manifestations of presidential power, questions of constitutionality, and under Butler at least, something admirable. The characters involved faced a unique and difficult set of circumstances. Still, under the pressures of the greatest crisis in the history of the United States, the military rulers of New Orleans did manage to muddle through. In various ad hoc ways they rebuilt a great city's shattered legal system, without, in the end, fundamentally altering it.

48. "An Act to Provide for the Suits, Judgment, and Business of the United States Provisional Court for the State of Louisiana, and for Other Purposes," 1865 La. Acts 134–6; Peabody, "Provisional Court," 210; Minutes, Provisional Court, 2: n.p., entry of 25 July 1865; *The Grapeshot,* 76 U.S. (1 Wall.) 129ff (1869); *Mechanics' and Traders' Bank* v. *Union Bank of New Orleans,* 89 U.S. (1 Wall.) 276ff (1874); *United States* v. *Diekelmann,* 92 U.S. (1 Wall.) 520ff (1876).

Part III

LAW AND SOCIETY

There are in this territory two classes of servants, to wit: Free servants and the slaves.

> James Brown and Louis Moreau Lislet, comps., *A Digest of the Civil Laws Now in Force in the Territory of Orleans* (New Orleans, 1808)

[F]ree people of colour ought never to insult or strike white people, nor presume to conceive themselves equal to the white; but on the contrary that they ought to yield to them in every occasion, and never speak or answer to them but with respect, under the penalty of imprisonment according to the nature of the offense.

> 1807 La. Acts 188–90

LAW, in its most general and comprehensive sense, signifies a rule of action, and this term is applied indiscriminately to all kinds of actions, whether animate or inanimate, rational or irrational. . . . In its more confined sense, law denotes the rule, not of actions in general, but of human action, or conduct.

> John Bouvier, comp., *A Law Dictionary, Adapted to the Constitution of the Laws of the United States of America, and the Several States of the American Union* (Philadelphia, 1839), 2:7

Law and society embrace each other warmly. Whether by custom, judicial decree, or by statute, law signifies accumulations of cultural assumptions about the right ordering of any society that gather from the experiences of the ages. Society's possessions—beliefs and family, property and reputation, life and liberty—lie within its ample fold, and it establishes how polity ought to be fashioned to guard those most precious assets. Its shapes and its rituals stand as reminders to all and sundry that it is the arbiter of their conduct. In turn it reflects shifting perceptions of governance and economics, or class, gender, and race, that invest political and social conversation. Law ultimately delineates culture because it expresses the composite singularities that set one society apart from another.

The concluding set of essays are suggestive of the nature of the intimacy between law and society in antebellum Louisiana. Each finds intellectual sustenance in the techniques of social history. All are therefore indicative of insights that flow when the methods of social history are joined to those of legal history. They are also suggestive of results that will inevitably proceed from similar investigations of other topics and other periods in Louisiana's past.

"FOREVER FREE FROM THE BONDS OF SLAVERY"

Emancipation in New Orleans, 1855–1857

On the morning of 6 March 1857, Chief Justice of the United States Roger B. Taney began reading his lengthy opinion in the case of *Dred Scott* v. *Sandford*. More than eleven years before that day, a slave named Dred Scott had sued for his freedom on the grounds that his master had taken him to free soil. When the chief justice finished reading, two hours later, Taney's decision meant that Dred Scott would remain in slavery. On the same day, eleven hundred miles away, the Louisiana legislature passed a one-sentence act that totally prohibited slave emancipation in the state from that day forward.[1]

Throughout the antebellum period, Louisiana law reflected an odd ambivalence with slave emancipation. Although Louisiana remained the easiest Deep South state in which to free a slave—at least until 1857—lawmakers fretted over the consequences of increasing the population of free people of color. Nevertheless, throughout most of the antebellum pe-

---

1. *Dred Scott* v. *Sandford,* 19 U.S. (1 How.) 393 (1857). Don E. Feherenbacher, *Slavery, Law, and Politics: The Dred Scott Case in Historical Perspective* (New York, 1981), 3–4; Kenneth Stampp, *America in 1857: A Nation on the Brink* (New York, 1990), 93–4. "An Act to Prohibit the Emancipation of Slaves," 1857 La. Acts 55.

riod, a number of New Orleans slaveholders voluntarily and legally freed their slaves with permission to remain in Louisiana. The state district courts in New Orleans also freed a number of slaves who claimed their freedom on the very basis that Dred Scott had—that they had been taken by their owners to free soil. But as the decades passed, the state legislature gradually placed more restrictions on owners wishing to free their slaves. As the law made manumissions more difficult, demands for individual exceptions increased. These petitions often succeeded, as did those to police juries, to judges, juries, and even to lawmakers themselves. Finally, with the dockets of the New Orleans district courts filled with petitions for emancipation, the legislature passed the act of 1857 that slammed shut the door to freedom for the state's approximately 300,000 slaves. Although the total prohibition of emancipation in Louisiana reflected the national political crisis over slavery in the 1850s, the sudden and dramatic increase in emancipations in the courts of New Orleans in 1855 and 1856 served as a catalyst in persuading the legislature to stop allowing the emancipation of slaves.[2]

Slaves in American Louisiana had two unique rights. State law allowed them to contract for their freedom and to initiate a lawsuit for their liberty. Article 174 of the *Civil Code of the State of Louisiana* (1825) allowed slaves to enter into only one form of contract—for their freedom. This right was quite limited, but unknown in other slave states. Slaves could not compel their owners to sell them if they managed to acquire their appraisal price, but if their masters or mistresses consented to the contract, the slave obtained the price the slaveholder set, and the contract was pre-

2. Laurence J. Kotlikoff and Anton J. Rupert, "The Manumission of Slaves in New Orleans, 1827–1846," *Southern Studies* 19 (summer 1980): 172–81. Kotlikoff and Rupert found that the Orleans Parish Police Jury (the governing body of the parish) allowed each slave whose emancipation they approved between 1827–1846 to remain in the state. In 1846 legislators abolished the Orleans Parish Police Jury and transferred responsibility for hearing emancipation petitions to newly created Emancipation Courts of the Councils of the Three Municipalities of New Orleans. "An Act to Abolish the Police Jury in the City of New Orleans," 1846 La. Acts 104. Each petition requested that the slave have permission to remain in the state, and the councils allowed these requests. "Slaves Emancipated by the Councils of Municipality No. 1, No. 2, and No. 3, 1846–1851," City Archives, New Orleans Public Library, Main Branch. E.g., *Marie Louise, f. w. c. v. Marot,* 8 La. 475 (1835); *Smith, f. w. c.* v. *Smith,* 13 La. 441 (1839); *Arsène, f. w. c. v. Pignéguy,* 2 La. Ann. 620 (1847); Ira Berlin, *Slaves without Masters: The Free Negro in the Antebellum South* (New York, 1974), 188–9, 139n. Kenneth Stampp, *The Peculiar Institution: Slavery in the Antebellum South* (New York, 1956), 232–4.

pared in the proper form for the transfer of real estate (slaves were considered real estate in Louisiana), slaves and owners entered into an enforceable contract by which slaves could purchase their freedom.[3]

The *Civil Code* also permitted slaves to sue for their freedom. In most common-law states, slaves who wished to sue for freedom had to proceed through the use of a legal fiction. Usually the common-law states prohibited slaves from suing directly for their freedom without the aid of a free person, a court-appointed guardian *ad litem*—a "Near Friend" (as it was called in Tennessee or "Next Friend" as some other southern courts termed it). In some states neither slaves nor free persons could directly initiate suits for freedom, even with the aid of a court-appointed representative. Instead, the guardian of the slave, or the slave himself or herself, had to begin an action of trespass against the master or mistress, who would respond that the plaintiff was a slave and could not sue, whereupon the plaintiff would claim to be free. The court would then ignore the assault issue and agree to rule on the issue of freedom.[4]

The *Civil Code* explicitly permitted owners to emancipate their slaves: "A master may manumit his slave in this State either by an act *inter vivos* [during life] or by a disposition made in prospect of death, provided such manumissions be made with the forms and under the conditions prescribed by law." The "conditions prescribed by law" became increasingly more stringent as the national crisis over slavery intensified.[5]

At first the procedure to free a slave seemed fairly simple. An 1807 law required slaves to have exhibited "honest conduct" for four years before the emancipation—specifically that he or she had not run away or committed a criminal act—and that the slave had reached the age of thirty years. If the slave had saved the life of the slaveowner or the slaveowner's family, slaveowners could dispense with both restrictions. The age requirement presented a formidable obstacle to emancipation. Slaves under thirty years had no recourse. This restriction prevented a slaveholder from freeing a slave woman with her children. It also stopped a free man or woman of color who purchased an underage spouse from effecting an emancipation until the slave reached the specified age. Children born to

---

3. *Civil Code of the State of Louisiana* (New Orleans, 1825), Art. 174, 27; Art. 461, 468.
4. Ibid.
5. *Civil Code,* Art. 184, 28–9.

slave women while owned by their free black husbands remained slaves by law for at least thirty years, because the child took the status of the mother. Although the free black purchaser would not have treated their spouse and children as slaves, if the free parent died, the spouse and children fell into the succession as any other property and faced judicial sale to satisfy the deceased's debts.[6]

Slaveowners petitioned the legislature, often with success, to make individual exceptions to the age requirement. In 1823 the legislature granted permission for a free woman of color to emancipate her two children, aged twenty-six and twenty-four. The following year lawmakers allowed seven slaveowners to free fifteen underage slaves; in 1825 legislators allowed five slaveholders to free eight more. Thirteen slaves under thirty gained their freedom from seven owners during the legislative session of 1826. Of the thirty-eight slaves who received their freedom by legislative emancipation from twenty owners, eleven slaves gained their freedom from seven free women of color, most often their free black mothers. Most of these acts contained a statement that the emancipation take place "as if the slave had attained the age required by law." A few required that the emancipating owner provide maintenance until the age of thirty years.[7]

6. "An Act to Regulate the Conditions and Forms of the Emancipation of Slaves," Orleans Territorial Acts (1807), 82–8; *Civil Code,* Arts. 183, 185–6, 28–9. The Supreme Court of Louisiana stated that if slaveholders could free their slave children, it would "flood the community with a class of persons who are totally incapable of supporting and taking care of themselves," *Carmouche* v. *Carmouche,* 12 La. Ann. 721 (1857).

7. "An Act to Authorise the Manumission of Certain Slaves," 1823 La. Acts 36; "An Act to Dispense Certain Slaves Therein Named with the Age Required by Law for the Emancipation of Slaves," 1824 La. Acts 42–6; "An Act to Dispense Certain Slaves Mentioned with the Age Requirement by Law for the Emancipation of Slaves," 1824 La. Acts 22; "An Act to Dispense Certain Slaves Therein Mentioned with the Time Prescribed by Law for the Emancipation of Slaves," 1825 La. Acts 132; "An Act to Emancipate Certain Slaves Therein Mentioned," 1825 La. Acts 150; "An Act to Authorize the Emancipation of the Slaves Therein Mentioned," 1825 La. Acts 198; "An Act to Authorise the Emancipation of Certain Slaves," 1826 La. Acts 32; "An Act to Dispense Certain Slaves Therein Mentioned with the Age Required by Law for the Emancipation of Slaves," 1826 La. Acts 40; "An Act Supplementary to the Act Entitled 'An Act for the Relief of Catherine Moreau,' Approved March 18, 1820," 1826 La. Acts 64–6; "An Act to Authorize the Emancipation of the Slaves Therein Mentioned," 1826 La. Acts 110–12. We have no way of knowing if the legislature rejected any petitions to free underage slaves or how many petitions came before the legislature. Journals of the Louisiana legislature in the 1820s have not survived. The legislature did not grant

In 1827, tired of the stream of petitions for exceptions, legislators made the age requirement less strict. Slaveowners wishing to free a slave under thirty could petition the parish judge and the police jury (the governing body of a parish) to allow an underage emancipation provided that the slave at issue was born in the state.[8]

The statewide population of free people of color grew by 53 percent between 1820 and 1830, from approximately 10,000 to 16,000. Louisiana legislators responded by passing a draconian measure against free people of color in 1830, not only to ensure that their numbers would not grow, but also to rid the state of some of the new arrivals. This act required all free persons of color who had come to Louisiana after 1825 to leave the state within sixty days or face a sentence of imprisonment at hard labor for one year. Failure to depart within thirty days of the end of the jail term imposed a penalty of imprisonment *for life* at hard labor. These provisions also applied to free blacks who came into Louisiana after passage of the act. The law required those wishing to emancipate their slaves to post a one-thousand-dollar bond to guarantee that the newly freed slave would leave the state within one month of emancipation. Lawmakers also ordered all free people of color legally allowed to remain in the state to register themselves in the office of their parish judge, recording their ages, gender, color, occupation, place of birth, and the date of their arrival in Louisiana. It cost fifty cents per person to register; failure to do so could result in a fine of $50 and imprisonment of one month. Legislators also directed the 1830 act against white people who wrote or printed statements that might "destroy that established line of distinction . . . between the several classes of this community." Whites who used incendiary language could incur a sentence of six months to three years in jail and a fine of $300 to $1,000. Free people of color violating this provision faced hard labor from three to five years, and perpetual banishment from the state after serving the sentence.[9]

---

emancipations before 1823 except in one instance, when lawmakers freed two slaves as a reward for revealing an insurrection plot. That act also provided financial compensation for the owners of the slaves. "An Act to Emancipate Certain Slaves and for Other Purposes," 1813 La. Acts 100.

8. "An Act to Determine the Mode of Emancipating Slaves Who Have Not Attained the Age Required by the Civil Code for Their Emancipation," 1827 La. Acts 12–14.

9. "An Act to Prevent Free Persons of Color from Entering into this State, and for Other Purposes," 1830 La. Acts 90–6. This violation of the First Amendment right of free speech was not as

The following year, lawmakers softened the rule that required freed slaves to leave the state within thirty days of their emancipation, although it kept the harsh penalties concerning those who had entered the state after 1825. By a three-fourths vote, parish police juries could allow newly emancipated slaves to remain in the state. And any slave freed for "meritorious conduct" could bypass the restrictions altogether. A study of the actions of the parish police juries indicates that from 1831 to 1846, the Orleans Parish Police Jury did not require even one emancipated slave to leave the state.[10]

The clash between the French-speaking population and the more prosperous Americans had resulted in a division of New Orleans into three separate municipalities in 1836, and each municipality established its own emancipation courts. The records that have survived—which are all in French—indicate that without exception freed slaves in Orleans Parish did not have the obligation to leave the state (sans qu'elle/qu'il soit obligée/obligé de quitter l'état).[11]

In the late 1830s and during the 1840s, Louisiana lawmakers began to pass acts once more granting legislative emancipations, requiring some free people of color whom police juries freed and allowed to remain in the state to post bond that they would not become a public charge. They also

---

egregious as it might seem, as the Supreme Court later ruled in *Barron* v. *Baltimore,* 7 Pet. 243 (1833), and *Permoli* v. *The City of New Orleans,* 3 How. 589 (1845), that the Bill of Rights did not apply to laws enacted by the states. A conviction for "failure to record" usually resulted in a fine of twenty-five dollars and court costs that averaged about eight dollars and twenty-four hours in jail. See First District Court of New Orleans, *State* v. *Thomas Powell,* No. 10,876, May 19, 1846. A conviction for "Convention" cases (being in the state of contravention to the law) resulted in an order to leave the state within sixty days for Mary Ann Martin, f. w. c. Martin did not leave as ordered, and on 4 October 1846, the First District Court of New Orleans sentenced her to one year in the state penitentiary at hard labor. *State* v. *Mary Ann Martin,* No. 299, 4 October 1846.

10. "An Act to Amend an Act Entitled 'An Act to Prevent Free Persons of Color from Entering This State,'" La. Acts 96–8; Kotlikoff and Rupert, "Manumission of Slaves," 172–81. In 1839 the legislature passed an act allowing the police juries of West Feliciana and Livingston Parishes to free several slaves owned by free persons of color, but required a bond to insure that those freed would not become a public charge ("An Act to Authorize the Police Jury of the Parishes of West Feliciana and Livingston to Emancipate Certain Slaves Therein Mentioned," 1839 La. Acts 78).

11. "An Act to Amend the Act Entitled 'An Act to Incorporate the City of New Orleans Approved February the Seventeenth, Eighteen Hundred and Five'" 1836 La. Acts 28–37; (New Orleans) *Daily Picayune,* 25 July 1846; Counseil de la Municipalité No. Un, 1 July–7 July 1851 (Emancipation Court), City Archives, New Orleans Public Library.

continued to make exceptions to the age requirement for emancipation, and began to make exceptions for free people of color required by law to leave the state to allow them to remain.[12]

By 1852 the mood in the Louisiana legislature had shifted against increasing the population of free people of color through emancipation with permission to remain in the state. Early in the legislative session Representative François Arceneaux of Lafayette Parish introduced a bill to prohibit all slave emancipations and Francis DuBose Richardson of St. Mary Parish sponsored a bill that required all liberated slaves to depart the state for Liberia. In the initial debate over this measure, Richardson cited the need for change in the emancipation law of the state:

> The constant increase of free negroes in this State, and their intercourse with slaves, tending to corrupt and poison them, was a crying evil, and in fact an absolute nuisance. It was a sore on the body politic . . . there was no humanity in liberating a good slave, and thus condemning him to drag out an irksome and precarious existence. The purpose of this bill was to send the black man in this case to the only spot on the globe where he can attain all the advantages and rights which are compatible with his mediocrity of intellect.[13]

Representative Uriah Burr Phillips of West Feliciana argued against the measure, stating that although he understood the "evils accompanying a free negro population," he believed that Richardson's bill would cause "an entire prohibition of all emancipations." Representative E. Warren Moise of Plaquemines Parish claimed that Richardson's measure was

12. "An Act to Authorize the Police Jury of the Parishes of East Feliciana and Livingston to Emancipate Certain Slaves Therein Mentioned," 1839 La. Acts 78; "An Act to Allow Harriet Mitchell, a Free Woman of Color, to Reside in the State," 1846 La. Acts 19; "An Act for the Relief of Julie Vigoureux and Tulie Morrow, f. w. c.," 1846 La. Acts 19; "An Act for the Relief of Jacob A. Norager, a Free Man of Color," 1847 La. Acts 4; "An Act to Dispense the Statu-Liber, Louis, A Mulatto Man Aged About Twenty-Eight Years, with the Time Prescribed by Law for the Emancipation of Slaves," 1848 La. Acts 104; "An Act for the Emancipation of the Slave Florestine and Children," 1848 La. Acts 34; "An Act to Emancipate the Slave Aspasie," 1848 La. Acts 62; "An Act to Allow Nancy Flournoy and her Son, Thomas Jefferson Flournoy, Free People of Color, to Remain in the State," 1848 La. Acts 90; "An Act for the Relief of Jane Graves, Free Woman of Color," 1848 La. Acts 95.

13. *Journal of the House of Representatives of the State of Louisiana* (New Orleans, 1852), 18, 36; *Report of the House of Representatives of the State of Louisiana* (New Orleans, 1852), 7.

aimed at New Orleans: "Its object was to take away from the Municipal Council the power to emancipate slaves with permission to remain in the State." Moise proposed an amendment requiring newly freed slaves to depart the state within ten days of their emancipation. He expressed his reasons for supporting the bill:

> [I]f the members of the House would take the trouble to examine the late census and compare it with the previous one, they would find that the free population of New Orleans had increased in a greater ratio than any other city of the Union. And this state of thing [*sic*] had arisen from the lac [*sic*] manner in which the municipal authorities had granted emancipations. The presence of so numerous a free colored population was injurious in the highest degree. It corrupted the morals of the slave, tended to make him dissatisfied with his condition, and formed a constantly augmenting nucleus of mischief and evil.

No one corrected Moise, but the population of free people of color in New Orleans had actually declined dramatically from a high of 19,226 in 1840 to 9,905 in 1850. This shrinking of the free black population resulted from the enforcement of the statute forcing free people of color to leave the state if they had entered after 1825. This act no doubt deterred many free people of color from moving to Louisiana and inspired others to leave. During the same period the free black population of Charleston more than doubled, as did those of Louisville and Washington, D.C. Of southern cities, only New Orleans and Norfolk, Virginia, experienced a decline in the population of free people of color, and Norfolk's declined from 1,026 to 956, a net loss of only seventy persons. Furthermore, the percentage of free people of color in the total population of the city declined as Irish and German immigration swelled. By 1850 the foreign born comprised 49 percent of the city's population.[14]

Representative Tillinhurst Vaughan of Claiborne Parish suggested that legal complications might arise from the passage of the bill. He expressed a desire to see abuses in the present law eliminated, rather than a

14. *Report of the House,* 7–8; Richard C. Wade, *Slavery in the Cities: The South, 1820–1860* (New York, 1964), 325–7.

wholesale deportation of freed slaves. "Under our present statute," he noted, "the slave had a right to contract for his liberty, while his [Richardson's] bill would cut off the right of those who have made such contracts and which are not yet perfected. He did not know how the law worked in the city, it might be liable to many abuses for ought he was aware of, but as far as its operation in the country was concerned, he knew it had worked well."[15]

The representatives from Orleans expressed the most opposition to Richardson's measure. C. C. Lathrop gave an impassioned speech, in which he stated that because he remained a staunch advocate of African colonization, he opposed this bill because under its provision, "to ship off indiscriminately all emancipated slaves to Liberia. . . . By doing so we would foist vicious subjects on that colony and thus tend to destroy its usefulness." Concerned with imposing "the scum of the colored population of the United States on Liberia," Lathrop also questioned the logistics of the act, as the American Colonization Society in Louisiana had but one ship to send to Liberia once each year. No one questioned his argument, despite the requirement that slaves emancipated in Louisiana had to establish that they had been of "honest conduct" for at least four years before the emancipation, specifically that they had never run away or committed a criminal act. And was Lathrop suggesting that freed slaves of bad character—"the scum of the colored population"—stay in Louisiana?[16]

William S. Campbell of Orleans expressed his objections to the provision requiring freed slaves to leave the state as well as the requirement to post a one-thousand-dollar bond, and he indicated that he would vote against the bill if these requirements remained.

> He considered it a very great case of hardship to take away from the master the right to liberate a faithful and deserving slave, one perhaps who had saved the life of his owner and had rendered other valuable services. Suppose a man had but one slave who had toiled with his master for many years, and had conferred lasting and enduring benefits on his owner, and he desired to liberate him, why he

15. Wade, *Slavery in the Cities,* 325–7.

16. *Report of the House,* 8–9. "An Act to Regulate the Conditions and Forms of the Emancipation of Slaves," Orleans Territorial Acts (1807), 82–8.

would be met full in the face by this law, which says you shan't
emancipate him because you cannot give a bond in the sum of $1000
. . . the feeling towards slaves is not of that hostile character which
should compel them to go abroad, for by doing so you tear them
away from all kindly associations and family ties.

Campbell finished his argument equating this measure with prohibiting
emancipation altogether, saying "he could not vote for a law taking away
from the people the right to emancipate their slaves."[17]

With feelings running high in the house, Campbell's colleague from
Orleans, J. G. Sever, recommended keeping the ten-day requirement for
freed slaves to leave the state. He warned the legislators that they must
protect the state from "this fanatical notion of abolition at the North."
Sever told his fellow representatives "it is no humanity, no favor, no mercy
to set a man free in a white community. If it was in his power, he would
make every black man in the country a slave and would engraft this on
the Constitution of the United States. He hoped the gentlemen would reflect and remember that we are under a necessity as pressing and inexorable as that which compels mortal man to bow to the grim king of ter-
ror."[18]

Lathrop then gave a glowing account of the success of the Liberia
colony, and stated that "the negro race would find a home in that land;
that for their own good and their safety, they must be removed to Liberia."[19]

Early in February 1852 the house and senate appointed a joint committee to consider "the further protection of slave property in this State,
for the greater restriction of the emancipation of slaves, and for the removal of emancipated slaves from the State." Early in March, Representative Richardson sponsored a successful resolution to turn over the
house chambers to the Reverend J. M. Pease to deliver a lecture on
the benefits of American colonization. A few days following the lecture,
the house passed a resolution supporting African colonization, a cause
which "deeply involves the best interest of the State." The resolution

17. *Report of the House,* 8.
18. Ibid.
19. Ibid., 8–9.

called for an appropriation of state funds to aid in removing free people of color *with their consent* to Liberia.[20]

At the same time as the house debated restricting the emancipation of slaves to those who would go to Liberia after receiving their liberty, the legislators continued to hear individual petitions for legislative emancipations. On March 11 the Louisiana legislature passed an act freeing the slave Nanny "for faithful and meritorious services during the long and painful illness of her said master, any law to the contrary notwithstanding." However, the act ordered Nanny to leave the state within three months of her liberation, "never to return," but it did not compel her to go to Liberia.[21]

Between March 15 and 18, lawmakers passed four important but conflicting bills, an indication of the deep divisions in feeling concerning slave emancipation. The first clarified an 1842 act that required parish authorities to imprison all free black sailors whose ships arrived in a Louisiana port until the ship departed. The 1852 act allowed them to remain on board their ships as an alternative to incarceration. Ship captains had the duty to register and describe free black sailors to a competent authority. Discovery of a free black crew member on shore illegally resulted in imprisonment for the sailor and a fine of one thousand dollars for the captain and owners of the ship.[22]

The second act passed freed the slave Eloy Barabino, allowing him to remain in the state. The third freed a slave family—Ben; Clarissa, his wife; and their three children—with the requirement that they leave the state (but not necessarily for Liberia) within three months of the date of the act or risk reenslavement.[23]

The fourth statute added a formidable obstacle to the manumission

20. *Journal of the House* (1852), 56, 144, 164.

21. Ibid., 30, 85, 121, 161, 166; "An Act to Authorise the Emancipation of the Slave Nanny for Meritorious Services to Her Master," 1852 La. Acts 122.

22. "An Act to Amend an Act Entitled 'An Act More Effectually to Prevent Free Persons of Color from Entering This State and for Other Purposes, Approved Sixteenth of March, Eighteen Hundred and Forty Two,'" 1852 La. Acts 193.

23. "An Act to Emancipate Eloy Barabino, a Slave Belonging to the Estate of the Late Stefano Barabino," 1852 La. Acts 198; "An Act to Emancipate the Slaves Ben, Clarissa, Edward, Susan and Mary, for Meritorious Service Rendered Their Late Master, Samuel Estelle, Deceased, Late of the Parish of Carroll," ibid., 200.

procedure. Lawmakers required all persons freeing slaves to send them to Liberia within one year of manumission. The emancipator had to pay the slave's passage of $150, and former slaves who did not depart, or who returned to Louisiana, forfeited their freedom and became slaves of their former owner once more. Slaveholders besieged the legislature with requests for individual exceptions, and the number of legislative emancipations with permission to remain in the state increased. Legislators responded in 1853 by passing five acts freeing eleven slaves without forcing them to leave the state, and in 1854 with four acts liberating seven slaves, all with permission to stay in Louisiana.[24]

Governor Paul Octave Hébert gave an address at the opening session of the legislature of 1855 on January 17. Responding to a petition to emancipate the slave Caroline and her children, with permission to stay in the state, which appeared on the legislative agenda even before his address, Hébert stated that the bill created an exception to the law of 1852.[25]

Before the end of January members of the house introduced petitions to emancipate several other slaves, and the bill to free Caroline and her children appeared once more for the members of the house to consider. Early in February, Representative Slaughter of Caddo Parish introduced an act to allow a free woman of color, Mary Amelia, to remain in the state; Representative Dennis Cronan of Orleans introduced yet another bill to free a slave woman and her child; and D. E. Beecher of Orleans petitioned to allow Philip Claiborne, f. m. c., to emancipate his slave family. The house referred these acts to the House Judiciary Committee, which reported unfavorably on all of them or tabled them. In all, the Judiciary

24. "An Act Concerning the Emancipation of Slaves in This State," 1852 La. Acts 214–5; "An Act to Emancipate Jane Mary, the Slave and Daughter of Patsy, f. w. c.," 1853 La. Acts 162; "An Act to Enable Baptist Dupeyre, or His Legal Representative, to Emancipate the Slave Zoe, With removing Her from the State," 1853 La. Acts 163–4; "An Act to Emancipate the Slaves Belonging to the Estate of the Late J. B. Cajus, of the Parish of Orleans," 1853 La. Acts 273–4; "An Act to Manumit or Emancipate Marie Melandy, Slave of Moise Hébert, of the Parish of St. Landry," 1853 La. Acts 276; "An Act to Emancipate Henrietta, Slave of Rebecca Coleman, of the Parish of East Baton Rouge," 1853 La. Acts 277; "An Act Authorizing W. C. Wilson to Emancipate His Slave David," 1854 La. Acts 34–5; "An Act to Authorize John Cousin, of the Parish of St. Tammany to Emancipate the Slave Frances and Her Three Children," 1854 La. Acts 35; "An Act to Authorize Mrs. S. A. Withers, Wife of Joseph M. Kennedy, to Emancipate Her Mulatto Slave, Clarisse, with Permission to Remain in the State," 1854 La. Acts 36.

25. *Journal of the House of Representatives of the State of Louisiana* (New Orleans, 1855), 9–10.

Committee heard and denied petitions of more than a dozen slaves for freedom and three previously freed slaves to remain in the state.[26]

Louisiana legislators passed a revision of the Black Code in 1855, titled "An Act Relative to Slaves and Free Colored Persons." Although the act reiterated most of the criminal stipulations of the Black Code, it contained a sweeping revision of the requirements and procedure for the manumission of slaves. The legislature, weary of the continuous pressure from citizens of the state to make exceptions to the 1852 act, turned the responsibility for emancipations over to the state district courts. The 1855 act required slaveholders to sue the state in a district court. The legislation charged the district attorney "to represent the State, and to urge all legal objections, and to produce such proofs as may be in his power to defeat plaintiff's demand." For this service, district attorneys received $20 for each slave freed; the emancipating owner had to pay not only that fee, but all court costs, regardless of the outcome of the suit. Slaveholders wishing to free slaves had to state the age, sex, and color of those they would free; provide an authenticated act of sale and a certificate from the registrar of conveyances to prove clear title to the slave; and produce a certificate from the recorder of mortgages that no one held a mortgage on the slaves. The act also required the slaveholder to prove that the slaves were "of good character and sober habits," by producing character witnesses. Furthermore, the act required proof that the slave in question had no criminal convictions. Before filing suit against the state, the person seeking to free a slave had to advertise in a local newspaper in accordance with the law of judicial sales at least five times during the thirty days before filing suit and subsequently prove that no one had made opposition to the intention to emancipate. The notices appeared under the heading of judicial sales, because freeing a slave represented a transfer of property from the owner to the slave. The owner also had to post a bond of one thousand dollars before filing the suit that the slave, if freed and allowed to remain in the state, would not become a public charge.[27]

26. Ibid., 9–10, 15, 18–19, 29, 48, 53, 56, 69–70, 81, 100–1. The reason the exact number cannot be ascertained is that one act involved "Certain Slaves," no names given; one was for a free man of color's family, no number of children given; and one was for a slave woman's children, again with no number given.

27. The Black Code is the name usually given to the 1806 act of the Legislative Council for the

After these requirements were fulfilled, the 1855 act required a jury trial for all suits for the emancipation of slaves as an adversarial procedure against the state. Jurors would decide not only whether the slave should go free, but also whether he or she should remain in the state. Slaves freed but not permitted to remain in the state could not be considered free until they left the state, and would become slaves once again if they returned.[28]

The 1855 act went into effect on April 28, and it had an immediate and dramatic effect in New Orleans. Despite the prerequisites needed for filing a freedom suit—the thirty-day advertisement, certificates from the mortgage and conveyance offices, evidence of good character, and the one-thousand-dollar bond per slave, the first suits for freedom in the First Judicial District Court of New Orleans appeared on the docket book during the first week of July 1855. They continued at a steady rate in this court, and later in the second, fourth, and fifth judicial district courts of New Orleans.[29]

The Presbytere, a building adjacent to the St. Louis Cathedral on the Place d'Armes (now known as Jackson Square), housed all of the district courts of the city of New Orleans. A visitor described the atmosphere of the building in 1847:

> I cannot forget the curious scenes I occasionally saw when in the New Orleans courthouse. . . . Applewomen take possession of its lobbies. Beggars besiege its vault like offices. The rains from heaven

---

Territory of Orleans that constituted the first slave code of American Louisiana. "An Act Prescribing the Rules and Conduct to Be Observed with Respect to Negroes and Other Slaves of This Territory," Orleans Territorial Acts (1806), 150–90; "An Act Relative to Slaves and Free Colored Persons," 1855 La. Acts 387–8. An "Act of Sale" is a civil law term used to describe real estate transfers. As the Black Code and the *Civil Code* classified slaves as real estate, Louisiana law required all sales of slaves to follow the form for real estate sales, including that the act be notarized, witnessed, and registered in the conveyance office. Black Code, Orleans Territorial Acts (1806), 154; *Civil Code,* Art. 461, 72. Judith Kelleher Schafer, *Slavery, the Civil Law, and the Supreme Court of Louisiana* (Baton Rouge, 1994). 185.

28. *Civil Code,* Sec. 73–4, 387–8.

29. 1855 La. Acts xiv; the Supreme Court of Louisiana ordered the First Judicial District Court of New Orleans to cease hearing civil cases and confine itself to its criminal docket. The case that inspired this ruling involved a contested election for the office of district attorney for the Parish of Orleans. Although the case had nothing to do with the emancipation cases in progress, the election may have been contested because the office of district attorney had suddenly become more lucrative. *State* v. *Judge of the First District Court of New Orleans and Benjamin S. Tappan,* 11 La. Ann 187 (March 1856).

sport among its rafters. It has everywhere a fatty, ancient smell, which speaks disparagingly of the odor in which justice is held. And yet in this building . . . are held from November to July, six courts whose officers brave damp and steam enthusiastically and persever- ingly . . . you turn . . . into a narrow alley, and brushing past a greasy crowd are soon within the criminal court, where a judge, perched in a big box, wrangles hourly with half-crazed witnesses; zealous, full- lunged lawyers; and audacious criminals ranged in boxes, very much to the satisfaction of a mustached district attorney and the merry- looking keeper of the Parish jail.[30]

Despite the Hogarthian-sounding conditions of the courts building, the trial records generated by these freedom suits give an in-depth view of attitudes toward slavery and freedom in New Orleans in the 1850s and much more. None of these cases appears in published court reports, as dis- trict courts did not publish reports of their decisions in the antebellum pe- riod and—since not one of them failed—none reached the Supreme Court of Louisiana on appeal, in which case it would have appeared in the court's printed reports. These transcripts are not on microfilm, and they have lain untouched among the records of the main criminal court of New Orleans and three other civil district courts since 1856. Using them is a daunting task, as the records of the first district court are not indexed ei- ther by subject or by proper name, and they are therefore only retrievable by docket number. One must therefore scan the docket and minute books page by page to find cases that the clerk recorded as *Smith* v. *State of Louisiana* rather than the usual form of criminal cases, *State of Louisiana* v. *Smith.* Almost all of the emancipation cases have survived intact, usually

---

30. A. Oakley Hall, quoted in Leonard V. Huber, *The Presbytere on Jackson Square: The American Period, 1803–Present* (New Orleans, 1970), 40–1, 43–4. There were complaints that juries of the first district court were not properly supervised. In *State* v. *Brunetto,* a trial for wilful murder, the sheriff took the jury to a restaurant for dinner during the jury deliberations. During the course of the din- ner, which lasted for two hours, jurors consumed cocktails of both absinthe and anisette, six bottles of claret, half a bottle of brandy, and a bottle of champagne. The jury returned to the jury room after dinner and resumed their deliberations, finding the defendant guilty. The defense attorney won on appeal to the Supreme Court of Louisiana. In a classic understatement, Justice Albert Voorhies de- clared "one or more of the jurors were not in possession of that unclouded intellect which the accused had a right to demand." *State* v. *Brunetto,* 13 La. Ann. 45 (1858); Robert C. Reinders, *End of an Era: New Orleans, 1850–1860* (New Orleans, 1964), 73–4.

tied up in the same red tape (now faded to brown) with which the clerk bound them when the cases ended more than 140 years ago. They constitute a fabulous find, a whole new body of evidence about slavery. The volume of these cases—159 individual suits to free 289 slaves in just over sixteen months—indicates that the suits would have continued—perhaps up to the beginning of the Civil War—had not the supreme court and the legislature intervened. These cases present compelling evidence of a pent-up desire to free slaves without forcing them to go to Liberia. Indeed, several of these records specifically state that the slaves seeking freedom would rather remain as slaves than live free in Liberia. And in the only freedom suit in which the jury freed the slave—Simon, a drayman and bricklayer—but denied him permission to remain in the state, the plaintiff sued the state again and in the second trial won both the slave's freedom and permission to stay. In her petition the owner of the slave Marianne declared that she wanted her slave freed "provided the jury grants her permission of remaining in the State of Louisiana after her manumission and not otherwise." Indeed, the standard wording of the judgments freeing the 289 slaves was usually "released from the bonds of slavery, and that she be entitled to all the rights and privileges of a free colored person and further that she be allowed to remain in the state." The overwhelming majority of these slaves were truly African-Americans, not Africans—almost all native-born Louisianians. Furthermore, many of those seeking to free them were blood relatives who sought to free them with permission to remain in the state.[31]

31. Five cases have disappeared and their outcomes cannot be determined: in the First Judicial District Court of New Orleans, *Babette Robin, f. w. c.* v. *State of Louisiana,* No. 10796 (Hannah), filed 7 January 1856; *D. S. Dewes, testamentary executive* v. *State of Louisiana,* No. 10918 (Zabel and Clem), filed 31 January 1856, transferred to Sixth Judicial District Court on 14 May 1856; *Thomas Askew* v. *State of Louisiana,* No. 10967 (Hannah), filed 15 February 1856; *Eugene Ducatel* v. *State of Louisiana,* No. 11053 (?), filed 6 March 1856, transferred to ? 10 April 1856. Second Judicial District Court of New Orleans: *Corrine Fabre* v. *State of Louisiana,* No. 10196 (Elizabeth Belsamine), filed 24 June, 1856; First District Court of New Orleans, *Joseph Adams alias Napoleon, f. m. c.* v. *State of Louisiana,* No. 10770, 11084 (Simon), 28 March 1856; Second District Court of New Orleans, *Eloise Laby Duvernay, f. w. c.* v. *State of Louisiana,* No. 9824 (Marianne), 13 February 1856; see also First District Court of New Orleans, *Widow John Clay* v. *State of Louisiana,* No. 10764 (Justine), 3 December 1855. For an example of the wording of a standard judgment see First District Court of New Orleans, *Denis Prieur* v. *State of Louisiana,* No. 10508 (Harriet Rollis), 3 December 1855. All dates contained in case citations are dates of the final judgment unless otherwise noted.

In each case, the district attorney for Orleans Parish, Benjamin S. Tappan, answered each petition for freedom with exactly the same phrase: "The State pleads a general denial and demands strict proof." No evidence exists in any of these suits that the district attorney made any other effort to impede the process. But the 1855 act put Tappan in a difficult position. If he did his job well, and obstructed emancipations, he lost the $20 fee for each slave freed. Suing the state to gain freedom for a slave was an adversarial procedure to violate the policy of the state to keep the population of free people of color from growing. Why did Tappan fail to fight these suits more vigorously? Could it have been that those suing for the freedom of their slaves assembled all of the documents and followed all of the procedures so as to make a defense useless? Could the $20 per slave freed—not $20 per suit but $20 per slave—have been an incentive to the district attorney, who made a salary of approximately $600 a year for a part-time position? If Tappan collected the $20 fee for each of the slaves freed by the district courts of New Orleans, he would have made $5,780 in fees at a time when the salary of the chief justice of Louisiana was $6,000 and that of the district court judges $2,500.[32]

Who were the jurors who seemed so unconcerned about increasing the population of free people of color? We know that jurors who served in the First District Court of New Orleans received $1.00 per day for their services. But jurors serving in the other district courts of New Orleans received $1.50 *per case* in which they rendered a verdict. Could the jurors of the second district court, which heard the second highest number of freedom suits, and who often ran a number of them through in a day, have been motivated at least in part to haste by the jurors' fees? The records kept by the clerks of the district courts of the city make an extensive study

32. Benjamin S. Tappan was not of the same family as the Tappan brothers, who were famous abolitionists. The New Orleans Tappan, a native of Tennessee, lived in New Orleans with his wife, Jane, according to the federal census of 1860. Benjamin Tappan, the abolitionist, was a native of Massachusetts. He died in 1857. Bertram Wyatt-Brown, *Lewis Tappan and the Evangelical War against Slavery* (Cleveland, 1969). Benjamin S. Tappan participated in the Louisiana secession convention in January 1861 and voted for the ordinance of secession (*Journal of the Proceedings of the Convention of the State of Louisiana, 1861* [New Orleans, 1861], 4, 231, 233); *Journal of the House* (1852), Report of the Auditor of Public Accounts, 10. As the "Committee on Retrenchment" recommended that district attorneys serve a larger jurisdiction with no raise in pay, Tappan's salary probably did not rise substantially by 1855. Salary of district judges is given in Constitution of 1852, Tit. III, Art. 63.

of the jurors difficult because they consistently entered the names of the jurors in the minute books by surname and first initial—such as W. Thompson. The city directory might show a Walter, William, and Warren Thompson, making it difficult to know which person served. But of those whose names are unambiguous, all seem to be working people, some skilled, some clerical, and some manual laborers. The 1850 and 1860 United States census indicate that an accountant, a trader, a laborer, two carpenters, and a tailor served on the emancipation juries. As the clerks of the district courts drew the names of jurors from the voting rolls, and Louisiana law required American citizenship and a one-year residency in the state to vote, those who served on juries were not new immigrants. Why were these men so willing to set free the slaves who came before them?[33]

One explanation may lie in the changing demographics of New Orleans in the 1850s. Because of the waves of German and Irish immigration, the white population grew dramatically from 1850 to 1860, from 89,459 to 144,601. In contrast, the population of free persons of color, which had declined precipitously from 1840 to 1850, from 19,226 to 9,905, grew only slightly between 1850 and 1860. These two factors meant that while in 1850 free people of color comprised 8 percent of the city's population (down from 18 percent in 1840) by 1860, despite a rise in actual numbers, the free black population had fallen to 6 percent of the total. Rural legislators' fears of a rapidly increasing free black population failed to materialize in New Orleans or in the rest of the state. Indeed, while the statewide population of whites grew by about 200,000 and the slave population by just under 100,000, the statewide population of free people of color rose by just over 1,000. By 1850, however, 49 percent of New Orleans's white population was foreign born, and in the Vieux Carré, supposedly the enclave of the French-speaking Creoles, 56 percent. Little wonder that the white Creoles felt more solidarity with the mostly Catholic, French-speaking Creoles of color than with the new immigrants.[34]

Perhaps even more importantly, there was a place in New Orleans so-

33. "An Act Relative to Juries in the Parish of Orleans," 1855 La. Acts 342–3; *Cohen's New Orleans Directory for 1855* (New Orleans, 1855); federal censuses of 1850 and 1860.

34. Joseph G. Tregle, Jr., "Creoles and Americans," in Arnold R. Hirsch and Joseph Logsdon, eds., *Creole New Orleans: Race and Americanization* (Baton Rouge, 1991), 164–6; Wade, *Slavery in the Cities,* 326.

ciety, both socially and economically, for those who gained their freedom that would not have existed in a rural parish. This was the crucial difference—the house divided, although Abraham Lincoln did not make that famous speech until 1858. The people of New Orleans, accustomed to relating with free people of color, did not fear increasing the free colored Creole population. Emancipation throughout the South tended to occur much more often in the cities than in the countryside. One Virginian noted that cities "naturally became liberalized on the subject of emancipation before the interior agricultural communities." This trend was accelerated by the influx of thousands of Irish and German immigrants in New Orleans. Creoles, black and white, felt besieged. The overwhelmingly French-speaking, Catholic free Creoles of color had much more in common with their white counterparts than they did with the newly arrived, often desperately poor Irish and German immigrants. The free black community in New Orleans, as the *Daily Picayune* reported in 1859, "are a sober, industrious and moral class, far advanced in education and civilization, far from being antipathetic to whites." The free people of color represented some of the most skilled masons, tailors, carpenters, tradesmen, and merchants in the city and monopolized several trades, such as plastering and ironworking. Unlike some of the country parishes, with large slave populations and very small or nonexistent free black communities, freed slaves in New Orleans had a place in the community. A newly freed slave in an overwhelmingly agricultural parish such as Tensas Parish, which in 1858 had 1,255 whites, 13,285 slaves, and 7 free people of color, would have had a difficult time making a living or fitting in with the free population composed of mainly planters, small farmers, and overseers. In New Orleans in 1850, free people of color owned an average of $3,800 in real estate alone; by 1860, they held an average of $4,500.[35]

Evidence that those freed in New Orleans could support themselves exists in most trial transcripts, as the 1855 act required that any slaves

35. Quoted in Berlin, *Slaves without Masters,* 143; quoted in David Rankin, "The Impact of the Civil War on the Free Colored Community of New Orleans," *Perspectives in American History* 11 (1977–78): 382; *Report of the Secretary of State of the Census of the State of Louisiana* (Baton Rouge, 1859), 7. Federal censuses, 1850, 1860. Average real estate holdings for Orleans Parish in 1850 and 1860 were calculated from figures given in Loren Schweninger, "Antebellum Free Persons of Color in Postbellum Louisiana," *Louisiana History* 30 (1989): 362–3.

freed under its provisions must not become a public charge. In one case a witness testified, "He has been supporting his wife and family a long time, besides paying his mistress for his time." In another, "he has a wife and has always supported her." A character witness testified that the slave, Agenon Martin, worked "as a waiter in the large hotels of this city . . . I have no doubt he is entitled to his freedom." The man who sold Martin to his present owner had wanted to free him, but did not because Martin wished to stay in the state. A second district court jury freed François Naba, who had run a grocery store worth $200 to $300 for more than two years. Naba testified he had paid for two-thirds of the stock and that he sold between $300 and $400 in groceries each month. He said about himself, "I can calculate and write a little. I need to go to night school." This is remarkable testimony, as Louisiana law prevented slaves from owning any kind of property and forbade teaching them to read. Naba had paid his master $900 to free him, but he had refused, and the court allowed him to sue for his own freedom. A witness for another slave before the fifth district court described the slave Eugene Aram Smith as a clerk worth $600 a year, "he can read and write."[36]

Several trial transcripts indicate that twenty-one slaves freed by the district courts had purchased themselves. Some slaveowners required that slaves purchasing themselves not only reimburse their owner for their value, but also with interest on their value. A few who freed their slaves did not require the slave to pay for themselves, but required them to pay court costs and attorney's fees, both of which could be quite expensive by the standards of the day. For each slave freed, there was the $20 fee for the district attorney, the $12 jury tax, and assorted other court costs, such as a fee for filing the petition and recording the judgment. Usually court costs for the freeing of one slave ran about $50. The docket books do not enu-

36. First District Court of New Orleans, *Widow Pierre Bouny* v. *State of Louisiana,* No. 10735 (Gaston Delille), 3 December 1855; *Agnes Stewart, f. w. c.* v. *State of Louisiana,* No. 10785 (William), 1 February 1856; First District Court of New Orleans, *Rivière Gardère* v. *State of Louisiana,* No. 10957 (Agenon Martin), 20 February 1856; Second District Court of New Orleans, *François Naba* v. *State of Louisiana,* No. 9252, 9723 (François Naba), 13 February 1856; Fifth District Court of New Orleans, *John G. Cocks* v. *State of Louisiana,* No. 11129 (Eugene Aram Smith), 27 May 1856; "An Act to Punish the Crimes Therein Mentioned, and for Other Purposes," 1830 La. Acts 96; James Brown and Louis Moreau Lislet, comps., *Digest of the Civil Law Now in Force in the Territory of Orleans* (New Orleans, 1808), Tit. VI, Chap. III, Art. 17, 40; *Civil Code,* Art. 174–5, 27.

merate attorney's fees, but the record in one case indicates that the attorney charged $50. At a time when a dollar a day was the standard pay for laborers, court costs and attorney's fees could be a formidable obstacle for a newly freed person.37

As the 1855 act required slaves to have exhibited "good character and sober habits," many cases contain testimony to prove this requirement. A first district court jury heard this testimony concerning the slave Harriet: "She was the favorite and confidential servant of my niece." Another testified, "she was treated in my family as a servant entrusted to more than the ordinary confidences." In another case, first district court jurors heard a witness testify that the slave Nicolle "is the pet of Mr. Verret's family." One character witness stated that he believed the slave Maranthe "incapable of doing anything wrong." A witness who knew the slave Damas Bonsignac described his relationship with his master, who "treated him more like a friend than a slave. He voluntarily followed his master from St. Domingo. He can oversee a small sugar plantation. . . . He is remarkably honest and faithful." A witness told the jury of Justine's care of her master while nursing him through a long illness with "remarkable devotedness and self-sacrifice." In his suit to free Lucille, Paul Luciani stated: "I am not a married man. My purpose in giving freedom to Lucille is for treating me so well when I was Sick with yellow fever and other sickness." The attorney for the slaves Louis and Titine, who was also Titine's godfather, described her as "a perfect subject," but another witness said Louis had done "some little grifting stealing." Despite this damaging testimony, the jury voted to free them both. Jurors of the fifth district court freed a slave who had run away, believing that she was already entitled to her freedom, hardly evidence of good character. Two character witnesses attempted to reassure jurors that if freed the slaves in two cases would not

37. See First District Court of New Orleans, *Marie Laurette Lambert Laribeau* v. *State of Louisiana,* No. 10681 (Overton), 3 December 1855; Second District Court of New Orleans, *François Naba, f. m. c.* v. *State of Louisiana,* No. 9252, 9723 (François Naba), 13 February 1856; Fifth District Court of New Orleans, *Priscilla Dunbar, f. w. c.* v. *State of Louisiana,* No. 11311 (Annah), 25 August 1856. The manumitting mistress charged 8 percent interest to John, who purchased himself in the second district court case, *Elizabeth Nicols Lathrop* v. *State of Louisiana,* No. 10437 (John), 3 July 1856; John also had to pay court costs and fees. One slave had to pay the attorney's fees, first district court case *Alexandre Peieira* v. *State of Louisiana,* No. 10678 (Zulmé), 3 December 1855. The $50 fee is listed in the *Naba* case; Wade, *Slavery in the Cities,* 42.

provide a bad example to the Creoles of color or the slaves in the city. One testified that the slave Nancy Watkins "would give good example to the slave population"; another stated that if freed with permission to stay in the state, the slaves Zélime and Eugène "would not be a bother to the community."[38]

The jurors of the New Orleans district courts probably saw little difference between the status of a slave owned by one of the seventy free persons of color who won suits to free their slaves and the newly freed slaves; as if their owners were their relatives, their new status would probably make little change in their day-to-day lives. Except for the legal ramifications of possible sale for the debts of the owner, slaves owned by their family members would live as free. Of course, not all slaves freed before the district court in 1855 and 1856 had relatives as owners. In those cases, the effect of the emancipation would result in as dramatic a change in status as for those owned by whites.

Two cases demonstrate the strength of family ties among the free Creoles of color, the solidarity of the free black community, and the genuine concern of some whites for their welfare. In the first, James Ross, the executor for a deceased free man of color named Richard Green, sued for the freedom of Green's slave wife Suzan and their three children, Henry, Luda, and Gardiner. Green, a barber, had left instructions in his will for Ross to free his wife and children as soon as they could remain in the state. Green died after the 1852 act became law, and Ross held the succession open because he could not comply with the terms of the will to free them and have them remain in the state. After the act of 1855 passed, Ross filed suit to free Suzan and her children. Ross and the attorney in the case, Frank Haynes, put up the $4,000 bond required by law to insure that

38. First District Court of New Orleans, *Henry McCulloch* v, *State of Louisiana,* No. 10663 (Harriet), 3 December 1855; *François Schmitt* v. *State of Louisiana,* No. 10682 (Damas Bonsignac), 29 November 1855; *Fercy Verret* v. *State of Louisiana,* No. 10933 (Nicolle), 16 February 1856; *Widow John Clay* v. *State of Louisiana,* No. 10764 (Justine), 3 December 1855; *Paul Luciani* v. *State of Louisiana,* No. 10808 (Lucille), 3 February 1856; *Oscar and Alfred Livaudais* v. *State of Louisiana,* No. 10772 (Louis and Titine), 20 February 1856; Fifth District Court of New Orleans, *Peyton Skipworth* v. *State of Louisiana,* No. 11133 (Hilsey or Elsay), 30 May 1856; Fourth District Court of New Orleans, *Richard Everard* v. *State of Louisiana,* No. 11068 (Nancy Watkins), 5 May 1856; First District Court of New Orleans, *Widow Antoine Abat* v. *State of Louisiana,* No. 11029 (Zélime and Eugène), 5 March 1856.

Suzan and her children would not become a public charge. Witnesses described Suzan as sober and industrious and able to support herself as a nurse. Two physicians testified as to her character. The first district court jury freed Suzan and her children with permission to remain in the state.[39]

The other case involved a slave mother's willingness to give up her daughter so that the daughter could gain her freedom. In 1850 Eugène Ducatel gave his five-year-old slave girl Marie Felicité to Justine Boisblanc, a childless free woman of color, to raise. Ducatel recorded this donation with a notary public, stating that he made the donation with the express condition that Boisblanc free the slave girl as soon as possible. The slave girl's mother, who belonged to Ducatel, consented to the donation to have her daughter freed. Witnesses testified that Boisblanc raised the child as her own, and one stated, "I do not believe there is a better woman in the State. Felicité is very well brought up by Justine." Another witness stated, "Felicité is a very good little girl, She waits at table." On 3 March 1856, a first district court jury freed Felicité with permission to remain in the state.[40]

Despite their small numbers in the population of the city, free people of color made up nearly half of those who freed their slaves in New Orleans under the Act of 1855. The trial records describe almost 60 percent of those freed as mulattoes, reflecting the demographics of the city in which the overwhelming majority of free people of color were mulattoes. Females outnumbered males almost two to one in the total number of slaves freed and three to one if only adult slaves are counted. These lopsided figures also reflect the population of slaves and free people of color in the city as a whole, wherein the number of women made up 67 percent of the free black population and 66 percent of the slave population. And to demonstrate the effect of the act of 1852, which required manumitted slaves to depart the state for Liberia, the owners of least one- fourth of the slaves freed in 1855–56 had sold them after the passage of the 1852 act

39. First District Court of New Orleans, *James Ross, Testamentary Executor of Richard Green, f. m. c. v. State of Louisiana*, No. 10413 (Suzan, Henry, Luda, Gardiner), 13 November 1855. The record does not indicate why Green did not emancipate Suzan and her children between the time he purchased her in 1837 and the passage of the 1852 act.

40. First District Court of New Orleans, *Justine Boisblanc, f. w. c. v. State of Louisiana*, No. 10965 (Marie Felicité alias Evelina), 3 March 1856.

with the express condition that their emancipation not take place until they could remain within the state. Every slave freed by the New Orleans district courts received permission to remain in the state; this permission became so routine that the fifth district court printed a form that had blank spaces for the clerk to fill in the name of the emancipating master and the name of the slave, but with the words "with permission to stay in the state" in print.[41]

Many of the trials held in the second and fifth district courts give evidence of their pro forma nature. When put into a national context, this seems extraordinary. Proslavery fervor intensified, as white southerners denounced emancipation as harmful to slaves. A Tennessee legislator exclaimed, "the responsibilities of freedom are too great for them, hence the man that emancipates his slave entails upon him a curse." At a time when the political crisis over slavery was at its height and many people in the South considered manumission outright sedition, juries of twelve men in New Orleans methodically and swiftly freed hundreds of slaves and allowed them to remain in the state. In several instances the courts ran through several cases in rapid succession on the same day. For example, essentially the same jury in the second district court heard nine cases on 7 May 1856. This is the same month that proslavery elements sacked the antislavery town of Lawrence, Kansas, and John Brown and his followers retaliated by murdering five proslavery settlers at Pottawattomie Creek; the same month in which congressional debate over the civil war in Kansas reached such a hostile level that Congressman Preston Brooks of South Carolina beat Senator Charles Sumner until he fell, bleeding and unconscious, to the floor of the United States Senate. During the summer of 1856, as the national crisis deepened, twelve jurors in New Orleans gave

41. David C. Rankin, "'The Tannenbaum' Thesis Reconsidered: Slavery and Race Relations in Antebellum Louisiana," *Southern Studies* 18 (spring 1979): 21; Wade, *Slavery in the Cities,* 329–30; e.g., First District Court of New Orleans, *Cyrille Labiche* v. *State of Louisiana,* No. 10489 (Marie Louise), 30 August 1855; Second District Court of New Orleans, *Jean Jacques Montreuil* v. *State of Louisiana,* No. 9820 (Louise), 2 December 1856; Fourth District Court of New Orleans, *Placide Forstall, testamentary executor of Marie Fontin Forstall, f. w. c.* v. *State of Louisiana,* No. 9614 (Mary), 24 January 1856; Fifth District Court of New Orleans, *John Hagan* v. *State of Louisiana,* No. 11074 (Lucy Ann Chateur and her two children and William Loundes), 23 May 1856. John Hagan was a prominent slave trader who had slave pens in Charleston and New Orleans. Hagan had purchased these slaves for fifty dollars on 19 January 1856 and promised to free them within three months. The form appears in the Fifth District Court of New Orleans, *James Goines, f. m. c.* v. *State of Louisiana,* No. 11310 (Marthe), 18 August 1856.

the Independence Day holiday a new meaning. On the two days before the fourth of July 1856, they decided twenty cases that freed forty-two slaves. Almost all of these had essentially the same jury and the same foreman, an accountant named Charles Lafitte. In all of these trials, the clerk's notation in the minute book reads: "After hearing the evidence and argument of Counsel, the Jury received a charge from the Court, and without leaving their seats, rendered the following verdict, to wit; Verdict for the slave [name], with permission to remain in the state." In all, the second district court juries decided twenty-seven cases freeing forty-two slaves "without leaving their seats." The fifth district court heard ten suits on 18 August 1856, that freed twenty-two slaves without retiring to the jury room to deliberate. Seven of these trials, which freed seventeen slaves, had the petition filed, the testimony heard, the certificates presented, and the judgment all on the same day, during which the jurors did not leave their seats to deliberate.[42]

Two 1856 decisions of the Supreme Court of Louisiana affected the emancipation proceedings taking place under the 1855 act in the district courts of New Orleans. In April 1856 the court decided *State* v. *Judge of the First District Court of New Orleans*. Although this decision did not quash the freedom suits already filed but not concluded in the first district court, it ordered the court to confine itself exclusively to its criminal docket. The clerk of court transferred all of the emancipation cases in March and April to the other district courts of New Orleans. In all, four went to the second district court, six to the fourth district, and six to the fifth district. All of the reassigned cases resulted in the freedom sought for the slaves and permission to remain in the state. And those who still wished to free their slaves began to file freedom suits in the other district courts. In all, seventy-four suits involving 127 slaves originated in the other district courts, all of which freed the slaves brought before them, with permission to remain in the state.[43]

The second decision of the Supreme Court of Louisiana destroyed

42. Quoted in Berlin, *Slaves without Masters,* 368; e.g., the Second District Court, *Joseph Henry* v. *State of Louisiana,* No. 10152 (Eliza), 2 July 1856; *John Fox, f. m. c.* v. *State of Louisiana,* No. 10153 (François alias Peggy), 2 July 1856; Fifth District Court, *Mary Walker, f. m. c.* v. *State of Louisiana,* No. 11309 (Lucinda), 18 August 1856; *A. W. Brewerton* v. *State of Louisiana,* No. 11314 (Delia), 18 August 1856.

43. *State on the Relation of M. A. Fonte, Praying for a Writ of Prohibition* v. *The Judge of the First District Court of New Orleans and Benjamin S. Tappan,* 11 La. Ann. 187 (1856).

those cases in progress when the court pronounced its decision and prevented slaveowners from bringing new actions to free their slaves. On 8 December 1856, the court rendered a decision, *State v. Harrison,* an appeal of a conviction of a slave for murder. Although not a response to the emancipations in the New Orleans district courts, the supreme court declared the 1855 statute, "An Act Relative to Slaves and Colored People," unconstitutional. The court based its decision on the Louisiana constitution of 1852, which forbade legislative acts from encompassing more than one object. Justice Alexander Buchanan explained the court's reasoning in a remarkable defense of the status of free persons of color: "Its [the Act of 1855] title expresses two distinct objects, to wit, slaves and colored persons. . . . Slaves and free colored persons embrace two classes, which it is impossible to confound in legal parlance; for in the eyes of the Louisiana law there is, with the exception of political rights, social privileges, and the obligations of jury and militia service, all the difference between a free man of color and a slave, that there is between a white man and a slave." Buchanan noted that the decision did not create any substantial void in the law of slavery in Louisiana, as most of the 1855 act represented a reiteration of preexisting statutes "with the exception of sections 71, 72, and 74, which treat of the mode of proceeding for the emancipation of slaves."[44]

How did Buchanan's ruling affect those emancipation suits already in progress, and did it mean that the 289 already freed must return to slavery? In an editorial on December 10, the *Daily Picayune* recognized that the decision in *Harrison* would result in "the greatest importance to the community." The *Picayune* addressed the implications for those freed under the 1855 act and those whose suits had not yet concluded: "In Consequence, the new process of emancipating slaves falls to the ground, is null, and with it all suits now in progress for the emancipation of slaves. How it will affect those already free, is more than we can at present determine."

44. *State v. Harrison,* No. 4464, 11 La. Ann. 722 (Dec. 1856); Constitution of 1852, Article 115 stated: "Every law enacted by the Legislature shall embrace but one object, and that shall be expressed in the title," Wayne M. Everard, "Louisiana's 'Whig' Constitution Revisited: The Constitution of 1852," in Warren M. Billings and Edward F. Haas, eds., *In Search of Fundamental Law: Louisiana's Constitutions, 1812–1974* (Lafayette, La., 1993), 37–51.

The docket books of the second, fourth, and fifth districts reveal that the district courts ceased to process all freedom suits in progress on the day of the supreme court's decision. This left seventeen suits for the freedom of thirty-seven slaves in limbo, and left those wishing to free slaves in the future without recourse.[45]

Rumors of an interstate slave insurrection circulated in the lower South during the Christmas holidays in 1856. Although most southern newspapers maintained a policy of suppressing news that might inspire slaves to revolt, the *Picayune* broke with this practice two days before Christmas by taking notice of rumors circulating around the South of unrest among slaves and placing the blame for a possible slave revolt on the Republican Party. Warning of the possibility of an imminent slave uprising, the *Picayune* published a front-page editorial that began a campaign to encourage the legislature to pass stricter laws concerning slave discipline:

> We have abstained thus far from giving publicity in detail to the many reports which have been sent to us . . . of slave disturbances in various parts of the Southern States . . . from the various quarters in many States, there are evidences of a very unsettled state of mind among the servile population—a vague impression among them that a critical change in their condition is at hand, to be effected by a powerful party in the United States, which temporarily defeated at the polls, is ready to give them the help of arms and troops when they shall undertake to rise on their own account . . . all the disclosures have fixed upon the same day everywhere, as that upon which an undefined effort is to be made against the whites. The day is the 24th of December, or more generally, about the Christmas holidays; and the same notion prevails in Kentucky, Arkansas, and Tennessee, as well

---

45. *Daily Picayune,* 10 December 1856. In the same issue, the editor printed without comment this item: "STAMPEDE OF FREE NEGROES. The *Nashville Patriot* of the 2nd inst. says: The free negroes at Murfreesboro took a compulsory stampede from that place last week. Their depredations had become insufferable to the citizens, and their pernicious influence among the slave population made them a serious grievance. Self-preservation compelled the whites to stringent measures to get rid of them, and a general stampede was the consequence." E.g., Second District Court of New Orleans, *Juliette Avegno, f. w. c.* v. *State of Louisiana,* No. 11106 (Therèsa), filed 21 November 1856; Fifth District Court of New Orleans, *Jean Baptiste Petron* v. *State of Louisiana,* No. 13337 (Josephine and four children), filed 26 August 1856.

as in Mississippi, Louisiana, and Texas. . . . When the legislature meets the whole subject of the Black Code will doubtless be taken up, with a view to adapting it more efficiently to the wants and developments of the times.[46]

The *Picayune* called for stricter laws to control free persons of color and slaves, and for the enforcement of those laws already in force:

> The latitude of privilege which they [whites] have heretofore given to free blacks and slaves, and the mildness with which they have administered, and of late, even neglected to enforce their own restrictive laws, exhibit the feeling of kindness and indulgence which has hitherto prevailed among them . . . a return [is] called for, back to the strictest rigor of police law . . . it has become highly expedient for the slave States to revise their codes . . . for the maintenance and subordination among the blacks, and the keeping of them from the contaminating influences . . . at work for mischief. . . . We have in New Orleans a large amount of the class of population, most likely to be influenced by these evil counsels. . . . They form, a facile medium of communication with the slaves.[47]

On the second day of 1857 in an article titled "The Negro Rumors," the *Picayune* admitted that the holidays had passed and with no trouble in the black community and claimed "there was never any fear of a concerted attempt to rise, or a general insubordination." Indeed, the *Picayune* bragged, the slave population was "in general, contented, cheerful and happy, beyond the laboring classes of any other nation under the sun." However, the *Picayune* warned that the weakness of slaves' minds demanded new and stricter law to keep them from going astray:

> They [slaves] are weak, and need his [the master's] parental support, against the machinations . . . to unsettle their minds, and to draw them into projects of which the issue is certain to be adverse to them. . . . It is the greatest mercy to the negro . . . to preserve him from

46. *Daily Picayune,* 23 December 1856; Judith Kelleher Schafer, "The Immediate Impact of Nat Turner's Insurrection in New Orleans," *Louisiana History* 21 (1980): 369–76.

47. *Daily Picayune,* 23 December 1856.

contact with these adversaries, who would mislead him to his inevitable ruin; and the time has evidently come for putting the whole system of slave police and slave discipline into a new order. . . . The whole black code of the State needs to be revised, in view of the late development. . . . A short and terrific doom should be made to fall, with certainty, on every man who . . . lends himself to the promotion of discontent and insubordination among the blacks, or wantonly disturbs the peace of Southern communities.[48]

On 19 January 1857, the Louisiana legislature convened in regular session. Governor Robert C. Wickliffe addressed a joint session of the house and senate, and his address indicated an increased hostility to free people of color as well as slaves. He warned against increased immigration of free people of color from other states, and he asked for passage of a law to remove all free blacks from the state because of their "pernicious effect on the slave population." On January 28, Senator Henry H. Hyams of Orleans introduced a bill to prohibit all emancipations of slaves. Hyams stated that passage of the act would "destroy at one full [*sic*] swoop, the power which the law confers on courts and juries." The *Picayune* expressed its delight that no strong opposition to the bill surfaced because "the necessity for preventing the further accumulation of a worthless and dangerous free black population was recognized by all." Senator G. W. Munday of East Feliciana Parish asked for an amendment allowing slaves who reported insurrection plots to gain an exemption from the prohibition of emancipation. Hyams disagreed, stating that he would accept only saving the life of the master or the master's family as an exception. Senator Munday noted that "it was but a few short months ago that a conspiracy existed among the servile population," and only the "timely information given by a faithful and devoted servant" prevented its success.[49]

Senator M. Ryan of Rapides Parish stated that although he would place "every possible legal check in the way of indiscriminate emancipation," he favored making an exception for slaves who revealed insurrection plots. Furthermore, he blamed the actions of the courts of New

---

48. Ibid., 2 January 1857.

49. *Official Reports of the Senate of Louisiana: Session of 1857* (New Orleans, 1857), 11; *Official Journal of the House of Representatives of the State of Louisiana: Session of 1857* (New Orleans, 1857), 7; *Daily Picayune,* 30 January 1857.

Orleans for making Hyams believe that only a total prohibition of emancipation could safeguard the state.

> The courts and juries of New Orleans, in this matter of emancipation, may be all in point of laxity and official morality, which the gentleman described them; but the picture would certainly not apply to his parish—the Parish of Rapides. What is the fact in reference to that parish? It is this, that since in 1855 the law went into effect placing the power of emancipation in the courts—not a single slave has been manumitted there thus showing how eminently conservative of their rights slave-holders are in that portion of the state.

Ryan went on to complain that Hyams's act did not prohibit legislative emancipation, a return to a practice that he described with contempt:

> a system of log-rolling will be introduced; those halls will be crowded with interested parties . . . the regular course of legislation will be impeded, and in short there will be a return to that state of things which might be witnessed here previous to the passage of the law of 1855—a state of things so harassing and annoying that the legislature, to escape from it, threw the power of emancipating into the hands of the courts . . . he would think it far safer and more conservative to place it in the hands of a jury.

Ryan also warned against adding an exception for slaves who performed meritorious services for their owners: "For the smallest service, on the part of a slave, rendered the State—even the preservation of a snag boat—some cunning attorney might claim that he was entitled to his freedom." The bill to prohibit all emancipation of slaves except those who informed on slave conspiracies passed the senate on January 27. On the same day Senator Henry W. St. Paul of Orleans Parish introduced a bill to allow slaveowners whose slaves the New Orleans courts had freed under the act of 1855 to file suits for reclaiming them as their slaves. He explained the rationale for this bill: "The judgment of the supreme court rendered some legislation necessary to settle the status of the slaves emancipated from the time of the passing of the act to the rendering of the judgment." The senate sent this act to the Judiciary Committee, over the strenuous objections of Senator St. Paul. "A pile of bills," he said "had already been referred to that committee. There they seem to lie entombed, and whether they would break the cerements of their resting place before the day of general resurrection, was a question of which he entertained some doubt." The bill died in committee, and those freed under the terms of the act of 1855 remained free. We have no record of the Judiciary Committee's reason for not recommending the bill, but as Article 189 of the *Civil Code* held that "An emancipation, once perfected, is irrevocable," St. Paul's bill would have been in conflict with the code.[50]

The house of representatives moved more slowly, waiting to introduce a bill to prohibit slave emancipations except in cases in which slaves saved the lives of their masters or their masters' families or revealed a slave conspiracy. Immediately house members began to argue for the bill. Representative Julien T. Hawkins of St. Martin Parish proposed an amendment requiring any slaves freed for saving the lives of their owners to leave the state rather than increase the population of free people of color. "The emancipation of negroes," he said, "is spreading and shedding its blighting influence, like the Upas tree, over Louisiana and the whole South. It is time that some check should be applied to this rapid increase of free negroes. I hold, Sir, that the negro is not benefitted by emancipation . . . by turning him loose upon the world in his old age to subsist by his own exertions. I am in favor of putting a full stop to all emancipations." Representative Haynes objected to the amendment forcing any freed slave to leave the state: "The master feels a sentiment of gratitude toward the slave who has rendered these acts of fidelity." Representative Thomas Jenkins Semmes of Orleans also disapproved of requiring freed slaves to depart for Africa, saying that he believed

> slavery to be the best condition for the African race. If the freedom of that race is a boon, then our slavery system must be a lie. . . . If you repeal the laws on the subject, and have the Legislature to act on these cases, one-third of our time would be occupied with such matters . . . the evil would be increased by flooding the Legislature with applications for emancipation. . . . Slaves do not regard freedom as a

---

50. *Official Reports of the Senate, 1857,* 12, 18. Snag boats were used to free Louisiana's bayous and rivers from snags. *Civil Code,* Art. 189, 29.

boon if they are to be sent away. They have a repugnance to wooly-headed government.

Hawkins argued that he preferred flooding the legislature with petitions for emancipation to making exceptions to the prohibition against emancipation. In fact, he stated, he would drive all free people of color from the state—people he termed "a nuisance, and operating insidiously upon our slave population"—but for the protection given them in the Louisiana Purchase treaty.[51]

Representative D. L. Beecher of Jefferson Parish suggested that the wholesale emancipations in the courts of New Orleans under the 1855 act called for a total prohibition of emancipation.

> Under the former law granting the courts the authority to emancipate, our courts were crowded, especially in the City, and hundreds upon hundreds of slaves were emancipated—1500 are said to have been emancipated—notwithstanding the guard thrown around it and the heavy costs to be incurred. I was informed by a gentleman from New Orleans that a negro woman who had been sent from Virginia for poisoning her mistress was emancipated in New Orleans, and the District Attorney told me that, despite of everything, the juries would emancipate. If the owner wants to emancipate under this law [an exception for saving the life of the owner or the owner's family] let the baby tumble down the stairs, the negro run and pick it up, toss it in her arms and quiet it, and the emancipation is had. The provisions of this bill will not check the evil. Let us repeal the laws entirely on this subject.[52]

The following day, Representative George C. Lawrason of Orleans amended the act to prohibit all emancipations with no exceptions for saving the life of the owner or for revealing slave plots. Hawkins spoke in favor of this amendment, citing the "blighting effects of emancipation . . . over the whole State." Representative E. Wooldridge of Orleans Parish asked his fellow legislators to address the problem of *statu liberi,* that is

51. *Journal of the House* (1857) 81. Upas tree, a member of the mulberry family, is extremely poisonous.

52. Ibid., 81.

slaves who had acquired the right to be free but whose owners had not yet freed them. He spoke eloquently of a "faithful old shoeblack" in New Orleans who had saved the life of his master's child, and who would find himself without recourse if the legislature prohibited all emancipation.

> Here in Louisiana, where we properly appreciate slavery, where we know how to treat our slaves, and where we understand the institution . . . better than elsewhere, let us be right. We cannot pass a law to impair the validity of contracts. The Supreme Court has said that slaves can contract with their masters for freedom. I ask the lawyers of the House to consider this. This law impairs hundreds of contracts with slaves now *statu liberi*. Hasty action of this subject . . . would furnish rich food for Northern abolitionists—would be trumpeted over the whole land.

At the end of the day, the house voted 45–17 to pass the bill stripped of all amendments. A joint house-senate committee agreed on the house version, and on 6 March 1857, the same day that Dred Scott discovered that the Supreme Court of the United States considered him enslaved for life, the possibility of legal emancipation ended for Louisiana's approximately 300,000 slaves. Although the legislature could have passed a new emancipation law that put into place the same provisions for slave emancipations as the 1855 act, the mood of the lawgivers had hardened against making freedom possible for persons of color. The freeing of 189 slaves in New Orleans must have contributed to their determination to prohibit all emancipations.[53]

The *Daily Picayune* praised the *Dred Scott* decision: "It is settled to be the law of the land that the constitution recognizes and guarantees to every State the right of the master to property in slaves." The editorial realized the significance of the decision.

> Generally the government of the United States was made for free whites, and Africans and descendants of Africans are not part of the "people" of the United States, and cannot constitutionally become citizens. . . . The bulwark which the Supreme Court has erected for

---

53. Ibid., 83–4; "An Act to Prohibit the Emancipation of Slaves," 1857 La. Acts 55.

the rights of the South is not to be easily broken down. . . . The really
considerate and patriotic in the free States cannot fail to see the hope-
lessness of effecting anything legally and constitutionally . . . it be
[*sic*] for them to decide [whether] to array the North and South
against each other as irreconcilable foes, engaged in domestic strife,
of which the fruits of a Northern triumph must be the total ruin of
the South, or the destruction of the government.[54]

In the 1858 term of the state legislature, lawmakers introduced five petitions for the emancipation of slaves. The Judiciary Committee gave each
of them an "adverse report" or "laid them on the table indefinitely."
Henry St. Paul, chair of the Judiciary Committee, explained the committee's actions: "[We] must sternly adhere to the present wise policy of this
and [the] preceding Legislature, in refusing to increase the number of free
colored people residing in this State."[55]

In 1859, legislators, overjoyed at having stopped all emancipations of
slaves, proceeded to pass an act that showed how proslavery logic had con-
quered the legislature, an act to allow free people of color to choose a master and voluntarily enslave themselves. Six other southern states passed
similar laws between 1857 and 1860: Alabama, Florida, Maryland, Tennessee, Texas, and Virginia. South Carolina and Georgia allowed free people of color to enslave themselves by special legislative acts. Nothing
would have reinforced proslavery arguments more emphatically than if
hundreds of free people of color volunteered to enslave themselves. A
Richmond newspaper noted that voluntary enslavement gave undeniable
evidence "in favor of the comfortable and contented condition of the
Southern slave." J. D. B. DeBow, editor of *DeBow's Review* agreed, "The
negroes know what their own best interest is." In New Orleans at least
twelve free persons of color filed petitions to enslave themselves under the
terms of this act. As the law considered slaves real estate in Louisiana, the
act required the recording of the transaction enslaving free persons of
color in the conveyance office. Despite a thorough search of the conveyance records from March 1859, when the act went into effect, to April

54. *Daily Picayune,* 20 March 1857. A nearly identical editorial appeared on 22 March.
55. *Official Journal of the Senate of Louisiana: Session of 1858* (Baton Rouge, 1858), 11, 19, 24, 58,
40, 88, 104. In the only vote reported to table a petition for emancipation indefinitely, legislators voted
17–2 in favor of the motion.

1862, when Union forces captured New Orleans, no such registrations appeared. But the docket books of the district courts indicate an actual judgment in only three of the twelve suits filed. The others seem to have gone
no further than the petition and citation of the chosen master. What are
we to make of this? One historian states that age and/or illness motivated
those who wished to enslave themselves. Yet the available information
about the persons filing these suits in New Orleans does not indicate age
as a factor, since four of the individuals were in their twenties and one
aged forty. Advanced age as an explanation makes little sense, because it
fails to explain why any chosen master would voluntarily assume the financial burden of supporting an elderly or infirm slave, unless inspired by
humanitarian motives or a desire to reinforce "positive good" beliefs in
the benefits of slavery. Another historian asserts that some free people of
color, fearing the outbreak of war between the North and the South,
sought a guardian to protect them, but none of the New Orleans cases
supports that motivation. One of the five cases about which we have more
detailed information indicates that Joseph Thomas, a twenty-nine-year-
old free man of color, selected as his master a man "with whom he has
been acquainted for many years." Another free man of color, William
Gray, age twenty-five, petitioned to become the slave of the same master.
Mary Walker, a twenty-nine-year-old free woman of color, petitioned to
enslave herself and her nine-year-old daughter to George W. Whittaker,
"a man of good standing and character with whom she had been acquainted for many years."[56]

56. Quoted in Berlin, *Slaves without Masters,* 367; "An Act to Permit Free Persons of African
Descent to Select Their Masters and Become Slaves for Life," 1859 La. Acts 214–5; Berlin, *Slaves
without Masters,* 367; Thomas D. Morris, *Southern Slavery and the Law, 1619–1860* (Chapel Hill, N.C.,
1996), 31–6; Fourth District Court of New Orleans, *Joseph Thomas, f. m. c.* v. *State of Louisiana,* No.
11318, filed 1 October 1859; *William Gray, f. m. c.* v. *State of Louisiana,* No. 13320, filed 1 October
1859; *Mary Walker, f. w. c.* v. *State of Louisiana,* No. 13319, filed 1 October 1859. Other cases, all of
which have vanished, include: Sixth District Court of New Orleans, *Jane Moore, f. w. c.* v. *State of
Louisiana,* No. 7589, 11 January 1859; *Amelia Stone, f. w. c.* v. *State of Louisiana,* No. 8465, 9593, 28
August 1861; *Jesse Nells, f. m. c.* v. *State of Louisiana,* No. 8647, 15 September 1860; *Austin Lloyd, f. m.
c.* v. *State of Louisiana,* No. 8648, 15 September 1860; *James Stewart, f. m. c.* v. *State of Louisiana,* No.
9158, 13 February 1861; *John Wells, f. m. c.* v. *State of Louisiana,* No. 9593, 15 September 1859. It cannot be determined whether Emilia Stone is the same person as Amelia Stone. Neither appears in the
1850 or 1860 census, and in their suits, Emilia Stone chose pharmacist John H. Pope as her prospective master; Amelia Stone chose the recorder of the fourth district, Lucien Adams. One free man of

A New Orleans newspaper gives an account of John Clifton, a forty-year-old free man of color, petitioning to become the slave of Green Lee Bumpass. The New Orleans *Daily Delta* reported that suits for voluntary enslavement made up "a very heavy docket of this class of cases," placing a burden on the district attorney, whom the law required to act as amicus curiae for the person requesting enslavement. A dozen cases does not support that conclusion, but the *Delta* used Clifton's case as proslavery propaganda. It reported that Clifton, who had lived in Louisiana for ten years, stated in his petition, "Having long since become satisfied that the rights, liberties, and free agency exercised by persons of the African descent, it being the status of your petitioner, is merely theoretical and has no foundation in point of fact. Therefore, your petitioner who was born in the South, and wedded to its institutions, has selected under the act of the legislature approved March the 7th, 1859, for his owner and master Green Lee Bumpass." Clifton's attorney, Thomas J. Earhart, commented on the petition in typically racist proslavery logic.

> John Clifton is evidently a philosopher. He has the sagacity to perceive and the courage to avow that with a kind and gentle master his *status* as a slave would be preferable to the mockery of freedom with which those seek to delude him, who pretend he can ever sustain himself as the equal of the white man, when nature and circumstances have had him his inferior. John Clifton naturally seeks a protector and guardian, and the law furnishes him one of his own choice, who by acceptance of this guardianship incurs the obligation to protect and support him. Such is the operation of our act of the legislature permitting free people of color to elect [*sic*] their owners and become slaves [italics in original].

As in much proslavery rhetoric, Earhart's logic defies reason. How can Clifton be so smart as to earn the term "philosopher" and yet be so "inferior?"[57]

---

color chose a master and enslaved himself by notarial act. Joseph Johnson chose Frederick John Hyatt, a member of the city police, as his master. James Graham, notary public, vol. 21, No. 4909, 20 May 1861.

57. Sixth District Court of New Orleans, *John Clifton, f. m. c.* v. *State of Louisiana,* No. 8465, 18 May 1860; (New Orleans) *Daily Delta,* 18 May 1860.

These twelve cases give few clues regarding the motivation for voluntary enslavement. Conceivably some of those seeking enslavement proved
unable to support themselves. Or perhaps they chose a particular master
because he owned their spouse, parent, or child. If true, these persons considered separation from family more devastating than being enslaved.
Mary Walker's and John Clifton's petitions state that they had been in the
state for only three and ten years, respectively, and therefore lived there illegally; perhaps they feared deportation under the state's draconian laws
prohibiting free people of color from entering the state and ordering the
deportation of those who arrived after 1825. Joseph Johnson, whom the
petition described as a twenty-six-year-old native of Kentucky, therefore
could not have resided in Louisiana legally either. The docket books of
the New Orleans criminal court from 1859 to 1862 show an increased
number of arrests and convictions of free people of color who had entered
the state in "contravention" of the law of 1830. These convictions may
have encouraged some free blacks in the city illegally to leave before being
apprehended and may have encouraged others to enslave themselves
rather than leave family and friends. The correct answer may never be
known.[58]

58. "An Act to Prevent Free Persons of Color from Entering into this State," 1860 La. Acts 90–6.
For examples of contravention cases see: First District Court of New Orleans, *State* v. *Hannah
Cornelius, f. w. c.,* No. 15325, 2 July 1861; *State* v. *Samuel Golding, f. m. c.,* No. 15518, 8 November
1861; *Julia Elliot, f. w. c.* v. *State,* No. 15514, 29 November 1861; *State* v. *Henry Waters, f. m. c.,* No.
15523, 8 November 1861.

DEFIANT WOMEN AND THE SUPREME COURT OF LOUISIANA IN THE NINETEENTH CENTURY

It is always risky business to defy social norms. Any real or imagined undermining of a community's social fabric threatens the established order and inevitably invites the wrath of those who maintain the status quo. As it was for women of earlier centuries, female recalcitrance was especially hazardous in nineteenth-century Louisiana. Antoinette Boullard, Fannie Roos, and Josephine Decuir provide excellent examples of the manner in which three women defied the conventions of their times and paid a price for their defiance. A hooch-trader, a harlot, and a plantation mistress—although each of different temperament and social circumstances—all three women sought relief through Louisiana's legal system when their unwillingness to adhere to the social norms and customs of their society threatened the community's way of life.

Antoinette Boullard ran afoul of Meredith Calhoun (1805–1866?), a wealthy planter who settled in Rapides Parish after 1830. After purchasing 14,000 acres of land fronting the Red River from his father-in-law, state senator William Smith, Calhoun divided the tract into four plantations: Smithfield, Farenzi, Mirabeau, and Meredith, where he cultivated cotton and sugarcane. His home, Calhoun's Landing, became an important shipping point on the river, and eventually the small village that sprang up near the landing became the seat of Grant Parish, the town of Colfax.

Boullard was described in the record as a "tolerably old woman"—in reality she was only thirty-six at the time her suit was brought before the bar—and a "mere trespasser" on another of Calhoun's plantations in Natchitoches Parish. It was alleged that she was "in the habit of enticing his [Calhoun's] negroes away from the Plantation . . . and selling them liquor and making her place a place where negroes are at night gathered to drink and buy whiskey, and sell to her Stolen property . . . thereby destroying the proper discipline of his plantation and interfering . . . in the legal and proper management of said slaves, and against this affiant's rights and the peace of the community."

In an effort to halt the nocturnal activities of Boullard, a white woman described by witnesses as a notorious "Negro Trafficker, and decided nuisance to the neighborhood," twenty-nine of Calhoun's slaves and four white men in his employ went to Boullard's home sometime during the night of 19 May 1856. They dragged Boullard from her house and placed her, as well as her belongings and goods from her store, on her flatboat. They then cast the hapless, screaming woman, surrounded by her possessions, adrift on the Red River. Not satisfied that this drastic measure would ensure an end to Boullard's activities, the vigilantes set fire to her store and house.[1]

As Boullard drifted helplessly down the river, she cried out for help, all the while fearful she might be struck down in the dark by a passing steamboat. When morning came, trembling with fear and cold (witnesses testified she was clad only in a "calico dress loosely thrown on") and unable to speak (presumably the result of a combination of fear and hoarseness), Boullard was rescued when her craft finally ran aground two miles below her now fire-gutted home.[2]

---

1. The original transcript of the district court records may be found in the Supreme Court of Louisiana Collection, Docket #295, Department of Special Collections, Earl K. Long Library, University of New Orleans; *Antoinette Boullard* v. *Meredith Calhoun,* 13 La. Ann. 445–9 (1858), hereinafter abbreviated as Boullard MS; *Dictionary of Louisiana Biography,* s.v. "Calhoun, Meredith"; Mabel F. Harrison and Lavinia M. McNeely, *Grant Parish, Louisiana: A History* [Baton Rouge, 1969]); Boullard MS, 7, 131.

2. Boullard MS, 10.

Once sufficiently recovered from her ordeal, Boullard sued Calhoun in the Rapides Parish district court. The plaintiff maintained Calhoun was responsible for injuring her reputation and the loss of her property because the whites were his employees and the slaves were his property. Accordingly, she petitioned the court, requesting a jury trial and damages in the amount of $20,000.

The tormented woman's case was heard before a jury composed of twelve men. Testimony lasted for three days, and the jury deliberated an additional two days before declaring they could not agree on a verdict. Judge E. North Cullom[3] declared a mistrial. On retrial, a second jury awarded Boullard five thousand dollars in actual and compensatory damages. Calhoun appealed the lower court's finding to the Supreme Court of Louisiana, which heard the case at its Alexandria session in August 1858.

The facts in the case were not disputed: witnesses for the defendant openly admitted they had indeed evicted Boullard and set her adrift on the river. Rather, the question debated before the high court was whether Calhoun, who owned over seven hundred slaves, and who, according to Article 2300 of the civil code, could be deemed responsible for acts committed by his slaves, was indeed to be held accountable. The court ruled that Calhoun, although he did not order his slaves to molest Boullard in his behalf, was nonetheless liable for their actions because he failed to prevent them from taking such action. Having vindicated Antoinette Boullard, the judges, however, failed to sustain the lower court's award for exemplary damages. To do so, they wrote, exposed slaveowners "to ruin by the acts of a vicious slave, without any fault of his owner; and would thereby operate as the greatest of discouragements, to the holding of that species of property," a consequence the court felt was "at variance" with Louisiana law. Therefore, the lower court's award was reduced to one thousand dollars in property damages.[4]

3. A native of Opelousas, Cullom (1824–?) was admitted to the Louisiana bar on September 7, 1850, while the supreme court was sitting at Opelousas. In 1858 Cullom was elected judge of the Thirteenth Judicial District, comprised of Avoyelles and Rapides parishes. After the Civil War Cullom moved to New Orleans, where he served as judge of the fifth district court. At the end of Reconstruction, Cullom retired from the bench, returned to Opelousas, and edited the *St. Landry Democrat* until 1891.

4. 1850 United States manuscript slave census. Calhoun owned slaves in both Natchitoches and Rapides parishes; Boullard MS, 155.

This decision reflects the court's consideration of testimony offered during the trial concerning Boullard's occupation—testimony ruled inadmissable by the trial judge. The defense attorney argued that the actions taken against Boullard were justified because of the illegal nature of her business, and that these circumstances mitigated Calhoun's alleged actions or inactions and served to negate Boullard's claim for exemplary damages. The supreme court concurred, noting that persons attempting to claim "enormous" damages should be sure they came before the court with "clean hands" and that supplicants "should take heed that no habitual violations" on their part made them a "nuisance to the community" in which they resided. With these words the court implied that had Boullard not engaged in activities counter to prevailing social standards it might have sustained the jury's original monetary award.[5]

In September 1883 the supreme court heard the case of the *City of Shreveport* v. *Fannie Roos*. Fannie Roos kept a brothel in Shreveport, and she had been convicted of disorderly conduct. She had defied the law and social norms when she permitted the inhabitants of her house to occupy the gallery of her establishment on Parade Day in defiance of a special city ordinance that specified that prostitutes were to remain confined inside their houses during the parade. That a madam would publicly defend her right to keep a brothel is not particularly noteworthy for the period. The keeping of whorehouses was not illegal in Louisiana because Americans in Louisiana, as elsewhere, had not yet embarked on their crusade to rid the nation of prostitutes. Rapid industrialization accelerated changes in family life after 1865, which led to a steady increase in institutionalized prostitution, and by the turn of the century, prostitution was condemned, but not classified as a criminal offense. Social disapproval was expressed through sporadic and unofficial harassment by law enforcement agencies. This toleration reflected Victorian beliefs about women and men. Middle-class white women were generally perceived as sexless beings, while men were seen as possessing strong sexual drives that could prove destructive unless provided an outlet. To supply white men with an appropriate means to manage their seemingly unmanageable sexual appetites (since these passions could not be unleashed on pure, unadulterated white "ladies"), prosti-

---

5. Boullard MS, 156.

tution was tacitly accepted as a necessary social evil. Prostitutes thus served as protectors of delicate wives and genteel lady acquaintances, and, ultimately, the sanctity of home and family.[6]

Roos's house was located in a working-class section of Shreveport. Nearby were fish houses, a barbershop owned by an African-American, a saddlery, a furniture repair shop, livery stables, and another brothel. None of Roos's neighbors complained to authorities about her, her customers, or the women residing in her house. Seemingly, the house met all existing legal requirements governing such establishments: Shreveport ordinances decreed that bawdy houses located within the town were not to be conducted in an indecent manner, or in a manner defined as a "nuisance." However, the ordinance was silent as to what constituted "indecency" and a "nuisance." The charges against Fannie Roos arose from the alleged indecent conduct of some of her "girls" during a parade in May 1883.

Testimony offered at trial revealed that longtime chief of police Edward M. Austin was standing across the street from Roos's establishment on the day of the parade. Austin, who admitted in court he possessed a nude picture of Roos that had been handed to him while acting in his official capacity for the "investigation" of Roos's character, said he observed the women "exhibiting themselves to public view on the front galleries . . . making motions to men and firemen passing in procession while the streets were crowded with ladies and children." Austin's investigation revealed Roos's reputation as a notorious thief in Shreveport, Memphis, and Little Rock, as well as the "degraded character" of her house situated on Shreveport's main thoroughfare.[7]

Austin testified that he arrested Roos frequently for unspecified acts

6. Supreme Court of Louisiana Collections, Docket #124, Department of Special Collections, Earl K. Long Library, University of New Orleans, hereinafter cited as Roos MS; Ruth Rosen, *The Lost Sisterhood* (Baltimore, 1982), 3–4. On prostitution in the United States see Barbara Meil Hobson, *Uneasy Virtue: The Politics of Prostitution and the American Reform Tradition* (Chicago, 1987); Mary P. Ryan, *Women in Public, Between Banners and Ballots, 1825–1880* (Baltimore, 1990); Thomas C. Mackey, *Red Lights Out: A Legal History of Prostitution, Disorderly Houses and Vice Districts, 1870–1917* (New York, 1987); Richard Tansey, "Prostitution and Politics in Antebellum New Orleans," *Southern Studies* 28 (1979): 449–79; Karen Trahan Leathem, "A Carnival According to Their Own Desires: Gender and Mardi Gras in New Orleans 1870–1941" (Ph.D. diss., University of North Carolina at Chapel Hill, 1994), 212–17.

7. Carol Gates, *Shreveport and Caddo Parish Officials* (Shreveport, 1985), 111–3; Roos MS, 9, 10, 12.

committed in her house that violated city ordinances, and he swore he often saw Roos's employees "exposed to public view improperly dressed or 'en dishabille.'" Additionally, the sheriff remarked how during the parade, one of the women appeared on the gallery attired in her petticoat, another woman's dress was open "behind" as she turned to go inside, while still other women were observed with uncombed hair. He described the prostitutes as being "slatternly" dressed, and presenting such a "lewd appearance" that the chief of police considered the whole matter one worthy of investigation. Pauline Markham, one of Roos's "girls," testified, however, that "Lizzie had on a waist and skirt, Cora a little princess, Lottie a white lawn. I had on a little princess. None of the dresses were thin enough to expose [the] shape of [the] person[;] some opened before and some behind, none were opened on the day mentioned."[8]

On 8 May 1883, Fannie Roos was convicted and fined fifty dollars for operating a house of ill fame in an indecent manner. The next day, Mayor Andrew Currie ordered her and the other brothel "inmates"—Cora Boney, Lizzie Jones, Pauline Markham, and Lottie Rogers—to abandon the house within three days. Roos appealed Currie's decision to the mayor's court, but it denied her. Through her attorneys Roos then sought relief in the Supreme Court of Louisiana, which agreed to take her appeal. At the hearing her counsel argued that since the ordinance regulating whorehouses did not specify what acts rendered such establishments "indecent," the eviction should not stand. Furthermore, they contended, the mayor had neglected to sign the ordinance, and his failure rendered it invalid.[9]

The high court dismissed the latter contention and said of the former that the town fathers could not have delineated specific acts causing the establishment to be labeled indecent because they had no experience in

8. Roos MS, 9, 11, 16. In the late 1870s slim dresses, rather than the voluminous skirts of the 1860s and bustles of the early 1870s, were fashionable. Daytime skirts became so narrow that it was sometimes difficult to walk while wearing them. "White lawn" probably referred to a fabric of thinly woven cotton.

9. Currie (1843–1918), born in Ireland, became a deputy sheriff in Shreveport and later served as the town's first constable. A member of the Knights of the White Camellia, he was also the first Democratic mayor elected after the Civil War, and he served in that capacity from 1878 to 1890. As a member of the state senate, 1892–1896, Currie introduced a bill to establish Louisiana Tech University (*Dictionary of Louisiana Biography,* s.v. "Currie, Andrew").

doing so. Legal precedent established that ordinances regulating houses of prostitution did not have to specify various acts of indecency that could render its keeper liable. Indeed, Chief Justice Thomas Courtland Manning,[10] author of the decision, observed that the town fathers could scarcely be expected to specify the particular acts rendering Shreveport prostitutes "obnoxious to the law's denunciation . . . [because] the experience of the city fathers in that domain is doubtless so limited that in drafting an ordinance which would comprehend all the indecent convolutions of lascivious cyprians they would be forced to put fancy on the wing, and imagine postures they never beheld." In view of these exigencies, the high court ruled against Roos.[11]

While the defiance exhibited by Antoinette Boullard and Fanny Roos was overt in nature, that of Josephine Decuir was more subtle. Daughter of Antoine Dubuclet, a *gens de couleur* and Pointe Coupée Parish planter, Decuir and her husband Antoine were prosperous slaveowners before the Civil War. The war's disruptions threw the Decuirs on hard times, nearly bankrupting them. Such was the strain on Antoine that he died in 1871.[12]

On 20 July 1872, the widow boarded the steamboat *Governor Allen* at New Orleans. Because she was of mixed white and black racial background, a *femme de couleur*, Decuir was denied a stateroom in the so-called ladies' cabin, an area reserved for the exclusive use of white women. Instead, the cabin steward directed her to a stateroom set aside for freedwomen and freedmen located in an area called the "colored bureau." Decuir declined to accept such accommodations and spent the night sitting in a chair at the rear of a public area reserved for white women. She was not permitted to eat in the dining area with other cabin passengers; instead, her meals were brought out to her, and a second chair served as her table.[13]

10. Manning (1831–1887), a native of North Carolina, was appointed to the supreme court three times: 1864, 1877, and 1882. He also served as ambassador to Mexico and as a member of Louisiana's secession convention in 1861 (Warren M. Billings, ed., *The Historic Rules of the Supreme Court of Louisiana 1813–1879* [Lafayette, La., 1985], 47).

11. Manning's opinion does not survive in manuscript, but a printed text is in 35 La. Ann. (1883), 662–3.

12. Loren Schweninger, "Antebellum Free Persons of Color in Postbellum Louisiana," *Louisiana History* 30 (1989): 345–64.

13. Frederick Way, Jr., comp., *Way's Packet Directory, 1848–1983.* (Athens, Ohio, 1983), 193–4;

Louisiana's Constitution of 1868 prohibited racial discrimination in public conveyances, establishments serving the public such as confectioneries, and places of amusement. As such, the barring of Madame Decuir (as she was referred to throughout the case) from a stateroom in the ladies' cabin clearly breached her constitutional rights. Mere adoption of a constitution and its attendant statutes did not end a long tradition of discrimination; few of the necessary enabling laws were enforced. Although streetcars in New Orleans were integrated, blacks were not permitted to stay in hotels catering to white patrons, nor were they served at soda shops and saloons frequented by whites. In an attempt to enforce the antidiscriminatory laws, several African Americans filed suit to test their effectiveness.[14]

Decuir became one of these individuals when she filed suit in 1873 against the owner of the steamer, John G. Benson. Citing article 13 of the state constitution and a statute that forbade discrimination on public conveyances, Decuir sued in the New Orleans district court and sought damages for mental and physical suffering, seeking actual damages of twenty-five thousand dollars and exemplary damages in the amount of fifty thousand dollars.[15]

Testimony at trial reveals a treasure trove of social history. There is clear evidence of the deeply inculcated intrarace class prejudice exhibited by the affluent black witnesses toward newly freed former slaves. The *Decuir* case is thus an excellent example of efforts by wealthy Creoles of color, who constituted what might be termed a "middle" race in antebellum Louisiana society, to retain—and often regain—their prewar status and privilege.

When one of the witnesses for the plaintiff, Pierre G. Deslonde,

Mrs. Josephine Decuir v. *John G. Benson,* Docket #7800, Supreme Court of Louisiana Collection, Department of Special Collections, University of New Orleans, hereinafter cited as Decuir MS.

14. Charles Vincent, "Black Constitution Makers: The Constitution of 1868," in Warren M. Billings and Edward F. Haas, eds., *In Search of Fundamental Law: Louisiana's Constitutions 1812–1974* (Lafayette, La., 1993), 69–81; Roger A. Fischer, *The Segregation Struggle in Louisiana 1862–1877* (Urbana, 1974), 52–5; Germaine A. Reed, "Race Relations in Louisiana, 1864–1920," *Louisiana History* 6 (1965): 379–92; Howard N. Rabinowitz, *Race Relations in the Urban South* (Urbana, 1978), chapter 8; John W. Blassingame, *Black New Orleans 1860–1880* [(Chicago, 1963), 185–96.

15. A native of Baltimore, Benson (1824–1875) came to New Orleans in 1865.

Louisiana secretary of state, was asked why he did not stay in the "colored bureau" on steamboats he replied, "Because I deemed it not a place for a man of my standing." Responding to the question of whether he would permit his wife to go into the "colored bureau," he said he would not because she "was raised in another sphere from that to be classed as such." It is noteworthy that although there was a designated white women's cabin separate from the white men's cabin, there was no distinction made between the sexes in the area reserved for African Americans. Female and male black passengers were assigned rooms in the same area.[16]

In his evidence, one of the white steamboat captains revealed how he customarily reserved two cabins for the exclusive use of "particular" blacks because "there are some colored people who wouldn't associate with other colored people." This prejudice is not surprising when it is remembered that the Creoles of color perceived themselves diametrically at odds with a predominantly illiterate, Protestant, English-speaking, landless class of people only recently released from bondage.[17]

Witnesses also spoke by implication to the anomalous position of *femmes de couleur* in negotiating the white world of postbellum Louisiana. When confronted by a woman whose status as a "lady" was compromised by her race, white men became confused and uneasy. Chivalry and the idealization of women had previously been reserved solely for white women.

Southern white men defined middle and upper-class white women as physically weak and therefore dependent on and in need of male protection. Thus were born attitudes of male chivalry and paternalism. Those manners, in turn, produced the myth of the Southern Lady. This fragile creature required protection from the threat of attack and almost certain rape by lascivious black males. Madame Decuir's presence before the bar posed a dilemma. Here was an educated woman, described by the white trial judge—ironically the same man who had presided in the

16. Decuir MS, 191, 193. Deslonde (1824–?), a wealthy Iberville Parish planter, served as a delegate to the 1867 constitutional convention and was secretary of state from 1872 to 1876. After the passage of the federal Civil Rights Act in 1875, he sued a Lake Pontchartrain saloon owner who refused to serve Deslonde and his wife a glass of soda water. When Reconstruction ended, Deslonde published the *News Pioneer* in Iberville Parish.

17. Decuir MS, 193, 121, 169.

Boullard trial fifteen years earlier (E. North Cullom)—as a genteel "lady of color" who was modest, neat, and "quite fair for one of mixed blood" and whose facial features were "rather delicate." Decuir was never a slave, but the color of her skin defined her not as a "lady" but as a black woman. Were she white, there would be no question that Josephine Decuir fit the southern definition of an ideal "lady"; a woman of purity, modesty, and refinement, fully deserving of male protection—be they black or white.[18]

Of course, a white woman of Decuir's rank would never have been denied a berth in the ladies' cabin, thereby negating the necessity of a lawsuit such as this. One of her attorneys attempted to establish her claim to equal treatment, arguing that a lady such as Decuir plainly could not undress for bed on deck "on account of delicacy." Furthermore, he averred, she was shocked, shamed, and mortified when subjected to the vulgar conversation of the crew and everyone else on the boat who passed by her.

Such arguments evidently proved persuasive. Madame Decuir won the case and received a thousand dollars in actual damages. She failed to collect exemplary damages because Judge Cullom reasoned that too little time had elapsed since emancipation for the general public to accept the integration of public conveyances and accommodations. Benson appealed the award to the Supreme Court of Louisiana, but the court turned him aside. He then sought relief from the Supreme Court of the United States.[19]

The facts of *Decuir* v. *Benson* evidence an unvoiced fear. Just as sanctioning a woman for selling liquor and fenced goods to slaves, or women appearing in public immodestly dressed, seemed threatening to traditional southern and national mores, so too was Decuir's demand for equal accommodations on a steamboat so soon after the abolition of slavery. Moreover, the era of Reconstruction died in March 1877, when President

18. Jacquelyn Dowd Hall, "'A Truly Subversive Affair': Women against Lynching in the Twentieth-Century South," in Carol Ruth Berkin and Mary Beth Norton, eds., *Women of America: A History* (New York, 1979), 372; Decuir MS, 218.

19. Decuir MS, 5. A significant portion of the testimony attempted to establish whether the quarters assigned to crew were located a sufficient distance away from "the ladies" so that female passengers would not be subjected to the "indecent" language of deckhands.

Rutherford B. Hayes removed remaining federal troops from Louisiana. That May, the nation's highest court reversed Judge Cullom. In rendering its decision, the Court declared that the laws under which the suit was brought were unconstitutional because they regulated interstate commerce, a right reserved to Congress under the United States Constitution. It is likely that this Court too was not yet willing to sanction de jure integration so soon after Reconstruction was abandoned. The Court, however, wished to find a means to sanction de facto segregation. It did so by ruling that since the *Allen* traveled intrastate as well as interstate, her owner had the right to adopt such "reasonable regulations" as he felt appropriate to conduct his business.[20]

The hooch-seller, the harlot, and the plantation mistress all defied social convention. In an era when women were expected to be seen and not heard, to be passive rather than assertive, these women nonetheless used the Louisiana judicial system to uphold their presumed right to be heard, to be seen, and to be assertive. By the same token, they used the courts as a forum to advocate their social interests. Antoinette Boullard, a working-class white woman, sued one of the wealthiest planters in antebellum Louisiana to punish him for destroying her means of subsistence. Court records show that two weeks after being cast out on the Red River, Boullard was back in business, replete with furniture, stock, and a stand to ply her trade. Although she was not able to gain punitive damages from the high court, she won a pyrrhic victory nonetheless.

Fannie Roos, on the other hand, defied social norms when she permitted the inhabitants of her house to occupy the gallery of her establishment on Parade Day in defiance of a special city ordinance that specified that prostitutes were to remain confined inside their houses during the parade. Was the Roos case a foreshadowing of the Progressive era movement to outlaw prostitution in Louisiana? It is remarkable that Roos used the court system to test the validity of vaguely worded ordinances regulating prostitution.

Josephine Decuir, a woman of a different class and caste from Boullard and Roos, manifested her defiance when she tested pioneering antidis-

20. Decuir MS, "Reasons for Judgment," 218–40, "Judgment" 240–1.

crimination laws at a time when segregation of the races was a socially accepted norm. Like Roos and Boullard, Decuir ultimately lost her case.
Given the nature of the social conventions, mores, and powerful political foes they challenged it is easy to admire these three different women.
On one level, they dared to contradict an extremely wealthy planter in
the antebellum South; a mayor and police chief in an ultraconservative
area at the dawn of the Progressive Era; and a steamboat captain during
the heyday of steamboating, when Jim Crowism was being born in
Reconstruction Louisiana. However, in a much larger sense their defiance extended beyond individuals. Boullard, Roos, and Decuir assaulted
the social and political power structures of their time by taking actions
on their own behalf through the utilization of the state's judicial system.

The *Boullard* case reveals something of the complicated relationship
between master and slave and the overseer who enforced the master's (or
mistress's) orders, and about how slaves augmented their meager existence by trading with those who were willing to barter stolen merchan-
dise in exchange for goods that were forbidden to them by antebellum
Black Codes. Boullard was a white woman consorting with slaves who
undermined plantation discipline. Not only was she a nuisance, a woman
engaging in unladylike behavior, she was a threat to the plantation slave
system.[21]

The case of Fannie Roos and the city fathers of Shreveport documents
a manner in which nineteenth-century prostitutes could contest the social
limits placed on them. It paints a vivid picture of the distinctly different
standards and expectations demanded of "nice" middle-class white women
versus those of "bad" working-class white women, and yields information
about the clothing they wore.

Josephine Decuir's case provides bonuses. It tells us something about
the slippery definitions of womanhood in the late-nineteenth-century
South and augments our understanding of race relations between free
men of color and freed men of color during Reconstruction in Louisiana.
It provides an insight into the chivalric ambiance displayed by white men
when confronted by a woman whose status as a lady was challenged by

---

21. *Hall* v. *Decuir* 95 U.S. 485 (1878).

the color of her skin. Josephine Decuir and others who filed similar law-suits during the Reconstruction period support C. Vann Woodward's ar-gument that the years between the Civil War and the *Plessy* decision were indeed a window of opportunity in which race relations might have taken a different course before Jim Crow became law.[22]

22. For a discussion of a similar class of disorderly women in antebellum South Carolina, see Victoria E. Bynum, *Unruly Women: The Politics of Social and Sexual Control in the Old South* (Chapel Hill, 1992), and for additional commentary on issues raised by the Decuir case see Elizabeth Fox-Genovese, *Within the Plantation Household: Black and White Women of the Old South* (Chapel Hill, 1988); Anne Firor-Scott, *The Southern Lady from Pedestal to Politics, 1830–1930* (Chicago, 1970); Ira Berlin, *Slaves without Masters* (New York, 1974), chapter 4.

IMPERFECT EQUALITY

The Legal Status of Free People of
Color in New Orleans, 1803–1860

In 1803, New Orleans merchant Benjamin Morgan wrote to an associate
about Napoleon's sale of the province of Louisiana to the United States.
He expressed concern for possible changes in the status of Louisiana's
large free colored population as a result of this transition. "Upon what
footing," he asked, "will the free quadroon mulatto and black people
stand; will they be entitled to the rights of citizens or not?" Morgan remarked that they were numerous, that many were respectable, and that
"under this government [they] enjoy their rights in common with other
subjects." In the suddenly American climate, what rights would they retain, and what privileges would they surrender?[1]

Louisiana's free black population, as Morgan pointed out, was numerous. In 1810, free people of color comprised 28 percent of the New

1. American-born, Morgan moved to Louisiana before the Purchase. Thomas Jefferson ap-
pointed him to the Legislative Council of the Territory of Orleans in 1804, and he served on the
Court of Pleas of the Territory of Orleans. James Wilkinson to the president, July 1, 1804; William C.
C. Claiborne to Thomas Jefferson, 19 November 1804, in Clarence Edwin Carter, ed., *The Territorial
Papers of the United States* (Washington, D.C., 1940), 4: 251, 334; Minute book of the Court of Pleas,
Territory of Orleans, 1804, New Orleans City Archives, New Orleans Public Library; Morgan to
Chandler Price, 7 August 1803, in Carter, ed., *Territorial Papers*, 4: 8.

Orleans population. Shortages of skilled workers and frequent epidemics had long forced the city's whites to welcome any talented person, regardless of color. As a result, free blacks monopolized occupations such as carpentry, masonry, and shoemaking. Though most remained of modest means, the successful sometimes owned slaves, and a few became planters. Numerical weight and economic situation gave free people of color a certain amount of social influence, which in turn allowed them to enjoy many, but not all, of the legal privileges accorded to their white neighbors. In the decades after 1803, however, their position grew increasingly tenuous, and some liberties were eventually lost.[2]

In recent years scholars have produced a number of works on New Orleans's free blacks, many of which touch tangentially on legal restrictions imposed on the city's *gens de couleur.* A study of court cases, statutes, and ordinances shows that New Orleans leaders made little progress in curtailing free blacks at first. By midcentury, however, changing economic conditions, competition from white immigrant laborers, and heightened suspicion of free black support for the abolition movement accelerated the erosion of free African Americans' legal status. While the state's politicians undercut incrementally such freedoms as public assembly, education, and travel, they barely touched other rights. Thus, free blacks managed to cling to a quasi-citizenship down to 1860.[3]

2. In 1810, New Orleans had 4,950 free black inhabitants, approximately 28 percent of the entire population. By 1840, free blacks numbered 19,226 in New Orleans, representing 18.8 percent of the population. After that date, free blacks experienced a severe decline in numbers, and by 1850 they comprised only 6 percent of the city's inhabitants. Population figures taken from Richard C. Wade, *Slavery in the Cities: the South, 1820–1860* (New York, 1964), 326; Virginia R. Domínguez, *White by Definition: Social Classification in Creole Louisiana* (New Brunswick, N.J., 1986), 116–7; Ira Berlin, *Slaves without Masters: The Free Negro in the Antebellum South* (New York, 1974), 113–4; Donald Edward Everett, "Free Persons of Color in New Orleans, 1803–1865" (Ph.D. diss., Tulane University, 1952), 194; Laura Foner, "The Free People of Color in Louisiana and St. Domingue: A Comparative Portrait of Two Three-Caste Slave Societies," *Journal of Social History* 3 (1970): 410; Gwendolyn Midlo Hall, *Africans in Colonial Louisiana: The Development of Afro-Creole Culture in the Eighteenth Century* (Baton Rouge, 1992), 129; Jerah Johnson, "Colonial New Orleans: A Fragment of the Eighteenth-Century French Ethos," in Arnold R. Hirsch and Joseph Logsdon, *Creole New Orleans: Race and Americanization* (Baton Rouge, 1992), 53; Robert C. Reinders, "The Free Negro in the New Orleans Economy," *Louisiana History* 6 (1965): 282; Richard Tansey, "Out-of-State Free Blacks in Late Antebellum New Orleans," *Louisiana History* 22 (1981): 369–70.

3. Berlin's *Slaves without Masters* provides a look at legal restrictions in the slave states. Two general works that touch on Louisiana law and its effect on the free black population are Everett's "Free

Free blacks' limited success at defending their status can be examined by looking at the kinds of rights white leaders revoked or circumscribed and those that blacks managed to keep. When these clusters of liberties are studied in conjunction with some of the statutes, ordinances, and court decisions, they confirm an increasing desire on the part of state leaders to restrict the movements and influence of free blacks. At the same time, the undisturbed group of rights discloses the means free persons of color used to protect the status they had fought to preserve since the colonial period.

Despite a unique niche that free persons of color filled in colonial New Orleans, the French had taken steps to ensure the inferiority of free blacks through the Code Noir. First, the Code levied stiffer fines on free people of color than on whites for harboring fugitive slaves. If the free black offender failed to pay, he or she could be sold into slavery. Another prohibition prevented persons of color from marrying whites. Yet a third admonished manumitted slaves always to offer "a singular respect toward their former masters, toward their widows, and toward their children." After Louisiana's transfer to Spanish rule, the new governors of the colony allowed the provisions of the Code Noir to stand.[4]

When the Americans took possession of the Territory of Orleans, they expected to fill it with their own kind, but the free black population placed the newcomers in a quandary. White slave owners feared that the presence of such a large number of *gens de couleur* would plant ideas of freedom in their bondsmens' heads. In spite of the threat to security free persons of color represented, they possessed three things that Americans held dear: freedom, property, and economic status. Thus, economic and numerical strength worked against the enacting of swift changes in free blacks' legal standing.

Among the earliest infringements on that status was one designed to set free blacks apart from whites in all acts of legal record. Formalizing a custom practiced by the French and Spanish, a territorial statute of 1808

Persons of Color in New Orleans, 1803–1865," and H. E. Sterkx, *The Free Negro in Ante-Bellum Louisiana* (Cranbury, N.J., 1972).

4. Art. 1, Secs. 6, 33 and 34, *Edit du Roi, touchant l'état et la discipline des Esclaves nègres de la Louisiane,* popularly known as the Code Noir, in *Recueils de réglements, édits, déclarations et arrêts concernant le commerce, l'administration de la justice des colonies françaises de l'Amérique* (Paris, 1724); Sterkx, *Free Negro,* 36–7.

required all officials to apply the designation "free man" or "free woman of color" in legal documents or public notices. To segregate the vital records of whites and free blacks, the Legislative Council of the Territory of Orleans also decreed that separate books be kept for the births and deaths of free persons of color.[5]

Although the legislative council paid a great deal of attention to differentiating free black from white, it never defined the phrase "free person of color." That task instead was left to the superior court of the territory, and in so doing, the court drew a color line between mulattoes and persons of pure African descent. In *Adele* v. *Beauregard,* for example, Judge François-Xavier Martin described persons of color as descendants of Indians on both sides, from one white parent, or from mulatto parents in possession of their freedom. He declared that, "considering how much probability there [was] in favor of the liberty of those persons, they ought not to be deprived of it upon mere presumption." Pure Africans, however, were generally brought to the country as slaves, and their descendants "may perhaps fairly be presumed to have continued so, till they show the contrary." The Supreme Court of Louisiana relied on this presumption in several subsequent cases primarily concerning suits for freedom.[6]

As the lines for racial identification were drawn, so were the boundaries of racial behaviors. Expanding on the Code Noir, the legislative council admonished free persons of color never to insult or strike white persons, "nor to presume to conceive themselves equal to the white . . . and never speak or answer to them but with respect." Although the free African American's legal position was below that of a white, it was far above that of slave. That superior place gave birth to white anxieties that reached back to colonial times. Such fears found life in 1811, when a band of slaves revolted along the German Coast, just outside of New Orleans. Stories of free black planters aiding in the capture of the renegades temporarily diffused the

---

5. "An Act to Prescribe Certain Formalities Respecting Free Persons of Color," Orleans Territorial Acts (1808), 92; "An Act to Provide for the Recording of Births and Deaths," 1811 La. Acts 74.

6. *Adele* v. *Beauregard,* 1 Mart. (o.s.) 183 (La. 1811). Judith Kelleher Schafer, *Slavery, the Civil Law and the Supreme Court of Louisiana* (Baton Rouge, 1994), 20. Other cases in which the court cited *Adele* v. *Beauregard* include *State* v. *Cecil,* 2 Mart. (o.s.) 208 (La. 1812), which upheld the validity of testimony by a person of color. The court also referred to *Adele* v. *Beauregard* in several suits for freedom, including *Forsyth et al.* v. *Nash,* 4 Mart. (o.s.) 3 (La. 1816); *English* v. *Latham,* 3 Mart. (n.s.) 88 (La. 1824); *Sally Miller* v. *Louis Belmonti,* 11 Rob. 339 (La. 1845).

tension of the moment.[7] Nevertheless, despite a high percentage of free black slaveholders who lived in New Orleans and the surrounding parishes, whites always suspected free persons of color. Over the ensuing decades, mounting abolitionist sentiment only served to increase the unease.

Consider the impact of four free men of color who were arrested in 1830 in New Orleans and charged with circulating *Walker's Appeal in Four Articles Together with a Preamble to the Colored Citizens of the World.* The pamphlet called on slaves to revolt and urged free blacks to assist. This incident, coupled with news of the Nat Turner rising in Virginia, intensified whites' fears of slave rebellion. Suddenly the need to curb the city's free blacks took on a new sense of urgency. As a result, state legislators passed new restrictions, as the public pressured authorities to enforce those laws already on the books. New limitations were added to existing ones until free blacks found themselves, in many cases, governed by a set of regulations quite separate from that of the whites.[8]

Among the rights that free blacks never possessed were the privileges to vote and hold office. In 1805 the New Orleans city council members discussed the need for officially disenfranchising free black males, but they concluded that the city charter already required that *all* voters had to be *both* free and white. The Constitution of 1812 removed any doubt, however, because its framers specified that only free white male citizens of the United States, twenty-one years of age or older, could vote and hold office in Louisiana. Other slave states with large free black populations were not so quick. Free persons of color, for instance, voted in Maryland until 1810, in Tennessee until 1834, and in North Carolina until 1835.[9]

---

7. "An Act Prescribing the Rules and Conduct to Be Observed with Respect to Negroes and other Slaves of this Territory," 1806 La. Acts 202; James H. Dormon, "The Persistent Specter: Slave Rebellion in Territorial Louisiana," *Louisiana History* 18 (1977): 393.

8. Everett, "Free Persons of Color," 92; Sterkx, *Free Negro,* 98–9.

9. New Orleans City Council, Official Proceedings, 1 March 1805, New Orleans City Archives, Louisiana Division, New Orleans Public Library; Constitution of 1812, art. II, secs. 4 and 8, in Benjamin Wall Dart, ed., *Constitutions of the State of Louisiana and Selected Federal Laws* (Indianapolis, 1932), 499, 500; Thomas N. Ingersoll, "Free Blacks in a Slave Society: New Orleans, 1718–1812," *William and Mary Quarterly* 3d ser., 48 (1991): 197; Roger Wallace Shugg, "Negro Voting in the Ante-bellum South," *Journal of Negro History* 21 (1936): 358; Carter J. Woodson, *Free Negro Heads of Families in the United States in 1830: Together with a Brief Treatment of the Free Negro* (Washington, D.C., 1925), xxi.

Most other civic liberties, however, were not completely closed off. In contrast to the strict ban on suffrage, the legislature generally allowed free blacks to keep and bear arms, providing that they always carried a certificate from a justice of the peace attesting to their freedom. Without this license, their firearms were subject to seizure. These provisions were decidedly more liberal than those in slave states such as Virginia and Maryland. That liberality originated in the territorial era, when Governor William C. C. Claiborne continued the colonial practice of employing a free colored troop of militia, though the commanders of this battalion were white. Moreover, during the War of 1812, the Colored Battalion of New Orleans fought in the Battle of New Orleans. The battalion remained in existence until the late 1820s when, because of waning interest, its members chose to disband. Thereafter, no whites challenged blacks' entitlement to own weapons.[10]

Other rights, such as those dealing with marriage and family, bore tighter restrictions. The Code Noir's interdiction against interracial marriage was reiterated in the *Digest* of 1808 and the *Civil Code* of 1825, but it was not tested in the Supreme Court of Louisiana until 1855, in *Dupré* v. *Boulard.* That case arose out of a disputed succession, and the issue turned on the validity of a French marriage between a white man and a free woman of color. The children of Marie Elizabeth Boulard attempted to block Jean Pierre Michel Dupré from claiming any of their mother's estate because Dupré's and Boulard's marriage was illegal in Louisiana. Writing for a unanimous court, Justice Henry Spofford expressed his disapproval, calling the marriage an "unnatural alliance" and refusing to sanction an evasion of Louisiana law by legitimating the union. The fact that the first challenge to this law came so close to the Civil War is somewhat surprising. Because New Orleanians tended to overlook cohabitation between white men and women of color, perhaps the marital status of

10. "An Act Relative to Slaves and Free Persons of Color," 1855 La. Acts 63; Maryland legislators intermittently banned the keeping of firearms for all free blacks beginning in 1824. Virginia lawmakers did not allow free persons of color to carry firearms without a rarely granted license, and they authorized patrols to conduct forced searches of free black homes in search of weapons; A. Leon Higginbotham and Greer C. Bosworth, "Rather than the Free: Free Blacks in Colonial and Antebellum Virginia," *Harvard Civil Rights and Civil Liberties Law Review* 26 (1991): 27; Everett, "Free Persons of Color," 82; Ingersoll, "Free Blacks in a Slave Society," 193–4.

Marie Elizabeth and Jean Pierre Michel Dupré would have gone unnoticed had it not been for the dispute over an estate worth almost $23,000.[11]

Although white New Orleanians tacitly accepted interracial cohabitation, the *Civil Code* made it difficult for a concubine or natural children of mixed race to make substantial claims on a white man's estate. The law allowed bastards of color to prove descent only from a father of color. Unless a white father formally acknowledged his natural child of mixed race either at birth or at a later date, the child had no claim to inherit any portion from his natural father.[12]

Natural fathers had to maintain their acknowledged children by furnishing what the statute styled "alimony"—that is, money for nourishment, lodging, support, and education of the minor child, in proportion to the wants of the person requiring it, and the circumstances of the parent. But in the case of a natural child of color, the *Civil Code* obliged parents only for what was "absolutely necessary to ensure them their board and lodging, and to enable them to learn to read and write, and a trade." The obligation to provide alimony ceased once the child was able to earn his own subsistence. Judge E. A. Canon of the Second District Court for the Parish of Orleans relied on these code articles when Emma Litot, a free woman of color, attempted to collect an inheritance from the estate of her white natural father, William Liddle. Canon dismissed the plaintiff's suit because her father had seen to her training as a dressmaker. Thus, he had fulfilled his legal responsibility by providing Emma with a trade, and Canon ruled that her father owed her no more under the *Civil Code*.[13]

When confronted with the issue of interracial concubinage, the courts

11. James Brown and Louis Moreau Lislet, comps., *Digest of the Civil Laws in Force* (New Orleans, 1808), art. 8; *Civil Code of the State of Louisiana* (New Orleans, 1825), title 4, ch. 2, art. 95; Petition of Plaintiff and Opinion of Justice Henry Spofford, *J. M. Dupré* v. *The Executor of Boulard, f. w. c. et al.,* Supreme Court of Louisiana, 1855, Docket No. 3743, Supreme Court of Louisiana Archives, Department of Special Collections, Earl K. Long Library, University of New Orleans (in the same repository see also *Succession of Minvielle,* 1860, Docket No. 6447).

12. Civil Code, art. 221, 226; *Jung et al.* v. *Doriocourt et al.,* 4 La. 175 (1832); *Robinett et al.* v. *Verdun's Vendees,* 14 La. 592 (1840).

13. *Civil Code, 1825,*Civil Code, art. 221, 246, 247, 259 & 260; *Emma Litot, f. w. c.* v. *Anna Liddle, wife of Gilbert L. Hawkins,* Second District Court of New Orleans, 1848, Docket No. 1392, New Orleans District Court Records, New Orleans City Archives, New Orleans Public Library.

were quick to condemn it and to throw up as many obstacles to such unions as possible. For example, in 1821 the supreme court took an appeal from the First Judicial District Court in New Orleans involving white children who demanded alimony from their white father. The children refused to abide with their father because he lived with a free woman of color, and they sued for separate maintenance. Their father, Pierre Heno, refused them, claiming that they were welcome to live with him. Jurors found for the Heno children, and the defendants appealed. The supreme court ruled that Heno was obligated to provide alimony because, in Judge Alexander Porter's words, the fact that their father lived openly with a woman of color was "certainly a good reason why the court should not compel his daughter, a white girl, to return to his house . . . when it is shown that their father made them associate and eat with the woman with whom he lives, and her children."[14]

New Orleans politicians discouraged even the most casual contact between the races through ordinances against social intermingling in public places. Thus, free persons of color could not gamble with whites or slaves, nor could they associate with one another in coffeehouses or cabarets, or sit together at theaters or public exhibitions. An especially contentious form of interracial contact was the "quadroon balls," in which the city's free women of color attracted white suitors. White females' outcries against this practice became so heated that the city council adopted ordinances to forbid whites from entering balls for men and women of color.[15]

Bans on social intermingling applied to New Orleans's youths as well. Part of the white effort at maintaining racial separation involved keeping

14. Opinion of Judge Alexander Porter, *Heno et al.* v. *Heno,* Supreme Court of Louisiana, 1821, Docket No. 510, Supreme Court of Louisiana Archives, Department of Special Collections, Earl K. Long Library, University of New Orleans.

15. "An Ordinance Concerning the Public Exhibition and Theaters of New Orleans," New Orleans City Council Ordinances and Resolutions, 8 June 1816, New Orleans City Archives; "An Ordinance Concerning Cabarets, Coffeehouses and Grog Shops," New Orleans Common Council, 7 January 1857, New Orleans City Archives; "An Ordinance Concerning Gaming-Houses within the City of New Orleans," New Orleans City Council Ordinances and Resolutions, 21 October 1816, New Orleans City Archives; "An Act Relative to Slaves and Free Persons of Color," 1855 La. Acts 51; "An Ordinance Relative to Masked Balls," New Orleans City Council Ordinances and Resolutions, 4 January 1828, New Orleans City Archives; Robert Randall Couch, "The Public Masked Balls of Antebellum New Orleans: A Custom of Masque Outside the Mardi Gras Tradition," *Louisiana History* 34 (1994): 411, 412, 420, 426.

free black children out of the newly formed public school system, even though their parents paid taxes for the schools' upkeep. Unlike in other southern states, however, this move was not an attempt to limit free blacks' social status or economic potential by banning them from learning to read and write. The city's *gens de couleur* could attend private schools, and many did so either in Europe or in the schools established by free blacks in New Orleans. By 1860 the literacy level of the community's free black population probably exceeded that of the white population of the state as a whole.[16]

New Orleans's white citizens became just as concerned about associations between resident and out-of-state free blacks as they were about interracial relations. Whites feared that the city's free blacks were being corrupted by those from outside the state. To stem increases in the state's free black population, Louisiana lawmakers moved to bar free blacks from settling in the state. As early as 1807, a law banned immigration of free persons of color; it proved to be ineffective, and the issue lay dormant for several decades. Accounts of slave rebellions and the Walker pamphlet scare renewed public demands for laws barring black strangers from the state. Public pressure prompted the legislature to adopt a more restrictive measure in 1830. An Act to Prevent Free Persons of Color from Entering into this State decreed that any free black who entered after 1 January 1825 was subject to expulsion. Further, it subjected native-born blacks who left the state to its provisions. It likewise compelled all free persons of color who settled in Louisiana before 1825 to register with designated officials. The statute also applied to free black seamen who remained in port longer than thirty days.[17]

Stringent though it may have seemed, the act was more rigid in theory than in practice. Indeed, within a year of passage, the legislators mitigated the travel restrictions when they allowed free black residents who owned property or who were gainfully employed to come and go from most

---

16. Luther Porter Jackson, *Free Negro Labor and Property Holding in Virginia, 1830–1860* (1942; reprint, New York, 1969), 19; Loren Schweninger, *Black Property Owners in the South, 1790–1915* (Urbana, Ill., 1990), 129; Rodolphe Lucien Desdunes, *Our People and Our History,* trans. Sr. Dorothea Olga McCants (Baton Rouge, 1973), 106; Donald E. Devore and Joseph Logsdon, *Crescent City Schools: Public Education in New Orleans, 1841–1991* (Lafayette, La., 1991), 41, 42.

17. 1830 La. Acts 90–4.

other states and foreign countries. Thereafter lawmakers authorized municipal councils and parish police juries to permit free blacks to remain within their jurisdiction, provided they furnish proof of good character and give bond to ensure observance of the laws. To hinder illegal aliens further, the city's general council forbade publicans from harboring any free black who was in the state without proof of residency. All free persons of color were presumed violators unless they could produce satisfactory evidence to the contrary.[18]

New Orleans officials used the illegal residency ordinances frequently during the 1840s and 1850s in an attempt to control the movement and growth of the city's free black population. In 1841 alone the Third Municipality Recorder documented eighty-three convictions for violations of the residency law. One newspaper in 1852 stated that city officials had made seventy-five "contravention arrests" in a two-day period. The escalation in enforcement of immigration laws illustrates mounting white fears that outsiders were swaying local blacks with anti-white, pro-abolitionist sentiment. The magistrates' zealous pursuit of violators, however, was apparently short-lived. The editor of the (New Orleans) *Daily Delta* in 1854 complained that the laws had fallen into disuse. As a result, he warned, New Orleans had been "filled with a lot of very impudent persons from the free states, who have succeeded in making our legitimate colored population free as well as slaves, so saucy, that there is no getting along with them now. . . . The darkies should be forced to pay some respect to even the 'poor white trash' for which they express such unutterable contempt."[19]

Nonetheless, New Orleans businessmen welcomed resident alien free blacks, whose presence helped keep wages low. Police cooperated with the businessmen by not arresting the resident aliens, but by the 1850s the in-

18. "An Act to Prevent the Emigration of Free Negroes and Mulattoes into the Territory of Orleans," 1807 La. Acts 76; "An Act to Prevent Free Persons of Color from Entering into this State, and for Other Purposes," 1830 La. Acts 90–4; "An Act to Amend An Act Entitled 'An Act to Prevent Free Persons of Color from Entering into this State, and for Other Purposes,' Approved March 16, 1830," 1831 La. Acts 96; "An Act to Amend An Act Approved March 16, 1842 Entitled 'An Act More Effectually to Prevent Free Persons of Color from Entering into this State, and for Other Purposes," 1843 La. Acts 133; Acts of the General Council of New Orleans, 31 July 1841, 30, New Orleans City Archives.

19. (New Orleans) *Daily Delta,* 15 June 1852. For other accounts of such arrests, see ibid., 18 October 1845, 17 October 1846, 7 August 1852, 7 April 1853, 28 September 1854, 15 March 1857; (New Orleans) *Daily Crescent,* 8 December 1849; and (New Orleans) *Daily Picayune,* 25 August 1860.

creasing strength of abolitionists nationally, the emergence of the Republican Party, and the heightened political power of the white working class contributed to an escalation of arrests. An editorial in the *Daily Picayune* reflected the ambivalence of the New Orleans white community toward free blacks. It stated the desirability of excluding all free persons of color from the state, because "the unrestrained intercourse of the bond and free of the same color is an anomaly that is full of the promise of evil." Nevertheless, toward his conclusion the writer tempered his statement, owning that "there are others, whose industrious habits, thrifty life and regard for the duties of their station might well claim exemption from the extreme severity of the law. . . . Perhaps the past execution of the law has been too lenient; let not the present be too rigid."[20]

Although free persons of color could not control the progression toward more restrictive laws, they could still exert influence on how the laws were interpreted. An act of 1843 decreed that if a free black resident returned to Louisiana after living in a free state, authorities could expel him. Two free men of color who had recently returned from a trip north were arrested for breaking that law. On the day of the trial, one newspaper reported that "the avenues of the Criminal Court were . . . thronged with free people of color, who assembled there to ascertain the judgment of the court in a case deeply affecting their interests." The accused maintained that an absence of less than two years did not deprive them of their residency. Judge Alphonse Canonge agreed, thus maintaining the city's free blacks' rights to travel to other parts of the Union without losing their claims to residency.[21]

In tandem with restrictions on the movements of resident free blacks, lawmakers also attempted to discourage free black visitors. The greatest number of such persons were seamen, and according to an act of 1842, none was to enter the state on board any vessel or steamboat as either passenger or crew member. Authorities could jail any such individual aboard a vessel anchored in Louisiana waters until she sailed. The law required

20. Tansey, "Out-of-State Free Blacks," 376–7; (New Orleans) *Daily Picayune,* 4 September 1859.

21. "An Act to Amend the Act Approved March 16, 1842 Entitled 'An Act More Effectually to Prevent Free Persons of Color from Entering into this State, and for Other Purposes,'" 1843 La. Acts 254; (New Orleans) *Daily Crescent,* 14 October 1843.

the skipper to post bond for every free person of color he brought into the state, and to pay the court costs.[22]

A clash of interests among local merchants, levee workers, and the general public prompted lawmakers and enforcement officials to vacillate. Restrictions placed on the free black seamen caused an outcry from northern states, France, and Britain, and as a result of these protests, a statute of 1852 supplanted imprisonment with a system of bond and registration. It permitted free black mariners to remain on their vessels if the masters or owners registered each man with the mayor's office. Those relaxations ceased when officials received reports that free black seamen came to New Orleans to work on the levees, thus displacing local laborers. This fact caused legislators to reinstate the practice of jailing seamen until their vessel was ready to leave port. They also imposed a five-hundred-dollar bond and a charge of forty cents per day for maintenance of each incarcerated seaman.[23]

As the cost of bringing free black crew members into the port became more prohibitive, ship captains sought ways to avoid the fees. From 1836 to 1852, New Orleans was divided into three sectors under one mayor, but with separate economic structures. Businessmen in these three municipalities vied for maritime interests by persuading their magistrates to overlook the collection of bonds and fines for the black mariners. Although the permissiveness of the police force benefitted white businessmen, lax enforcement angered other whites. Reacting to pressure from its constituency, the legislature wrote ever more stringent laws. Because of the bond requirements, however, free blacks were more inclined to stay aboard ship to avoid arrest. This meant that they took shipboard jobs away from white levee workers, and discontent among local laborers ignited racial violence along the waterfront.[24]

22. "An Act More Effectually to Prevent Free Persons of Color from Entering into this State, and for Other Purposes," 1842 La. Acts 308.

23. Everett, "Free Persons of Color," 109, 117, 120; "An Act to Amend An Act More Effectually to Prevent Free Persons of Color from Entering the State and for Other Purposes, Approved Sixteenth of March, 1842," 1852 La. Acts 193; Carol Wilson, *Freedom at Risk: the Kidnapping of Free Blacks in America, 1780-1865* (Lexington, Ky., 1994), 58–63; "An Act Relative to Free Persons of Color Coming into the State from other States or Foreign Countries," 1859 La. Acts 70; Everett, "Free Persons of Color," 112.

24. Tansey, "Out-of-State Free Blacks," 372–4.

To appease the public, an act of 1859 did away with the bond and pass system and required local officials to jail all black seamen until their vessels departed. This provision drew a legal protest by two free black seamen who questioned its constitutionality. The plaintiffs argued before the supreme court that the statute called for illegal imprisonment, because they had committed no crime. Justice Albert Voorhies, who had written the court's opinion, relied on a provision in the Constitution of 1852. The appellants' offense, he wrote, was not punishable by death, imprisonment in the penitentiary, or imposition of a fine exceeding three hundred dollars, which were the constitutional grounds for appealing a criminal conviction. Thus, the supreme court refused to hear the case, claiming it lacked the power to take the appeal.[25]

In most criminal cases, the courts generally considered free persons of color entitled to trial by jury, and most convictions carried the same punishment as for whites. Penalties for some crimes, however, were more severe for free blacks than for whites. Death was mandatory for free persons of color convicted of felonies such as poisoning any person, house burning, or raping a white woman. (The law against rape applied to white women only.) Punishment was at the discretion of the court for other crimes like burning or attempting to burn stacks of corn, wheat, or other produce.[26]

Within the penal system itself, authorities segregated free persons of color from white prisoners. The New Orleans city council required free black convicts to work separately from white criminals and to wear different colored uniforms. City leaders forbade free persons of color from leading or overseeing chain gangs of black prisoners, and they dismissed

25. Opinion of Justice Albert Voorhies, *State of Louisiana ex rel Cook et al., f. m. c.* v. *Keeper of Parish Prison,* Supreme Court of Louisiana, 1860, Docket No. 6007, Supreme Court of Louisiana Archives, Department of Special Collections, Earl K. Long Library, University of New Orleans; "An Act Relative to Free Persons of Color Coming into the State," 1859 La. Acts 70; Constitution of 1852, art. 62, in Albert Voorhies, comp., *A Treatise on the Jurisprudence of Louisiana: Embracing the Criminal Statutes of the Territory of Orleans, and of the State of Louisiana, from the Year 1805 to the Year 1858, inclusively, and Having Copious References to the Decisions of the Late Court of Errors and Appeals, and of the Present Supreme Court, up to the Thirteenth Volume of Louisiana Annual Reports, Inclusively* (New Orleans, 1860), 39; Everett, "Free Persons of Color," 112.

26. "An Act Prescribing the Rules and Conduct with Respect to Negroes and Other Slaves of this Territory," 1806 La. Acts 132; "An Act to Amend the Act Entitled the Black Code or 'An Act Prescribing the Rules and Conduct with Respect to Negroes and Other Slaves of this Territory,'" 1816 La. Acts 148; "An Act Relative to Slaves and Free Persons of Color," 1855 La. Acts 50, 51.

free blacks employed as overseers at the public works, where many black prisoners labored. The council members appointed a jail physician to visit the sick slaves and free persons daily, but they required free black prisoners to pay for these services before they were released, whereas they did not require whites to do so.[27]

Most free persons of color were merely concerned about conducting their businesses and earning their livings. Increased competition for jobs and whites' fears of their rising economic power slowly diminished free blacks' economic freedom, as state and city officials threw obstacles in their way. In 1833, for instance, after the state legislature chartered the Citizens' Bank of Louisiana, two prominent New Orleans free men of color, François Boisdoré and John Goulé, bought stock. Three years later the legislature amended the charter to exclude free blacks from owning bank shares, whereupon the directors refused to grant Boisdoré and Goulé their privileges as stockholders. Boisdoré and Goulé promptly sued on the grounds that the charter amendment should not apply retrospectively to them. The first judicial district court found for the plaintiffs, and the Citizens' Bank board appealed to the supreme court. Judge Henry Adams Bullard upheld the lower court's ruling. He defended Boisdoré and Goulé, stating that the intent of the legislature was not to prevent existing shareholders from exercising their rights, regardless of race.[28]

The freedom of *gens de couleur* to choose an occupation remained unchallenged until just before the Civil War, when the legislature denied them licenses for coffeehouses and cabarets. Additionally, in keeping with other laws limiting mobility, the legislature enacted a statute requiring all vessels navigating the waters of Louisiana to be captained by whites. Compared to the laws in other southern states, these restrictions came

27. Resolution of the New Orleans City Council, 29 October 1827, New Orleans City Archives; Resolution of the New Orleans City Council, 1 December 1828, New Orleans City Archives; Resolution of the New Orleans City Council, 21 August 1833, New Orleans City Archives.

28. Two of New Orleans's most prominent attorneys, Christian Roselius (1803–1873) and Judah Philip Benjamin (1811–1884) represented the plaintiffs in this case. Other lawyers of note, such as Charles Magill Conrad (1804–1878) and Alexander Buchanan (fl. 1830s) also handled cases for free persons of color. Plaintiff's petition and opinion of Judge Henry Bullard, *Boisdoré & Goulé, f. p. c.* v. *Citizens' Bank of Louisiana,* Supreme Court of Louisiana, 1836, Docket No. 2956, Supreme Court of Louisiana Archives, Department of Special Collections, Earl K. Long Library, University of New Orleans.

about rather late. Virginia and Maryland legislators began limiting free black employment opportunities at least twenty years before their Louisiana counterparts.[29]

One of the more significant results of the fear of increased abolitionist agitation were curbs on the right of black assembly. Although no statute banned blacks from holding public meetings, the New Orleans City Council passed several ordinances against them. Caught in the middle of this crackdown were three city congregations of the African Methodist Episcopal Church, which ten free men of color had organized as a private corporation. In 1858 the city council passed an ordinance requiring that all free black congregations be supervised by a white church, and banning assembly of the church members without the sponsorship of a white congregation. Soon thereafter, magistrates seized the churches on the grounds that they operated unlawfully.[30]

Members quickly challenged the constitutionality of the seizure. They sued the city on the grounds that its ordinance violated Article 105 of the Constitution of 1852. That article banned ex post facto laws, laws impairing the execution of a contract, or acts that stripped a party of vested rights. Because the ordinance had the effect of preventing church members from attending divine worship, it thus interfered with the church's inherent rights as a corporation. The church's claim of incorporation provided the second grounds for appeal; it challenged a statute that annulled corporations organized by free persons of color. Church members again

29. "An Ordinance Concerning Cabarets, Coffeehouses and Grog Shops," New Orleans Common Council, 13 December 1856, Ordinances and Resolutions, New Orleans City Archives; "An Act Requiring Vessels and Watercrafts, Navigating the Rivers, Bayous and Lakes in the State of Louisiana, to Have on Board a Free White Person as Captain," 1859 La. Acts 172. By 1834, Virginia legislators barred free blacks from procuring licenses to become vendors, or selling or administering medication of any kind. Maryland law banned them from navigating vessels on the state's waters and from trading in partnership with whites; June Purcell Guild, *Black Laws in Virginia: A Summary of the Legislative Acts of Virginia Concerning Negroes from Earliest Times to the Present* (New York, 1969), 114; Higginbotham and Bosworth, "Rather than the Free," 44; J. M. Wright, *Free Negro in Maryland* (Baltimore, 1921), 98–9.

30. Petition of plaintiff, *African Methodist Episcopal Church* v. *City of New Orleans,* Supreme Court of Louisiana, 1860, Docket No. 6291, Supreme Court of Louisiana Archives, Department of Special Collections, Earl K. Long Library, University of New Orleans; "An Ordinance to Prohibit the Assembly of Free Persons of Color for Worship or Any Other Purpose," New Orleans Common Council Ordinances and Resolutions, April 7, 1858, New Orleans City Archives.

claimed that the law violated the constitution, submitting that it was an ex post facto law, and thus could not apply to their corporation.[31]

The Supreme Court of Louisiana thought otherwise. In his opinion, Justice Alexander Buchanan turned aside the church members' claims of unconstitutionality. He stated that "the African race are strangers to our Constitution, and are the subjects of special and exceptional legislation." Therefore, the legislature could make exceptions to the constitution in cases involving persons of color, free or slave. While developing his point about the tenuous legal position of free blacks, Justice Buchanan carefully reaffirmed their individual right to hold property. It was the "pretended corporation," not the "person" holding property to which the court objected.[32]

In view of New Orleans whites' increasingly desperate efforts to preserve their slave society, it is not surprising that whites moved to degrade the status of free blacks. What is noteworthy, though, is the number of rights the blacks retained, as well as their nature. For example, free blacks kept an absolute right of petition and an unconditional liberty to sue in any court of law. They were not afraid to use these rights, as the records of New Orleans's parish and district courts clearly show. The case files for the years 1813 to 1860 contain upwards of 300 suits and petitions for redress of grievances brought by free persons of color. In 242 of the cases the defendants were white, indicating that free blacks had a certain amount of confidence that the court system would uphold their claims for relief. Their confidence seems well-placed, for in the 103 cases found in which decisions are extant, 95 free black plaintiffs won their suits against white defendants.

The most numerous suits were for debt. Although the bulk of these actions involved less than $300.00, over 20 percent amounted to sums above $1,000.00, the largest being a debt of $3,721.67, filed by Louis Cormié against R. L. Sejour, both free men of color. Cormié, who resided in Paris, employed Sejour as his agent in New Orleans. When that relationship

31. Petition of Plaintiffs, *African Methodist Episcopal Church* v. *City of New Orleans,* 1860, Docket No. 7291, Supreme Court of Louisiana Archives, Department of Special Collections, Earl K. Long Library, University of New Orleans.

32. Opinion of Justice Alexander Buchanan, *African Methodist Episcopal Church* v. *City of New Orleans,* 1860, Docket No. 6291, ibid.

ended, Sejour allegedly provided Cormié's new agent with false information, which resulted in a significant monetary loss. The suit was eventually settled out of court. More common were disputes like the one between J. H. Rinehart and Joseph Green, in which fourth district court
Judge George Strawbridge ordered the sale of Rinehart's furniture to pay
a $175 debt owed to Green.[33]

Free persons of color also aggressively pursued unpaid debts for their
services. In 1820 Charles Duplessis won a $280 judgment for unpaid work
on a chimney. Parish court Judge James Pitot awarded Pierre Estève $400
from Antoine and Luce Toca for outstanding debts on a house Estève
built for the Tocas.[34]

A number of the suits turned on disputes over slave purchases. In 1836,
for example, Robert Clannon sued to cancel promissory notes totaling
$980 when he discovered that a slave he purchased from Marie Olive was
addicted to theft and running away. Felicité Houssard won a judgment
for $1,200 that she claimed Mr. B. Nongonitte and others owed her for the
sale of slaves.[35]

Unlike in other southern states, free blacks also retained the right to
testify against whites. Louisiana's Civil Code considered free people of
color competent to serve as witnesses in any litigation, except where race
might, under certain conditions, undermine a witness's credibility. Slaves,
on the other hand, could not testify against free persons of color unless an
accused was implicated in a slave insurrection. These provisions stood
until the Civil War, though they weathered a challenge to their legality.[36]

33. *Cormié, f. c. m.* v. *Sejour, f. c. m.,* Orleans Parish Court, 1845, Docket No. 16593, Orleans
Parish Court Records, Louisiana Division, New Orleans Public Library; Judgment of Judge George
Strawbridge, *Green, f. m. c.* v. *Rinehart,* Fourth District Court of New Orleans, 1850, Docket No.
3885, New Orleans District Court Records, Louisiana Division, New Orleans Public Library.

34. *Duplessis, f. m. c.* v. *L. Michel,* Orleans Parish Court, 1820, Docket No. 2679, Orleans Parish
Court Records; *Estève* v. *Toca,* Orleans Parish Court, 1843, Docket No. 15536, Orleans Parish court
records.

35. Testimony of Robert Clannon, *Clannon, f. m. c.* v. *Marie Olive, f. w. c.,* Orleans Parish Court,
1836, Docket No. 8910, Orleans Parish Court Records; *Houssard, f. w. c.* v. *Nongonitte et al.,* Orleans
Parish Court, 1836, Docket No. 8946, Orleans Parish Court Records.

36. Guild, *Black Laws in Virginia,* 163; *Civil Code,* art. 2261, "An Act to Amend the Act Entitled
the Black Code or 'An Act Prescribing the Rules and Conduct with Respect to Negroes and Other
Slaves of this Territory,'" 1816 La. Acts 146; "An Act Relating to Slaves and Free Colored Persons,"
1855 La. Acts 391.

The test arose in 1850 when two whites, Henry Levy and Jacob Dreyfous, were adjudged guilty of larceny, largely through the testimony of a free man of color named Lajoie. They appealed to the supreme court, arguing that their convictions should be set aside because the legislature had made no provisions permitting free persons of color to give evidence in criminal cases against whites. Writing for the court, Justice George Rogers King forcefully turned that contention aside. He noted the difference between Louisiana's legislation and jurisprudence and that of other states with large free black populations. The difference, he opined, arose from the unique condition of Louisiana's free persons of color. He then praised the free blacks as respectable, educated, and industrious property holders, "far from being in that degraded state which renders them unworthy of belief, they are such persons as courts and juries would not hesitate to believe under oath." He went on to observe that the right to give testimony was vital to the free blacks' protection. King contended that, should they lose that privilege, "the gravest offenses against their persons and property might be committed with impunity, by white persons."[37]

Free persons of color also maintained their right to own property. In most states with large free black populations, landowning percentages were low, indicative of the blacks' general economic standing. In New Orleans, by comparison, property held by free persons of color in the late 1850s was estimated at around $2.5 million. The unrestricted ability to acquire land and slaves helped free blacks maintain the status and influence they needed to stave off wholesale diminution of their personal and civil liberties. As long as they had economic standing, they had a voice.[38]

The legislature also left untouched the right to remain free. The abduction of free blacks for sale into slavery was a common occurrence throughout the nation. As in most states, it was illegal to kidnap a free person of color and to bring him into Louisiana as a slave. Though many such kidnapings probably went uncontested, a particularly poignant example of the protection this law afforded was played out in the supreme

37. Bill of Exceptions and Opinion of Justice George Rogers King, *State* v. *Henry Levy and Jacob Dreyfous,* Supreme Court of Louisiana, 1850, Docket No. 1414, Supreme Court of Louisiana Archives, Department of Special Collections, Earl K. Long Library, University of New Orleans.

38. Jackson, *Free Negro Labor and Property Holding in Virginia,* 113; Wright, *Free Negro,* 185; Schweninger, *Black Property Owners in the South,* 99, 117, 81.

court in 1824. The plaintiff, a young woman named Delphine, had been born free in Hispaniola. In 1803 she embarked for Cuba under the care of her great aunt, who died en route. A man named Belzons took her in, brought her to Louisiana, and sold her into slavery. She sued her new owner for her freedom. The supreme court ruled that Delphine was free, even though she could not produce the required documentary proof of her freedom. Judge François-Xavier Martin rested his opinion on a provision in *Las Siete Partidas* that said "if a man be free, no matter how long he may be held by another as a slave, his state or condition cannot be thereby changed; nor can he be reduced to slavery, in any manner whatever, on account of the time he may have been held in servitude."[39]

Ironically, just before the Civil War, the legislature bestowed on free persons of color a last right, albeit one of dubious distinction. It permitted them to select masters and become slaves for life. A handful availed themselves of the offer and filed petitions to request that they be voluntarily enslaved. One of the few case files that still exists involves the petition of Thomas Joseph, a twenty-seven-year-old free man of color who petitioned to become the slave of John F. Florence. Thomas's petition was granted by the fourth district court, and Florence was ordered to comply with the court's judgment.[40]

By 1860, Louisiana's lawmakers had answered Benjamin Morgan's questions about the fate of New Orleans's free persons of color. They were neither entitled to full privileges of citizenship, nor had they lost all legal footing within the Americanized city. Free blacks retained key privileges such as property ownership and free access to the courts. They could not vote, but they were essential to the city's economic welfare, and thus kept some measure of de facto political weight. This was enough to delay the

39. "An Act to Amend the Several Acts Enacted for the Punishment of the Crimes and Misdemeanors, Committed by Free Persons, and for Other Purposes," 1819 La. Acts 64; Wilson, *Freedom at Risk*, 68; *Delphine* v. *Deveze*, 2 Mart. (n.s.) 650 (La. 1820); Louis Moreau Lislet and Henry Carleton, trans. *The Laws of Las Siete Partidas, Which Are Still in Force in the State of Louisiana* (New Orleans, 1820), 1: 387. See also *Sally Miller* v. *Louis Belmonti*, 11 Rob. 339 (La. 1845). In this case the plaintiff won her freedom in part because of her light complexion. In reaching its decision, the court relied on the presumption that mulattoes were free, a precedent set by *Adele* v. *Beauregard* in 1812.

40. "An Act to Permit Free Persons of African Descent to Select Their Masters and Become Slaves for Life," 1859 La. Acts 214; *Thomas Joseph, f. m. c., praying to become a slave*, Docket No. 13318, Fourth District Court of New Orleans, 1859.

erosion of their rights, but inadequate to keep whites permanently at bay. While free blacks were needed to help build the colony and territory, restrictions were mild and merely social in nature. Eventually, however, the economy stabilized and Americans gained dominance in the business and politics of the state. At that point, free blacks were no longer welcome additions to a burgeoning Louisiana. Instead, they were intruders who held jobs coveted by whites.

Legislation enacted after 1830 reflects whites' heightened desire to insulate their society from the influence of free blacks and to assure whites a superior position. At the same time, it became increasingly important to the city's whites to protect black New Orleanians, both free and slave, from contamination by abolitionist ideas from the outside. What began as rules that fixed social conduct became a daunting set of restrictions that hedged free blacks' influence during times of growing unrest. To white New Orleanians, the assurance of inferior status for free persons of color was no longer merely an issue of social segregation. It was a matter of maintaining their way of life. To free blacks, in spite of their ability to fight the rising tide of racial prejudice, legal changes made survival in a white world a formidable challenge.

Contributors

WARREN M. BILLINGS, distinguished professor of history at the University of New Orleans and historian of the Supreme Court of Louisiana, writes about seventeenth-century Virginia and Louisiana law.

MARK F. FERNANDEZ, associate professor of history at Loyola University of New Orleans, is the author of the forthcoming *"A Herculean Task": The Evolution of Louisiana's Judicial System, 1718–1862* and various writings on Louisiana legal history.

THOMAS W. HELIS earned a B.A. and an M.A. from the University of New Orleans and is currently employed as a computer systems consultant in St. Louis, Missouri.

FLORENCE M. JUMONVILLE is head of the Department of Archives, Manuscripts, and Special Collections in the Earl K. Long Library at the University of New Orleans and formerly librarian at The Historic New Orleans Collection. She has published extensively on printing and the history of the book in Louisiana. Her *Bibliography of New Orleans Imprints, 1764–1864* (New Orleans, 1989) is the definitive treatment of the subject.

KATHRYN PAGE, archivist at the Louisiana Historical Center, Louisiana State Museum in New Orleans, has curated exhibitions for the museum and wrote "A First-Born Child of Liberty: The Constitution of 1864," in Warren M. Billings and Edward F. Haas, eds., *In Search of Fundamental Law: Louisiana's Constitutions, 1812–1974* (Lafayette, La., 1993) and other papers on issues of race, gender, and constitutional law in nineteenth-century Louisiana.

ELLEN HOLMES PEARSON earned degrees from Spring Hill College and the University of New Orleans and is a doctoral student at the Johns Hopkins University in Baltimore.

CARLA DOWNER PRITCHETT is a law librarian on the staff of the Loyola University School of Law in New Orleans.

JUDITH KELLEHER SCHAFER, associate director of the Murphy Institute of Tulane University and adjunct professor of legal history in the Tulane University School of Law, is the author of *Slavery, the Civil Law, and the Supreme Court of Louisiana* and numerous essays on slavery and legal history.

SHERIDAN E. YOUNG holds an M.A. in history from the University of New Orleans, an MLIS from Louisiana State University, and a Ph.D. in higher education administration from the University of Tennessee. She is a librarian at the University of Tennessee, Chattanooga.

Index